THE OFFICIAL®
PRICE GUIDE TO
Collectibles
of the
'50s
and
'60s

THE OFFICIAL® PRICE GUIDE TO
Collectibles of the '50s and '60s

By Charles J. Jordan

FIRST EDITION

**THE HOUSE OF COLLECTIBLES
NEW YORK, NEW YORK 10022**

Important Notice. The format of *The Official Price Guide Series,* published by *the House of Collectibles,* is based on the following proprietary features: *All facts and prices are compiled through a nationwide sampling of information* obtained from noteworthy experts, auction houses, and specialized dealers. *Detailed "indexed" format* enables quick retrieval of information for positive identification. *Encapsulated histories* precede each category to acquaint the collector with the specific traits that are peculiar to that area of collecting. *An average price range* takes geographic location and condition into consideration when reporting collector value. *An inventory checklist system* is provided for cataloging a collection.

All of the information, including valuations, in this book has been compiled from the most reliable sources, and every effort has been made to eliminate errors and questionable data. Nevertheless the possibility of error, in a work of such immense scope, always exists. The publisher will not be held responsible for losses which may occur in the purchase, sale, or other transaction of items because of information contained herein. Readers who feel they have discovered errors are invited to *write* and inform us, so they may be corrected in subsequent editions. Those seeking further information on the topics covered in this book are advised to refer to the complete line of Official Price Guides published by the House of Collectibles.

Published by: The House of Collectibles
201 East 50th Street
New York, New York 10022

Distributed by Ballantine Books, a division of Random House, Inc., New York and simultaneously in Canada by Random House of Canada Limited, Toronto.

Manufactured in the United States of America

ISBN: 0-876-37548-4

First Edition: April 1987

10 9 8 7 6 5 4

Table of Contents

Acknowledgments

This book was produced under the direction of Charles and Donna Jordan, consulting editors for House of Collectibles. They would like to thank all who made it possible.

Special appreciation goes to two writers who provided informative articles on some of the hottest fields of '50s and '60s collectibles.

Scotia Jordan, who wrote: "Holy Cow, Batman! We're Collectable!"; "Collectors With a Cause"; "Dark Shadows—Tales From Syndication and Beyond"; "To Trap A Spy—Collecting 'The Man from U.N.C.L.E.' "; "Daytrippin—Collecting the Beatles"; "All Aboard For the 'Last Train to Clarksville' "; "Elvis Presley: The King of Rock 'n' Roll Collectibles."

Heather Mitchell Amey, who wrote: "In Pursuit of the Presidency"; "Kennedy Collectibles: Souvenirs of The New Frontier"; "Time to Light Up a Lucky"; "Collectibles That Are M'm! M'm! Good!"; "Coca-Cola Collectibles Are the Real Thing!"; "The Edsel: Beauty is in the Eye of the Collector"; "A Revolution in Juvenile Fiction"; "Little Golden Books Are Popular Again!"; "That Doll Ginny"; "Only You Can Prevent Forest Fires!"; "He's Your Dog, Charlie Brown!"; "The Tragedy of a Heroine"; "Say Kids, What Time Is It?"; "Happy Trails To You!"; "America's Number One Mouseketeer."

We also appreciate the efforts of Galina Kolev, who compiled the price listings found in this volume.

Thanks are also due to the collectors and dealers featured in this book. They graciously opened their collections to us, as well as shared with us their vast knowledge in their given areas of expertise. This book is dedicated to them.

Special thanks to collectors Dick Elliott (cigarette packs); Freddi Margolin (Snoopy items); Charles F. Rosenay (Beatles collector); and Bill Hutchinson (James Dean collector) for the photos featured in the color insert.

Thanks also to Cornelius J. Dwyer (J.F.K.'s eyeglasses); Don Rutledge (Eisenhower oil painting and Rolex watch); Sotheby's (Beatles Gold album and John Lennon's Rolls); and Charles F. Rosenay (Beatle memorabilia).

Introduction

"Everyone's Just Wild About Nostalgia"

nostalgia: a longing for something far away or long ago or for former happy circumstances.

—Webster's New World
Dictionary

Americans have long kept the souvenirs of their youth. Whether it be the saving of a school paper or a favorite toy car or doll that recalled the formative years of our lives, our society has been filled with pack-rat tendencies for generations. We never considered this form of saving as collecting, however. We were merely holding onto keepsakes for memories' sake.

For decades collecting was viewed as something we did as a hobby, a means by which we could pass idle hours. Stamps and butterflies were favorite themes. Collecting was also viewed as a practice indulged in by the wealthy patrons of the finer things in life; art, quality antiques and rare books were all popular "collectibles" during the first half of the 20th century. If we saved things as kids, Elvis Presley records or Brooklyn Dodgers baseball cards, for example, our parents would assure us that this was a phase we would someday outgrow.

During the 1960s and 70s, however, collecting began to

change as what we called collectibles changed. It was the birth of the "pop-culture revolution"—a force considered to be one of the strongest factors motivating the collecting world today. At the center of this force is one word: nostalgia.

Television had long been our greatest exponent of nostalgia, a fact which began out of necessity during television's early years. Stations were forced to buy up thousands of old films to fill in air time between early network programming. Consequently, yesterday's film favorites were to enjoy an entirely new audience in the form of 1950s TV viewers, who enjoyed the classic routines of the likes of Laurel and Hardy and the Little Rascals via the family Dumont television. It is little wonder that when the first generation of television-age youngsters began reaching college age in the mid '60s they adopted the images of Chaplin, Fields et al. as their own. (Campy posters of Charlie Chaplin, W. C. Fields and the Marx Brothers, etc., were all the rage on college dormitory walls during the mid-'60s.)

The message coming out of colleges was that old was chic. Interest in yesterday began reaching new heights by the early'70s. Within the period of a few weeks late in 1970 and early in '71, two national weeklies devoted cover stories to what was by now being called "the nostalgia boom." *Newsweek* reported on the nostalgia fad in an issue which showed a beaming Norman Rockwell Santa Claus on its cover. Meanwhile, *Life* captured the phenomenon with a cover story featuring a bevy of yesterday's film actresses along with the cover line: "Everyone's Just Wild About Nostalgia." "Old is in," the editors of *Life* announced. "We are happily awash in the sleek and gaudy period that stretched from the '20s through the '30s and into the '40s."

For its part, *Newsweek* sought to spotlight a few of the pioneer "nostalgia collectors." Among their gallery: science fiction collector Forrest Ackerman, Mickey Mouse buffs and doll collectors.

People who had quietly saved their Elvis Presley records

and Brooklyn Dodgers baseball cards all those years emerged from the shadows and became heroes. Meanwhile, a national treasure hunt began for all the items we had cast out as kids. America was searching the attic in hot pursuit of that Shirley Temple dish which only a few short years before was viewed as a sentimental keepsake of childhood —and little else. Now we were being told that it was a collectible—something to be brought back out into the light of day. And, best yet, it was something that someone might be willing to pay a premium price for!

Collecting clubs flourished during the '70s, and by decade's end leading auction galleries such as Sotheby's, Christie's and Phillips had established collectibles departments. In the years since, the collecting world has been rocked by major sales which have been established in the auction sales by these and other auction establishments. Sotheby's sells a Disney "Silly Symphony" poster for $7000. Christie's sells a pair of ruby slippers worn by Judy Garland in *The Wizard of Oz* for $12,000. A Chicago baseball card collector buys a Honus Wagner card for $27,000. A button picturing a young Franklin Roosevelt passes over the block for $30,000. Meanwhile, the first issue of *Action Comics* featuring the debut of Superman now prices over $20,000. Nostalgia has become a high-priced game.

Enter the '50s and '60s

The biggest development in the collectibles world since the establishment of pop-culture collectibles has been the major inroads being made by items of the '50s and '60s. In 1983, the head of Sotheby's Collectibles Department in New York was quoted as saying, "I think you will see some big money being paid for items from the 1950s and '60s at auction over the next ten years. Collecting is moving into the baby boom generation."

Evidence of this eventuality is reflected in the following

news items which recently flashed around the collecting world:

—An autographed paperback copy of "Giant" signed by actor James Dean sells for $1263.

—A Charles Eames' simple birch lounge chair from the '50s in fine condition carries a $550 price tag today.

—An original 1957 Elvis Presley Emene toy guitar now brings $500 to $700, and Beatle dolls that sold in 1964 for $2 to $3 now command $850 in New York City auctions.

Collecting experts are saying that we in the 1980s are witnessing the early stages of the second phase of the pop-culture phenomenon, the development of the post-war years collectibles. Of the latest trend, the *Boston Globe* recently wrote, "From the return of a number of 1950s television shows to the persistent success of 'oldies' radio stations, nostalgia has never been more popular or pervasive." It went on to say that the hit film *Back to the Future,* which told the story of a teenager who travels back to the '50s, was not only one of the most celebrated movies of the '80s, but "an epigram for an era."

The increased mining of the not-so-distant past is evident in all fields of collecting. For example, *Antique Market Report* wrote recently about the new popularity in '50s furniture, stating: "It was not until the early '80s that people started taking a closer look at the styles of the '50s—partly because antique sources were drying up, and partly because of a realization that there were many fine quality and lasting designs during that period."

The purpose of *The Official Price Guide to Collectibles of the '50s & '60s* is to provide the reader with an up-to-the-minute look at a rapidly developing field of collecting. Of course, as with any field in flux, many prices have yet to reach full maturity and it may be a number of years before the dust settles. While it would be impossible to list every item produced during the 20-year period which is the focus of this book, the pages which follow offer a cross-section of collectibles which have already established a footing in the collecting world. Look for the values to increase as '50s and '60s collectibles continue to attract new attention.

The Official Price Guide to Collectibles of the '50s & '60s also includes interviews with a group of collectors who are in the forefront of the many categories of this new wave of collecting. Many have been watching their respective fields develop and gain in recognition over recent years, and offer helpful insight into what is hot and what is not. A large number of photographs will also help the beginning collector to familiarize himself with the sort of memorabilia increasingly turning up at collector shows and flea markets.

While this book is designed for collectors, it is the hope of House of Collectibles that it will provide enjoyable hours to all readers who seek to recall those roller-coaster years. So get out your coon-skin cap, Fab Four guitar and poodle skirt. The '50s and '60s are here!

What the Prices Mean

The prices used in this book are based either on estimates through auction houses like Christie's, Sotheby's and Phillips, or on estimates from dealers and collectors across the United States. While the price ranges from auction galleries may not be wide-ranging between the high and low, the dealers and collectors have contributed the extremes. For example, a Snoopy cutting board (found in the "Peanuts" section of Kid's World) has sold for both $10.00 and $25.00.

The House of Collectibles publishes so many books on varying fields of interest that the author was able to utilize some of the many contributors to the series, like Dr. James Beckett who annually updates *The Official Price Guide to Baseball Cards.*

The reader should understand that all price estimates are based on quality and condition. Items such as comic books were meant to be used and likely will have tears or finger-print marks; however, the price estimates for items in this book are based on those found in good to excellent condition.

Americans in the '50s and '60s

Introduction

The post-war home, to Americans who had survived the Depression and were now emerging from the turmoil of the greatest global conflict in history, represented the pinnacle of civilization. We had dreamed of this time for so long. Magazine advertisements in the final months of World War II conditioned us to expect a world in which convenience would be the keystone. Americans would enjoy "extra hours of freedom for happier living," an ad for Hotpoint appliances proclaimed. This was the world we were promised during the New York World's Fair of 1939–40, via an exhibit of "The World of 1960."

While the reality of life in the 1950s and '60s could never measure up to the hype it had received in the years preceding and just following World War II, there was no doubt that life would be easier for most Americans. Rationings and shortages, so much a part of daily life in the '30s and '40s, were nonexistent as we entered the '50s. Indeed, with the abundance of electric refrigerators and other household appliances, faster and more streamlined cars, new television sets and stereos, the future certainly seemed bright.

The housing shortage which greeted returning veterans was soon replaced by the greatest building boom this country has ever seen. The year 1950 alone saw the construction of 1.4 million new homes. The great post-war baby boom resulted in soaring sales of baby cribs as we entered the new decade, and manufacturers worked overtime to come up with new lines of toys. Coon-skin caps sold like hotcakes midway through the decade when a character named Davy Crockett caught the under-10 set, and everyone was singing about the famous frontiersman "born on a mountaintop in Tennessee." Meanwhile, traditional toys became more sophisticated. Dolls now cried and cooed, and did practically everything else real-life infants could. Before the '50s ended, one doll in particular revolutionized the toy industry when Barbie first appeared on the market, looking not like an infant but a fully developed young woman. She was followed by Ken, Midge, Skipper and more accessories than could fill a miniature closet.

Our preoccupation with space travel resulted in the unleashing of a small galaxy of space-related toys during the '50s and '60s. At first came the spaceships. Then came robots. By the time man actually ventured into space, the farfetched space machines of the '50s vanished, to be replaced by authentic models of NASA rockets. One of the hotsellers of Christmas 1962 was a model kit of the Mercury spacecraft which had carried John Glenn into space earlier in the year.

As television became more and more a part of our lives, our reading habits changed. Picture magazines continued to spring forth in a steady profusion, while some of yesterday's great reading magazines, such as *Collier*'s and the *Saturday Evening Post*, battled for survival. The books we read also changed. Paperbacks, which first emerged in the '30s, flourished during the '50s. A testimony to the times was the fact that the fastest growing magazine during the 1950s was *TV Guide*.

The Official Price Guide to Collectibles of the '50s & '60s begins with a look into American life during the post-war years.

Around The House

DESCRIPTION: Decorative items found in the American home during the 1950s and '60s, a period now remembered as one of great experimentation. This period also saw a great increase in commercial packaging designed to be displayed for its aesthetic appeal around the home after use.

TYPES COVERED: Art pottery, Avon, furniture, Jim Beam, prints.

Art Pottery: The Modern Studio Movement

Thomas G. Turnquist has been collecting art pottery for about 10 years. "I started collecting elephants when I was in my twenties. I was very active in the Republican party and started collecting clay elephants. I found a Van Briggle elephant in a shop in Denver and started doing research on Van Briggle. Then I became so enamored with pottery itself that I just went into the collecting of pottery. I started out collecting Rookwood and Roseville—all the traditionals—and then ended up really becoming interested in studio pottery." (The information listed in the price guide section on art pottery is basically on studio potters who were popular during the 1950s and 1960s. They are considered to be part of the Modern Studio Movement.)

Art Pottery of the United States, written by Paul Evans and published by Everybody's Press in Hanover, Pennsylvania in 1974, is considered a classic in the field. Paul Evans cre-

(photo courtesy of Thomas Turnquist)

Stonelain bowl by Adolph Dehn

ated some definitions that have been very useful to art pottery collectors. He defines art pottery as "not identified by particular styles or techniques, specific operation or span of years, but rather by the philosophy or attitude of the individuals involved in its execution."

"What the American Art Pottery movement in a sense was, was aesthetically and artistically correct work produced basically in commercial settings—companies, corporations, etc.," says Turnquist. "And it was a great division of labor." While one person might do the decoration, another would do the casting, a third might be a chemist, and so on. "It was a balance between the artist and artisan—artisan defined as a technician—and to produce a fine piece of studio pottery the studio potters worked usually by themselves or possibly

(photo courtesy of Thomas Turnquist)

Bottle by Vivika and Otto Heino

with a partner, like the Heino's or the Scheier's. They were everything—the artist, the artisan and the chemist. They had total artistic control."

For every Vivika and Otto Heino, two popular potters, there were literally hundreds of potters from 1920 to 1969, but only a relatively small percentage, to coin an old phrase, grabbed the brass ring. "And only a small percentage are of the quality that was worth collecting," added Turnquist.

Hull china should be considered a part of Industrial Artware, as should Hall china. "I would think that Fiestaware would fall under Tableware and Industrialware. If you look at dinnerware, it's not American art pottery produced in that period as defined by Evans, and it's not studio pottery. So it's either under Industrial Artware or it's under Dinnerware," Turnquist said. "If you're talking about Hull vases and bowls and so forth, I think you can safely say that is within the definition of Industrial Artware."

"To emphasize the importance of the potter himself, the studio worker almost always incised his piece with his own name," wrote Evans. "Art pottery in contrast most often bore the formal cipher or mark of the works at which it was produced, sometimes with the added initials or other signatures of the various craftsmen, such as the potter, the decorator and the designer. Studioware, which tended to be a unique expression of the potter, was most often built or thrown instead of cast. Because there were few stock designs one rarely finds catalogs or the shape numbers which were commonly used in art pottery." Evans says that seldom did the studio potter attain the speed or proficiency of the specialist of the art pottery era. "Although highly skilled in his particular work, the specialist rarely had the studio potter's overall command of the art."

The studio potter was primarily interested in continuing the tradition of the artist potter rather than in the extensive production or application of a technique. "His primary intentions were to experiment and to instruct rather than to build an industry. As a result studio potters most often received their training in an art or ceramic school rather than serving an apprenticeship in a pottery plant."

(*Note:* Mr. Turnquist, who provided the listings which follow, is a writer on art pottery as well as a collector. His book, *Denver's White Pottery,* was published in 1980 by Homestead Press in Tulsa, Oklahoma. He has written for *Antique Trader, American Art Pottery Journal of the American Art Pottery Association,* and lectured at a symposium called "Women in Clay: The Ongoing Tradition," in 1984.)

Price Range

Andreson, Laura

☐ **Bottle,** 5½" x 3½", copper-red glaze on porcelain, c. 1963 . . . .   275.00

☐ **Bowl,** 6½" x 9", soft green, matte-glazed stoneware with narrow vertical stripes, 1953 . . . .   600.00

☐ **Bowl,** 5" x 7", yellow-orange, mesquite ash glaze, c. 1956 . . . .   500.00

Price Range

☐ **Vase,** 7½" x 6¼", soft yellow, matte-
glazed earthenware, c. 1962 . . . .   650.00

Black, Harding

☐ **Bowl,** rice-bowl form, footed, 4" high,
7" across, exterior-incised paneled-line
design, iron-blue with shaded white
highlights both interior and exterior,
stoneware body, signed, and dated 1956   200.00   300.00

☐ **Bowl,** rice-bowl form, footed, 3" high,
5" across, white crackle glaze, stoneware
body, signed and dated 1960 . . . .   100.00   175.00

☐ **Bowl,** altered free form, thick walls, 4"
high, 10" across, interior red chun glaze,
exterior natural stoneware body, signed
and dated 1952 . . . .   200.00   400.00

☐ **Bowl,** low, spherical form, 12" across,
"Flame Glaze," iron blue with oxblood-
red flames, stoneware body, signed and
dated 1954 . . . .   300.00   600.00

☐ **Vase,** bottle form, 7" high, copper-
reduction oxblood-red glaze, porcelain,
signed and dated 1950 . . . .   300.00   500.00

☐ **Vase,** spherical form with cylindrical
neck, 9" high, 8" across body, geometric
Viennese secession design, matte black
with inlayed white glaze, stoneware
body, signed and dated 1955 . . . .   500.00   700.00

Price Range

Deutch, Eugene

☐ **Bowl,** 3½″ x 2¼″, white matte glaze on exterior and speckled matte glaze in interior, c. 1952 . . . .   60.00

☐ **Bowl,** 6½″ x 4½″ x 2″, thrown and hand-formed bowl, black interior, rust-colored exterior, c. 1951 . . . .   75.00

☐ **Vase,** 10″ x 6½″, brown clay, triangular-shaped body with a swirled tan and brown glaze, c. 1955 . . . .   100.00

☐ **Pitcher,** 11″ x 4¾″, slightly mottled matte blue glass, piece has circular looped handle, c. 1950 . . . .   125.00

☐ **Vase,** 10″ x 6½″, brown clay, triangular-shaped body with a swirled tan and brown glaze, c. 1955 . . . .   100.00

Heino, Vivika and Otto

☐ **Bowl,** 4½″ x 3½″, cobalt-blue porcelain, c. late 1960s 80.00

☐ **Bottle,** 11¼″ x 5⅝″, dark brown glaze with white vertical stripes, a Heino classic, c. 1960 . . . .   650.00

☐ **Bottle,** 6″ x 4″, a black, blue and reddish, metallic-looking glass, c. late 1960s . . .   150.00

☐ **Bottle,** 8″ x 5″, ash glaze on stoneware body, glaze color is tan with mixture of black, rim is black, c. late 1960s 200.00

Martz, Karl

☐ **Communion Plate and Pitcher,** stoneware, plate is 16½" in diameter, pitcher is 12⅛" in height, c. 1956 . . . .   400.00

☐ **Floor Vase,** 53" x 16", lidded vase with buff glaze, brown knobs, c. 1961 . . . . .   1000.00

☐ **Vase,** 20½" x 18", unglazed stoneware with incised decoration, c. 1955 . . . . . .   500.00

☐ **Vase,** 11¼", unglazed stoneware with incised linear pattern, c. 1955 . . . .   300.00

McIntosh, Harrison

☐ **Bottle,** 5" x 5¼", stoneware with copper-green engobe and clear matte glaze, c. 1963 . . . .   250.00

☐ **Bowl,** 4½" x 9¼", hand-thrown stoneware, black and blue-green engobe, gray matte glaze, Mishima design, c. 1967   500.00

☐ **Lidded Jar,** 11½" x 9½", stoneware with brown, black and beige matte glazes, carved stripes, c. 1959 . . . .   750.00

☐ **Vase,** 15½" x 14½", stoneware, with blue-green and black engobe, gray matte glaze, Mishima line, c. 1967 . . . .   900.00

Nicodemus, Chester R.

☐ **Creche,** cast ceramic, nine pieces, c. 1969   200.00

Price Range

Pillin, Polia

☐ **Bowl,** 6½" x 1¾", decorated with two
fish in white, blue and black, c. 1960   175.00

☐ **Bowl,** 11" x 5", orange and black crater
glaze, a heavy body with a thick-
textured glaze, c. 1968 . . . .   200.00

☐ **Plate,** 7½" diameter, decorated with
woman with bird on her wrist in gray,
black, red-pink, white and light green
colors, c. 1968 . . . .   100.00

☐ **Vase,** 7" x 3½", decorated with a horse
on one side and a standing woman on
the other in blue, white, pink-red and
burnt orange colors, c. 1965 . . . .   125.00

Pitney, William

☐ **Bowl,** 5½" x 3¾", stoneware, with
granular illmenite in body, exterior cela-
don glaze, reduction fired in a sagger
within an oxidation kiln, c. 1968 . . . . .   125.00

☐ **Decanter** and Corked Stopper, 12¼"
(15" with stopper) x 2½", porcelain, slip
cast, colored slips (robin's-egg blue, yellow, black) frisketed application in
equal vertical divisions, c. 1960 . . . . . .   120.00

☐ **Shallow Bowl,** 12" x 2½", stoneware,
dark brown, frosty matte-glaze lining,
reduction fired, c. 1969 . . . .   150.00

Price Range

Sanders, Herbert H.

☐ **Lidded Jar,** spherical form, pointed knob on lid, gold crystalline glaze against a blue background, 8" high to top of lid, porcelain, signed, c. 1960 . . . .   1500.00   2500.00

☐ **Vase,** cylindrical form, 13" high, 7" across, incised design of human figures, black-stained stoneware body, titled "Evolution of Man," signed, c. 1950s   2200.00   3000.00

☐ **Vase,** small spherical form, 4" high, flash-luster glaze in orange-red, porcelain body, signed, c. 1950s 500.00   1500.00

☐ **Vase,** bottle form, 9" high, blue crystalline glaze on white background, porcelain, signed, early 1960s 700.00   2000.00

Stonelain

☐ **Plate,** 12" diameter, titled Frolic designed by Adolf Dehn, decorated with five horses in white, tan and black, c. 1952 . . . .   200.00

☐ **Plate,** 10½" diameter, designed by Aaron Bohrod, decoration consists of three weather vanes, in green and light maroon, c. 1950 . . . .   175.00

Strong, Harris G. (Tiles)

☐ **Wall Hanging,** 6" x 6", in a two-tile by six-tile tile configuration, the subject matter is a Picasso-like human figure, model #1202, c. 1965 . . . .   550.00

Price Range

☐ **Wall Hanging,** 41″ x 9½″, vertical three-tile configuration of a woman, tile mounted on 41″ x 9½″ walnut board, model #W-10, c. 1965 . . . .   275.00

☐ **Wall Hanging,** 11″ x 36″ W. Horizontal, five 6″ x 6″ tile configuration, the subject matter is a group of people in robes carrying flags, tile mounted on 11″ x 36″ walnut board, model #540, c. 1965 . .   325.00

☐ **Wall Hanging,** 9½″ x 41″ W. Horizontal, three-tile piece, each tile depicts prehistoric cave drawings, tile mounted on 9½″ x 41″ walnut board, model #W-26, c. 1965 . . . .   275.00

Avon

"Avon Calling!"

For more than 100 years Avon, the modern leader in the world of collectible non-liquor bottles, has been attracting collector interest in their decorative toiletries and cosmetic bottles. Since none of the figurals are extremely rare, a complete collection is not impossible, though it would certainly require hundreds of bottles.

Avon was founded as the California Perfume Company by D. H. McConnell, a door-to-door book salesman, who gave away perfume samples to prevent doors from being slammed in his face when trying to sell his books. There are bottles in circulation marked "C. P. C." that are very desirable, though they are hard to date because they were issued in very small quantities and have not been well preserved.

Avon ad from *Life* magazine

Many designs were used in the C.P.C. bottle preparation, and in most cases sales do not occur frequently enough to establish an accurate price level.

Now that Avon collecting has become so popular, all of its bottles and their boxes have been carefully catalogued in a book called *Avon-8,* published by Western World Publishing in Pleasant Hill, California. Everything from brochures to magazine ads (there are some beautiful ads in *Life* magazines from the 1950s) are being collected. Although it seems that every possible subject has appeared in the form of figurals, Avon continues to bring out original bottles in a variety of sizes, colors, designs, and scents with each passing year. The new figurals are often issued in limited edition, with the editions often large enough to accommodate the collector as well as the general public.

Avon stands as the oldest toiletry company issuing decorative bottles; however, the collecting interest did not become widespread until 1965, when Avon released an aftershave lotion in a stein decanter and a men's cologne in an amber boot.

By the late '60s, Avons were plentiful. They were beginning to turn up in antique shops, and values were rising. It was about that time that collecting clubs were established.

Western World Publishing not only published *Avon-8,* a softcover book spanning the late 1800s to the early 1980s; they also produce a bimonthly newsletter called the *Western World Avon Collectors Newsletter* for members of the Western World Avon Collectors Club. There are today over 5000 members of the WWACC. The single issue cost for the newsletter is three dollars, and a one-year subscription is $13.50. The newsletter includes a section on "Avon Around the World," a column by Phyllis Popham (who covers the latest news from Canada, England, and Brazil); Bette Mackay reports on New Zealand Avon products, and Mike Hayworth, the "Avon Amigo," writes on what is happening in the field of Avon from Mexico.

With information gathered from all corners of the nation, the *Avon-8* handbook secures many of its prices from its readers, as well as a large network of Avon buyers and sellers. The publishers are currently planning an *Avon-8* supplement, to be released shortly.

Besides trying to amass as many figurals as possible, Avon collectors also collect by subject matter, as well as by the type of product the figurals originally contained, such as perfume, or after shave.

For more Avon information, write to Western World Avon Collectors Club (not affiliated with Avon), P. O. Box 23785, Pleasant Hill, CA 94523. All prices are from *Avon-8* and appear courtesy Western World Publishing.

Avon Bottles

(Note: The original retail price is provided in parentheses just before each current estimate.)

Price Range

1950

☐ **Avon Blossoms Set,** 4 perfumes: "Cotillion," "Quaintance," "Golden Promise" and "Luscious," clear glass, plastic color caps, white label on front, ⅝ oz. each (2.00) 90.00   110.00

☐ **Doubly Yours Set,** "Cotillion" and "Flower Time" colognes, clear glass, white plastic cap, white label on front, 2 oz. each (2.10) 50.00   100.00

☐ **The Cotillion,** cream lotion and cologne, clear glass, white plastic cap, label on front, 6 oz. and 4 oz. (2.39) 50.00   100.00

Avon-8, published by Western World

	Price Range	
☐ **To A Wild Rose Perfume,** clear glass, large blue cap, flower around the neck, 2 dr. (4.50)	60.00	100.00

1951

☐ **Forever Spring Cream,** clear glass, yellow cap, lettering painted on front, 4 oz. (.95) 12.00   16.00

☐ **Fragrant Mist Set,** toilet water—clear glass, white plastic cap, pink and white label on front, 2 oz.; perfume—clear glass tube, black plastic cap, 1 dr. (2.35)   45.00   65.00

☐ **Gift Perfume,** clear glass, round, clear yellow glass stopper, gold neck cord with round gold label, 3 dr. (3.00) 100.00   120.00

Price Range

☐ **Gift Perfume,** clear designer-shaped glass, floral design clear glass stopper, gold neck cord with white label, 3 dr. (3.50) 90.00   110.00

☐ **Golden Promise Perfume,** clear glass, glass stopper with flat top, gold and white label, ½ oz. (3.95) 130.00   150.00

☐ **Special Set,** two 4 oz. hand lotion, clear glass, white plastic cap, blue & white label on front (1.18) 30.00   50.00

1953

☐ **Cotillion Enchantment Toilet Water,** clear glass, pink plastic cap, label on front, 2 oz. 30.00   50.00

☐ **Cotillion Cologne,** clear glass, silver glass stopper, long neck, no label, imprint on glass, label around neck, 4 oz. (2.00) 15.00   25.00

☐ **Cotillion Perfume Oil for Bath,** matte glass, pointed matte glass stopper, no label, imprint on glass, ½ oz. (4.00) ..   8.00   10.00

☐ **Cotillion Toilet Water,** clear glass, silver glass stopper, long neck, lettering painted on front, label around neck, 2 oz. (1.50) 15.00   20.00

☐ **Golden Promise Toilet Water,** clear glass, large dome-shaped cap, lettering painted on around shoulder, 2 oz. (1.50)   20.00   24.00

☐ **Precious Pear,** two 1-dr. perfumes, choice of fragrances, clear glass, gold cap. (2.75) 80.00   100.00

Price Range

☐ **Quaintance Toilet Water,** clear glass, ribbed corners, rose-shaped and colored cap, with green leaf neck band, green painted lettering on front, 2 oz. (1.25)   20.00   30.00

1954

☐ **Bright Night Cologne,** clear glass coated with white plastic, gold neck cord and white paper label, 4 oz. (2.50) 15.00   25.00

☐ **Bright Night Perfume,** clear glass, glass stopper, white label on gold neck cord, ½ oz. (7.50) 80.00   140.00

☐ **Cotillion Garland,** cream lotion and bath oil, clear glass, pink matted glass stopper, 4½ oz. each (2.15) 35.00   45.00

☐ **Jardin D'Amour Perfume,** clear glass bottle that sits in a blue and gold bucket with gold cord that ties around the top of the bottle, clear plastic cap, gold label, 1 dr. (15.00) 190.00   200.00

☐ **Jardin D'Amour Perfume Set,** larger bottle — 1½ oz., clear glass bottle that sits in a blue and gold bucket with gold cord that ties around the top of the bottle, jeweled-rim clear plastic cap, blue/gold label, smaller bottle—1 dr., clear glass flaconette, gold cap (15.00)   180.00   220.00

1955

☐ **Cupid's Bow Set,** four ½-oz. bottles of "Bright Night," "Quaintance," "Cotillion" and "To A Wild Rose," clear glass,

Price Range

square-shaped bottles, white plastic
caps, lettering painted in white on front
(2.50) 65.00   85.00

☐ **Pine Bath Oil,** clear glass, green cap,
paper label on front with pine needles
and cones, 4 oz. 25.00   45.00

☐ **To A Wild Rose Perfume,** white glass,
large domed pink cap, lettering painted
on front, floral border around base, ½
oz. (5.00) 100.00   140.00

☐ **Toilet Water,** clear glass, glass stopper,
gold neck cord with white label, 2 oz.
(2.00) 20.00   24.00

1956

☐ **Cologne with Atomizer,** triangular-
shaped clear glass bottle, white plastic
top, white imprint on glass, 2 oz. (1.25)   20.00   25.00

☐ **Cotillion Talc,** frosted glass, pink cap,
pink paper label, 3 oz. (1.00) 10.00   15.00

☐ **Elegante Cologne,** clear glass, silver cap
and neck tag, red ribbon, 4 oz. (2.50)   40.00   50.00

☐ **Elegante Perfume,** clear glass, silver cap
and neck tag, red neck ribbon, ½ oz.
(7.50) 120.00   160.00

☐ **Forever Spring Perfume,** clear glass,
glass stopper, blue ribbon and tag on
neck, 3 dr. (5.00) 70.00   100.00

☐ **Forever Spring Toilet Water,** clear glass,
yellow cap, blue bird on cap, lettering
painted on front, 2 oz. (1.50) 15.00   20.00

Price Range

☐ **Fragrance Rainbow Set,** four 3-dr. bottles of "Nearness," "Bright Night," "Cotillion" and "To A Wild Rose," round clear glass, long neck, white dome-shaped plastic stoppers, color ribbons around neck, lettering painted in white on front (2.75) 65.00   85.00

☐ **Magic Hours Set,** toilet water and cologne, clear glass, glass stopper, 2 oz. (3.50) 40.00   60.00

1957

☐ **Bright Night Gem Set,** clear glass, glass stopper, gold neck cord with white label, 2 oz. (3.50) 40.00   50.00

☐ **Cotillion Cologne,** clear glass, white cap, label lettering painted on front, 3 dr. 18.00   22.00

1958

☐ **Bright Night Cologne Mist,** clear glass coated with white plastic, gold-speckled gold cap, gold neck cord with white label, 3 oz. (2.75) 15.00   25.00

☐ **Cologne Mist,** clear glass, glass stopper, gold neck cord with label, 3 oz. (2.75)   20.00   28.00

☐ **Elegante Toilet Water,** clear glass, silver cap and neck tag, red neck ribbon, 2 oz. (2.00) 30.00   50.00

☐ **Here's My Heart Cream Lotion,** clear glass, white plastic cap with scalloped and beaded rim, lettering painted on front, 4 oz. (1.00) 4.00   6.00

Price Range

☐ **Spray Cologne,** clear glass triangular-shaped bottle, white plastic cap, 1½ oz. (1.59) 15.00   20.00

1959

☐ **Cotillion Gift Cologne,** (1959 only), clear glass, golden stopper, long neck, 4 oz. (N.Y. Pasadena label) (2.50) 50.00   100.00

1960

☐ **Cologne,** clear glass, white plastic cap, pink bow around neck, no label, imprint on glass, 2 oz. (1.35) 14.00   18.00

☐ **Cologne Mist,** glass bottle, white plastic cap, 2½ oz. (.89) 8.00   12.00

1961

☐ **Cotillion Cologne,** clear glass, silver glass stopper, long neck, lettering painted on front, label around neck, 2 oz. (1.50) 20.00   26.00

☐ **Cotillion Cologne,** matte glass, pointed matte glass stopper, lettering painted on front, 4 oz. (3.00) 10.00   15.00

☐ **Cotillion Cologne,** matte glass, pointed matte glass stopper, lettering painted on front, 2 oz. (2.00) 4.00   6.00

☐ **Somewhere Cologne,** clear glass, pink cap, sculptured bottle, lettering painted around shoulder, jeweled trim around cap, 2 oz. (2.00) 5.00   7.00

Price Range

☐ **Somewhere Perfume,** clear glass, pink cap, sculptured bottle, lettering painted around shoulder, jeweled trim around cap and base, 1 oz. (20.00) 50.00 70.00

1963

☐ **Topaz Perfume,** amber glass, amber jeweled glass stopper, faceted bottle, 1 oz. (20.00) 110.00 130.00

☐ **Topaz Perfume Oil For The Bath,** clear glass, gold cap, lettering painted on front, ½ oz. (4.00) 50.00 70.00

1964

☐ **Topaz Perfume Oil,** clear glass, gold cap, lettering painted on front, ½ oz. (4.00) 50.00 70.00

1966

☐ **Crystal Cologne,** clear patterned glass, matching plastic cap, gold trim at shoulder, 4 oz. (4.00) 4.00 6.00

1967

☐ **Blue Lotus After Bath Refreshener,** clear glass, blue cap, 6 oz. (3.00) 4.00 8.00

1968

☐ **Blue Lotus Cream Sachet,** blue frosted glass, blue cap, .66 oz. (2.50) 2.00 5.00

☐ **Bud Vase Decanter,** long neck, clear glass, oval-knob top, 4 oz. (4.50) 10.00 15.00

Price Range

1969

☐ **Cotillion Cologne,** clear glass, pointed matte glass stopper, no label, imprint on glass, ½ oz. (1.50) 1.00   3.00

Avon Gifts

☐ **A Man's World,** after shave lotion, Avon, 1969, globe-shaped and sculptured container, sharp-pointed cap, overall gold color, sits in a globe stand, 6 oz. (5.00) 5.00   10.00

☐ **Avon Calling,** phone-shaped figural, cologne in phone (6 oz.) and talc in receiver (1½ oz.), silver with black (8.00)   10.00   15.00

☐ **Defender,** Avon, 1966, after shave, cannon-shaped clear glass, gold cap, gold bottom cover, gold label around middle of bottle, sits on a dark brown plastic cannon stand, 6 oz. (5.00) 20.00   25.00

☐ **First Edition,** Avon, 1967, encyclopedia-shaped clear glass bottle, dark brown label on narrow side, dark brown plastic cap, in "Bay Rum," "Wild Country" or "Leather" after shave, 6 oz. (3.50) 6.00   10.00

☐ **Gavel,** Avon, 1967, after shave, gavel-shaped tan color glass, glass stopper, dark brown glass holder (4.00) 15.00   20.00

☐ **Scimitar in Windjammer After shave,** Avon, 1968, beautiful, jeweled, daggar-shaped, gold-colored figural, 6 oz. (6.00)   15.00   25.00

Price Range

☐ **Viking Horn in Spicy, Original or Blue Blazer After shave,** Avon, 1966, horn-shaped tan-colored glass, sculptured gold cap and gold cover on opposite end, 7 oz. (7.00) 20.00 25.00

☐ **Weather-Or-Not,** Avon, 1969, after shave, thermometer- and barometer-shaped, rust color clear glass, gold dome-shaped cap with eagle on top, 5 oz. (5.00) 5.00 10.00

Avon Gift Sets

☐ **Jewel Collection,** Avon, 1964, six ⅝-oz. gram flacons of perfume oil set in a beautiful jewel-like design over dark blue velvet, clear glass, dome-shaped clear glass stopper, "Somewhere," "Topaz," "Cotillion," "Persian Wood," "Here's My Heart" and "To A Wild Rose" (5.95) 55.00 75.00

☐ **Pyramid of Fragrance,** Avon, 1969, cologne, 2 oz., beautifully sculptured clear glass in the shape of crystal pyramid, gold pyramid-shaped cap (5.00) 5.00 10.00

☐ **Renaissance Trio,** Avon, 1966, ½ oz. colognes in a choice of 9 fragrances, clear glass, long neck, pointed silver cap, three renaissance figures on box (3.50) 15.00 25.00

☐ **Roll-A-Fluff,** 1969, roll-on dispenser and talc, 3½ oz., brocade in white (13.50) 15.00 25.00

Price Range

Avon Christmas Gift Sets

☐ **Golden Angel Foaming Bath Oil,** Avon, 1968, sculptured crystal-cut clear glass with wings, white plastic cap shaped as angel's head, 4 oz. (3.50) ...   10.00   15.00

red 8.00   12.00

green 8.00   12.00

Avon Products for Children

☐ **Away in a Manger,** 4 animal-molded soaps with a paper fold-out background (1.49), Avon, 1955 ....   135.00   140.00

☐ **Best Friend,** dog-shaped soap, blue (.59), Avon, 1956 ....   45.00   55.00

☐ **Casey Jones,** Jr., 3 soaps, boxed (1.19), Avon, 1956 ....   95.00   105.00

☐ **Circus Wagon,** 3 animal-shaped soaps in circus wagon box (1.25), Avon, 1957   95.00   115.00

☐ **Fire Engine No.5,** soap (.59), Avon, 1957   45.00   60.00

Avon Christmas Ornaments

☐ **Christmas Cologne,** Avon, 1969, oval-shaped flat floral design on front, oval-shaped neck, sharp pointed cap, 3 oz. (3.50)

red, "Unforgetable" 6.00   10.00

gold, "Topaz" 6.00   10.00

blue, "Occur!" 6.00   10.00

green, "Somewhere" 6.00   10.00

Price Range

☐ **Christmas Ornament Bubble Bath,**
Avon, 1967, 4 oz., ornamented ball-
shaped glass, gold cap with hook (1.75)

green	8.00	12.00
silver	8.00	12.00
gold	8.00	12.00
red	8.00	12.00

☐ **Christmas Sparkler Bubble Bath,**
Avon, 1968, crystal cut, round-shaped
glass with floral design on front and
back, gold cap with hook, 4 oz. (2.50)

blue	8.00	12.00
green	8.00	12.00
gold	8.00	12.00
red	8.00	12.00
purple	30.00	40.00

☐ **Christmas Tree Bubble Bath,** Avon,
1968, tree-shaped glass, cone-shaped
caps, 4 oz. (2.50)

silver	8.00	12.00
gold	8.00	12.00

☐ **First Down Set,** junior size rubber football and football soap-on-a-rope, 6 oz.
(3.95), Avon, 1965 .... 40.00   50.00

☐ **Freddie the Frog Floating Soap Dish,**
and 3-oz. soap (1.75), Avon, 1965 .... 20.00   25.00

☐ **Gaylord Gator,** 9½″ long, holds 3-oz.
soap (2.25), Avon, 1967 .... 12.00   15.00

☐ **Globe Bank,** bubble bath, plastic, 10 oz.
(2.50), Avon, 1966 .... 18.00   20.00

☐ **Humpty Dumpty,** bubble bath, 8 oz.
Avon, 1963 .... 15.00   17.00

Price Range

☐ **Jet Plane,** gel bubble bath, 3 oz. (1.50),
Avon, 1965 . . . .   17.00   20.00

☐ **Kiddie Kennel,** 3 dog-shaped soaps in
kennel-shaped box (1.49), Avon, 1955   135.00   145.00

☐ **Little Red Riding Hood,** bubble bath, 4
oz., with "Granny" glasses (1.50), Avon,
1968 . . . .   10.00   12.00

☐ **Monkey Shines Puppet Sponge,** and
soap, 3 oz. (3.00), Avon, 1969 . . . .   10.00   12.00

☐ **"Old 99" Train Engine,** soap (.69),
Avon, 1958 . . . .   40.00   50.00

☐ **Ring-Around Rosie,** elephant's trunk
holds 3-oz. soap (2.25), Avon, 1966 . .   25.00   30.00

☐ **Santa's Helpers,** 3 figure-shaped soaps,
Santa in red, two helpers in yellow and
green (1.19), Avon, 1955 . . . .   125.00   135.00

☐ **Speedy the Snail,** soap-on-a-rope, 4 oz.
(1.35), Avon, 1966 . . . .   20.00   30.00

☐ **Spinning Top,** bubble bath, 4 oz. (1.75),
Avon, 1966 . . . .   12.00   14.00

☐ **Spongaroo,** kangaroo foam sponge and
Baby Ru soap, 3 oz. (2.25), Avon, 1966   16.00   20.00

☐ **Three Little Bears,** soap, molded in three
bear shapes, boxed (1.10), Avon, 1954   125.00   135.00

☐ **Tin Man,** blue pipe, shampoo, 4 oz.
(1.50), Avon, 1967 . . . .   10.00   12.00

☐ **Toofie,** raccoon design, magenta tooth-
brush (1.25), Avon, 1967 . . . .   12.00   14.00

Price Range

☐ **Toofie on Guard,** green toothbrush
(1.25), Avon, 1968 . . . .   11.00   13.00

☐ **Toofie Tiger,** toothbrush (1.35), Avon,
1966 . . . .   15.00   18.00

☐ **Toofie Twosome,** clown design, tooth-
brush (1.25), Avon, 1964 . . . .   16.00   18.00

☐ **Toy Soldiers,** set of 4, lotion, shampoo,
bubble bath and hand lotion, 4 oz. each
(1.25 each), Avon, 1964 . . . . each 13.00   16.00

☐ **Tub Catch Fishing Rod,** and 3 plastic
fish, rod holds bubble bath, 6 oz. (3.50),
Avon, 1968 . . . .   15.00   16.00

☐ **Whitey the Whale,** bubble bath, 8 oz.
(1.69), Avon, 1959 . . . .   18.00   20.00

☐ **Yankee Doodle,** soap, 3 oz. (2.00), Avon,
1969 . . . .   11.00   13.00

☐ **Yo-Yo Set,** yo-yo and soap, 3 oz. (1.50),
Avon, 1966 . . . .   35.00   40.00

Jim Beam

Jim Beam bottles are unrivaled in their variety of styles, shapes, subjects, colors, and approach to modeling. With such a wide selection, a collector can choose them by topic according to such Beam specialties as "operas," "trophies" or "figurals."

The Beam bottles were first issued in the 1950s. The James B. Beam Distilling Company dates back to 1778, when it was founded by Jacob Beam. The company now bears the name of Colonel James B. Beam, Jacob's grandson. Beam whiskey was popular throughout the south during the 19th and 20th centuries, even though it was not widely distributed. The Northern Yankees often boasted of possessing "genuine Kentucky whiskey" after they had been able to purchase it.

In 1953, the Beam Distilling Company produced and sold bourbon in a special ceramic decanter for the Christmas and New Year season. Special packaging at that time by any spirits distiller was rare, and because these holiday decanters sold so well, Beam realized that more frequent creative bottling could increase sales. This decorative packaging led to a variety of series: Ceramics in 1953, Executive and Regal China in 1955, Political Figures and Customer Specialties in 1956, Trophy in 1957, and State in 1958.

The Executive series consisted of 22-karat gold decorated bottles issued to mark the corporation's 160th anniversary, distinguishing the Beam Distilling Company as one of the oldest continuing American business enterprises.

The Regal series proved one of the most popular of Beam bottles. They were issued to honor significant persons, places or events, based on Americana and the contemporary scene. The first Regal china bottle issued was the Ivory Ashtray.

In 1956, the Beam Political Figures series appeared with the traditional donkey and elephant, signifying the Democratic and Republican parties. They have been changed every four years with each presidential election.

Customer Specialties bottles were made on commission for customers who were usually liquor dealers or distributors. The first Customer Specialties bottle was created for the Foremost Liquor Stores of Chicago.

In 1958 and '59, the admittance of Alaska and Hawaii into the Union was commemorated with a Jim Beam bottle for each. The Beam Distilling Company continued to issue bottles in honor of the other 48 states.

Since 1953, over 500 types of Beam bottles have appeared. The ceramic bottles produced by the Wheaton Glass Company of Millville, New Jersey, have been more popular than the glass bottles.

Price Range

Jim Beam Bottles

1950

☐ **Pin Bottle,** short, 6-year-old bourbon, glass series 12.00

1953

☐ **Chateaux,** glass series 28.00

☐ **Cocktail Shaker,** glass series 12.00

☐ **Pin Bottle,** gold top, glass series 2.00

☐ **Pin Bottle,** white top, glass series 2.00

☐ **Royal Reserve,** glass series 4.00

1954

☐ **Pyrex Coffee Warmer,** glass series black 10.00

Price Range

gold	10.00
green	10.00
red	10.00
yellow	10.00

1955

☐ **Duck and Geese,** glass series 8.00

☐ **Royal Porcelain,** executive series 450.00

☐ **White Ashtray,** regal china series 20.00

1956

☐ **Black Foremost,** customer specialty ...   275.00

☐ **Democrat Donkey Ashtray,** political
series 17.00

☐ **Grey Foremost,** customer specialty ...   275.00

☐ **Pink Speckled Beauty,** customer specialty 500.00

☐ **Royal Gold Round,** executive series ..   130.00

☐ **Short Pinch Bottle,** glass series 30.00

1957

☐ **Mallard Duck,** trophy series 28.00

☐ **Man in Barrel,** #1, customer specialty   445.00

☐ **Royal Di Monte,** executive series 75.00

☐ **Sailfish,** trophy series 28.00

☐ **Silver Opal,** customer specialty 24.00

1958

☐ **Alaska Star,** state series 65.00

☐ **Grey Cherub,** executive series 350.00

	Price Range
☐ **Man in Barrel,** #2, customer specialty	225.00
☐ **Ram,** trophy series	120.00
☐ **Setter Dog,** trophy series	45.00
1959	
☐ **Colorado,** state series	38.00
☐ **Hawaii,** state series	44.00
☐ **Oregon,** state series	35.00
☐ **Tavern Scene,** executive series	67.00
1960	
☐ **Blue Cherub,** executive series	135.00
☐ **Kansas,** state series	59.00
☐ **Pheasant,** trophy series	22.00
☐ **Santa Fe,** centennial series	215.00
1961	
☐ **Civil War North.** centennial series	35.00
☐ **Civil War South,** centennial series	60.00
☐ **Golden Chalice,** executive series	73.00
1962	
☐ **Black Horse,** trophy series	24.50
☐ **Brown Horse,** trophy series	24.50
☐ **Flower Basket,** executive series	50.00
☐ **Marina City,** customer specialty	32.00
☐ **White Horse,** trophy series	24.50

Price Range

1963

☐ **Dancing Scot Short,** glass series 95.00

☐ **Harolds Grey,** customer specialty 185.00

☐ **Harrahs Grey,** customer specialty 600.00

☐ **Harrahs Silver,** customer specialty 950.00

☐ **Idaho,** state series 55.00

☐ **Montana,** state series 75.00

☐ **New Jersey,** state series 65.00

☐ **West Virginia,** state series 200.00

1964

☐ **Dancing Scot Tall Couple,** glass series   325.00

☐ **First National Bank,** customer specialty   3100.00

☐ **Harolds Club Nevada Silver,** customer
    specialty 185.00

☐ **Republican Elephant Boxers,** political
    series 17.00

1965

☐ **Green Fox,** trophy series 35.00

☐ **Harolds Club Pinwheel,** customer spe-
    cialty 62.00

☐ **Marbled Fantasy,** customer specialty   80.00

1966

☐ **Majestic,** executive series 36.00

☐ **Eagle,** trophy series 15.00

	Price Range
☐ **Oatmeal Jug,** customer specialty	50.00
☐ **Ohio,** state series	11.00

1967

☐ **Blue Fox,** club series	125.00
☐ **Blue Slot Machine,** customer specialty	15.00
☐ **Harolds Club VIP,** customer specialty	65.00
☐ **Kentucky,** black head stopper, state series	12.00
☐ **Kentucky,** brown head stopper, state series	30.00
☐ **Kentucky,** white head stopper, state series	25.00
☐ **Prestige,** executive series	16.00
☐ **Yellow Katz,** customer specialty	28.00

1968

☐ **Black Katz,** customer specialty	14.00
☐ **Broadmoore Hotel,** customer specialty	12.00
☐ **Cardinal,** trophy series	49.00
☐ **Harolds Club VIP,** customer specialty	75.00
☐ **Ruidosa Downs,** sport series	25.00
☐ **YUMA Rifle Club,** organization series	30.00

1969

☐ **Baseball,** sport series	12.00
☐ **Bell Scotch,** regal china series	18.00

	Price Range
☐ **Bell Scotch,** quart, regal china series . .	23.00
☐ **Blue Jay,** trophy series	10.00
☐ **Golden Nugget,** customer specialty . . .	40.00
☐ **Gold Fox,** club series	75.00
☐ **Harolds Club VIP,** customer specialty	300.00
☐ **Tall Pinch Bottle,** glass series	41.00
☐ **White Fox,** club series	45.00

Furnishings

Life With the Amoeba Chair

Furnishings and home decorations found in homes during the '50s and early '60s often reflected great experimentation. This, after all, was the era of American Modern (first called "moderne"), in which new synthetics developed during the war years abounded.

In the forefront of the new school of design was Russel Wright, who unveiled his first furniture line in 1934. Heavily upholstered and box-like, it was displayed at Bloomingdale's along with Wright's famous accessory line of curtains, carpets, lamps and tableware, attracting much curiosity but few buyers. It would be several years before the work of Wright and his contemporaries gained general public acceptance. As the *Antique Market Report* recently noted, "It was not until the '50s that these designs found popular acceptance, and hence became associated with that era." Until that time, "they had been viewed as elitist, designed by architects to complement a building's design concept and enhance the architect's reputation for innovation." The *Report* also pointed out that it wasn't until moderne dropped its pretentious final "e" that it finally "moved into the atomic age of tract houses, fiberglass draperies with geometric designs, and accessories in solid colors of pink, gray, lime, olive green, chocolate brown and black."

Partly through the exposure Wright's work gained during a 1983 exhibition at the Smithsonian (Wright died in 1976), and owing to what *Better Homes and Gardens* recently referred to as a new appreciation for "good design, sculptural beauty, and spare but sturdy construction," the works of Wright and others of his generation are starting to increase dramatically in value. A five-piece setting of Russel Wright dinnerware can now fetch $25 in New York, while a simple birch lounge chair made by Wright's contemporary Charles Eames carries a $550 price when found in top condition—an increase of hundreds of dollars in just a few years.

One of the most popular designs found in furnishings during the '50s and early '60s was the famous "amoeba" coffee table. Often copied, it traces its descent to sculptor Ismu Noguchi's original produced in 1944. One such original, with birch legs and long since out of production, recently commanded $3000 at a New York City store. Noguchi's design is again popular with home decorators seeking to emulate the '50s, as evidenced by the fact that the Herman Miller Company of Zeeland, Michigan, recently came out with a reissued version featuring either black or walnut legs for $995 retail.

The post-war years provided American designers with an opportunity to move into the limelight, while war-torn Europe (usually the leader in furniture designs) rebuilt. The coming of peace was reflected in the fresh, new looks which came from American designers during those years, with new materials developed during the war, such as plastics, plywood, tubular steel and aluminum, coming into frequent use.

Steve Starr, a collector of art deco and art moderne furnishings and accessories, says that current "hot" '50s furnishings are blond woods, which were very big in the '50s, along with wrought iron pieces and chairs with molded fiberglass seats and metal legs. Dark stained table legs are also common '50s touches. "So are atom shapes—as in a circular-faced clock surrounded by radiating spokes with balls at the tips," he was quoted as saying in *USA Today*. "The main thing about most '50s furniture is that it had a very casual look and was not easy to move around."

The designs of Wright, Eames, and others have lived on through collectors and historians. The '50s-'60s Modernist movement is an important period in an ever-changing and fickle America.

Price Range

Furniture and Accessories

☐ **Andirons,** brass, designed by Donald Deskey, c. 1955, height 19" 300.00   400.00

☐ **Bureau,** c. 1950, the dressing mirror of circular form surmounted on mirrored bureau with inset center section flanked by four drawers, 5'7" x 46" 600.00   900.00

☐ **Bedroom Suite,** manufactured by Aktlebolaget lggesunds Bruk, Sweden, 1956, each piece of concave form and raised on engaged sculptured openwork supports. Two nightstands, long chest, cabinet on a chest, headboard ..   1000.00   2000.00

☐ **Chairs,** set of two, "Potato Chip," designed by Charles Eames, molded plywood back and seat on U-shaped legs, height 29" 250.00   400.00

☐ **Chairs,** set of four, "Potato Chip," designed by Charles Eames for Herman Miller, metal U-shaped legs 400.00   700.00

☐ **Chairs,** set of six, walnut, designed by Gio Ponti for Singer Furniture, 1950, upholstered in brown checkered fabric   800.00   1500.00

☐ **Chairs,** set of two, lounge chairs designed by Swansky, 1960, fiberglass conical seat set on a culinical base and upholstered in brown vinyl, height 39"   300.00   600.00

☐ **Chest,** gray and cream lacquer, designed by Kittinger, 1950, rectangular with geometric design pulls 400.00   700.00

Price Range

- [ ] **China Closet,** by Gilbert Rohde for Herman Miller, 1950 .... 1000.00   2000.00

- [ ] **Floor Lamp,** aluminum, 1960, Knoll International, two vertical fluorescent tubes 300.00   500.00

- [ ] **Floor Lamp,** Barbieri, three-arm, 1950, tubular standard set with adjustable arms supporting enameled metal shades 300.00   600.00

- [ ] **Floor Lamp,** balance form, Italian, 1960, in gray and white 200.00   400.00

- [ ] **Hall Stand,** 1950s, tripod form with black tubular supports ending with spherical colored plastic coat balls 300.00   500.00

- [ ] **"Hollywood" Liquefier,** 1950, manufactured by the Hollywood Liquefier Company of California, molded in maroon and cream plastic 250.00   400.00

- [ ] **Mantel Clock,** circular, designed by George Nelson for Howard Miller, 1955, mounted on a brass stand 200.00   350.00

- [ ] **Occasional Table,** by Paul T. Frankl for Johnson Furniture Company, 1950, of oriental influence, raised on a mahogany frame 400.00   700.00

- [ ] **Pasta Set,** by Russel Wright, spun aluminum with rattan banding, casserole, two shakers and tongs 200.00   400.00

- [ ] **Sculpture,** by Mary Callery, 1960, contemporary metal sculpture composition piece, American 300.00   500.00

Price Range

☐ **Sculpture,** 1968, by Donovan Lee Coppock, contemporary sculpture from Wedge Series No. 11, American, model for large floor warp .... 200.00　400.00

☐ **Sculpture,** by David Weinrib, 1967, contemporary sculpture of two cast acrylic forms, one rose-amber the other yellow-amber .... 200.00　400.00

☐ **Side Chair,** Jaques Guillion, mahogany, 1950, veneered frame with a cord-strung seat and back rest .... 200.00　400.00

☐ **Table and Chairs,** by Frank Lloyd Wright, mahogany extension dining furniture, for Henredon, 1955, circular top edged with fretwork stamped copper band, four cross stretcher feet, eight chairs with octagonal padded backs and square seats upholstered in (original) green vinyl .... 5000.00　8000.00

Prints

The '50s and '60s saw a widespread vogue for Japanese art.

	Price Range	
☐ **Chaim Gross, "Martin Luther King,"** lithograph, 1968, signed in pencil, dated, inscribed "OK," image 18" x 15¾"	50.00	75.00
☐ **James Rosenquist, "See Saw,"** lithograph, printed in colors, 1968, signed in pencil, numbered ⁶⁷/₁₀₀, dated, sheet 24" x 34½"	200.00	250.00
☐ **Joan Miro, "Joan Miro Exhibition, Japan 1966,"** lithograph and poster printed in colors, signed in ink, sheet 22½" x 15½"	250.00	350.00
☐ **Karel Appel, "Untitled,"** lithograph, printed in colors, signed in pencil, numbered ¹⁹/₂₀₀, 26" x 19½"	200.00	300.00
☐ **Mark Chagall, "Abraham and Sarah,"** lithograph in color, from "The Bible," 1956, signed in crayon, 12½" x 9½"	300.00	400.00
☐ **Mark Chagall, "The Green Bird,"** lithograph and poster printed in colors, 1962, signed in pencil, poster 21" x 27½" ..	500.00	700.00
☐ **Maurits Cornels Escher, "New Year Cards,"** 4 cards printed for Eugene and Willy Strens, 1953–56, woodcuts, printed in color, sheets 7" x 6"	400.00	500.00

Price Range

☐ **Maurits Cornelis Escher, "Fish and Scales,"** woodcut, 1959, signed in pencil, inscribed 'eigendruck' on a japan paper, image 14¾" x 15" 1500.00 2000.00

☐ **Maurits Cornelis Escher, "Rippled Surface,"** linocut in black and gray/green, 1950, signed in pencil, on cream, thick paper, image 10" x 12½", taped to matte 2500.00 3000.00

☐ **Maurits Cornelis Escher, "Salamanders,"** woodcut, 1957, signed in pencil, on card, from 'Space Division,' earlier proof, image 9½" x 7" 400.00   600.00

☐ **Maurits Cornelis Escher, "Three Worlds,"** lithograph, 1955, signed in pencil, inscribed VAEVO, on cream Holland paper, image 14¼" x 9¾" . . .   1500.00 2500.00

☐ **Maurits Cornelis Escher, "Wild Dogs,"** woodcut, 1957, signed in pencil, on card, image 9½" x 7" 400.00   600.00

☐ **Paul Jenkins, "Abstract,"** lithograph printed in colors, 1969, signed in pencil, numbered ⁶/₁₀₀, dated, 13¾" x 10½"   150.00   200.00

☐ **Richard Lindner, "Nude in Art,"** lithograph and poster printed in colors, signed in pencil, 1964 . . . .   300.00   350.00

☐ **Richard Lindner, "Spoleto 1957–1967,"** color silkscreen, signed in pencil and numbered ⁶⁸/₁₀₀, sheet 39½" x 27" 300.00   400.00

Price Range

☐ **Tsuhuhary Foujita, "Two Friends,"** lithograph printed in colors, 1964, signed in pencil, annotated HC, image 22" x 18" 600.00   800.00

What We Bought

DESCRIPTION: Product-related memorabilia is one of the most popular forms of pop-culture collectibles. Some of the most creative talents of the '50s and '60s went into marketing the products we bought. To insure that everyone remembered a product, agencies came up with a multitude of catchy jingles and slogans. Remember what L.S.M.F.T. stood for? How about all those times we were told to "See the U.S.A. in Your Chevrolet?" And who can ever forget "You'll wonder where the yellow went when you brush your teeth with Pepsodent!"

TYPES COVERED: Automobiles, food products, cigarettes, premiums.

Automobiles

BACKGROUND: It was in 1896 that Henry Ford operated his first car—a twin cylinder, four-horse power quadricycle. Since then, collectors have specialized in everything from Edsels to auto advertising and auto literature. The nostalgia boom of the 1960s produced an increased interest in the "Classic Car" period.

BOOKS: *The Official Price Guide to Collector Cars,* House of Collectibles, New York, 1986.

Car Collectibles

Note: Prices quoted include "good" and "excellent."

	Price Range	
☐ **Alfa-Romeo 1900,** 1955, 4 cyl., coupe	5000.00	9000.00
☐ **Alfa-Romeo,** 1955, 4 cyl., coupe	3000.00	4000.00
☐ **Alfa-Romeo,** 1959, 3 litre, coupe	3300.00	6600.00
☐ **Amx,** 1968, 8 cyl. 2-passenger coupe . .	5000.00	7000.00
☐ **Amx,** 1969, 8 cyl., 2-passenger coupe . .	5000.00	7000.00
☐ **Asardo,** 1958, sport, coupe	6000.00	12500.00
☐ **Ascort,** 1959, corvair, gran turismo coupe	5500.00	9000.00
☐ **Ashley,** 1958, coupe	2000.00	7000.00
☐ **Ashley,** 1961, sportiva, coupe	2000.00	7000.00
☐ **Ashley GT 4 S,** 1961, sedan	2400.00	7800.00
☐ **Auburn 866 GP,** 1968, 8 cyl. (Ford), speedster	19000.00	28000.00
☐ **Austin A 40,** 1954, 4 cyl., coupe	5000.00	16000.00

Price Range

☐ **Austin Princess,** 1954, 4 cyl., sedan ... 5000.00 16000.00

☐ **Austin A 50,** 1955, convertible 6000.00 14000.00

☐ **Austin Princess,** 1958, 4 cyl., limousine 6000.00 13000.00

☐ **Bentley MK-VI,** 1951, sedan 7000.00 16000.00

☐ **Bentley S I,** 1958, convertible 36000.00 52000.00

☐ **Bentley S I,** 1958, sedan 12000.00 32000.00

☐ **Bentley S III,** 8 cyl., convertible 36000.00 70000.00

☐ **Bentley S III,** 8 cyl., sedan 18000.00 35000.00

☐ **B.M.W. Type 328,** 1953, drop head
coupe 4400.00 9800.00

☐ **B.M.W. 2000 CS,** 1965, coupe 6800.00 13000.00

☐ **Buick Super,** 1950, 8 cyl., hardtop 2550.00 7550.00

☐ **Buick Roadmaster,** 1950, 8 cyl., hardtop 3500.00 7500.00

☐ **Buick Special,** 1952, 8 cyl., sedan 2400.00 6200.00

☐ **Buick Super,** 1952, 8 cyl., convertible 4000.00 8000.00

☐ **Buick Century,** 1955, 8 cyl., convertible 4800.00 10800.00

☐ **Buick Special,** 1956, 8 cyl., hardtop ... 3000.00 6100.00

☐ **Buick Super,** 1957, 8 cyl., convertible 3100.00 8100.00

☐ **Buick Century,** 1958, 8 cyl., convertible 2150.00 6000.00

☐ **Buick Electra,** 1960, 4-door, hardtop
sedan 1000.00 1200.00

☐ **Buick Electra 225,** 1961, 8 cyl., convertible 3200.00 7600.00

☐ **Buick Electra 225,** 1963, 8 cyl., convertible 2500.00 7000.00

Price Range

☐ **Buick Electra 225,** 1966, 8 cyl., convertible 2800.00 7000.00

☐ **Buick Wildcat,** 1969, 8 cyl., convertible 3300.00 6600.00

☐ **Cadillac Coupe de Ville,** 1952, 2-door hardtop 4800.00 12600.00

☐ **Cadillac Eldorado,** 1953, convertible .. 14100.00 20000.00

☐ **Cadillac Fleetwood,** 1954, convertible 13575.00 22000.00

☐ **Cadillac Coupe de Ville,** 1956, hardtop 4600.00 11500.00

☐ **Cadillac Eldorado,** 1957, convertible .. 11500.00 27500.00

☐ **Cadillac 60-S Fleetwood,** 1958, sedan 2000.00 4900.00

☐ **Cadillac Coupe de Ville,** 1966, hardtop 2600.00 8000.00

☐ **Cadillac Eldorado FWD,** 1967, coupe 2400.00 7700.00

☐ **Cadillac Fleetwood,** 1969, limousine .. 5400.00 11300.00

☐ **Cadillac Coupe de Ville,** 1969, convertible 3800.00 9800.00

☐ **Chevrolet 210,** 1953, sedan 3000.00 4000.00

☐ **Chrysler New Yorker,** 1956, 4 door ... 3000.00 3500.00

☐ **Chevrolet Nomad,** 1955, 8 cyl., 2 door 8200.00 14000.00

☐ **Chevrolet Corvette,** 1955, 6 cyl., roadster 15000.00 31000.00

☐ **Chevrolet 210,** 1956, 8 cyl., hardtop ... 2200.00 4900.00

☐ **Chevrolet Corvette,** 1957, 8 cyl., roadster 13000.00 21000.00

☐ **Chevrolet El Morroco,** 1957, 8 cyl., hardtop 8200.00 14000.00

☐ **Chevrolet Bel Air,** 1958, 8 cyl., hardtop 8900.00 15000.00

Price Range

☐ **Chevrolet Impala,** 1960, 8 cyl., sport
coupe 3000.00 6200.00

☐ **Chevrolet Corvair,** 1960, 6 cyl., roadster
coupe 3300.00 6300.00

☐ **Chevrolet Corvair,** 1965, 6 cyl., sport
coupe 2800.00 5800.00

☐ **Chevrolet Nova SS,** sport coupe 1800.00 4100.00

☐ **Chevrolet Corvair,** 1967, 6 cyl., convert-
ible 3600.00 6700.00

☐ **Chevrolet Corvair,** 1969, 6 cyl., coupe 2900.00 5200.00

☐ **Chrysler Windsor,** 1951, 2-door hard-
top 2800.00 6500.00

☐ **Chrysler New Yorker,** 1951, 8 cyl., club
coupe 3200.00 7200.00

☐ **Chrysler New Yorker,** 1956, 8 cyl., con-
vertible 8400.00 21000.00

☐ **Chrysler New Yorker,** 1958, 8 cyl.,
sedan 4200.00 10400.00

☐ **Chrysler 300-D,** 1958, 8 cyl., hardtop 6500.00 16000.00

☐ **Chrysler 300-E,** 1959, 8 cyl., 2-door
hardtop 5600.00 16000.00

☐ **Chrysler 300-G,** 1961, 8 cyl., 2-door
hardtop 7600.00 16000.00

☐ **Chrysler 300,** 1964, 8 cyl., convertible 7000.00 14000.00

The Edsel: Beauty is in the Eye of the Collector

There is a story about a little old lady who owned a pink Citation—a top-of-the-line Edsel. She was ashamed to drive it around town because everybody teased her about owning the Edsel, "the ugliest car in the world." Finally she made a desperate phone call one night and asked if someone would come and get the Edsel—take it out of her garage, hide it so nobody would see it, and most importantly never tell anybody where he got it from. She sold it to an Edsel buff. Today the buff still smiles as he recounts the story—smiling all the way to the bank!

Perry Piper is proud to say that he's one of those early Edsel buffs, there at the beginning when the much-maligned lemon of the late '50s and early '60s could use a friend.

Edsel ad

Today, the Edsel Collector's Club is headed by Piper, who bought his first Edsel back in 1958, only because he couldn't get a Packard any more. "I tried to get one of those new Edsels that I knew would be around for a long time," he said, tongue-in-cheek, "but I had to settle for a '57 Ford that was a dog."

Perry tried to find a used Edsel to buy, but no one was trading. "Back in those days, the dealer would say, 'If you got an Edsel to trade, you keep the car and I'll give you $50.' "

There appeared to be no used Edsels, but Perry persisted in his search. "The owners who had them really were ashamed to admit to their neighbors that they owned an Edsel, or ever had.

"I wondered what had been the fate of the other 110,000 Edsel buyers, so I ran an ad in the car papers. It read, 'Edsel Owners Unite. Let's register our cars and share our woes.' Soon I had hundreds of letters coming in every week."

A fellow named Edsel Henry Ford (no relation to the giant car maker) called about the club, and Perry at once saw the publicity value. "I made him President *Pro Tem.* of the Edsel Owners Club. We were off and running."

A powerful and poignant question, "What went wrong with the Edsel?" is deep-rooted in the culture of the late '50s. The unfortunate answer lies in the definition of Edsel in The New American Dictionary: "the utmost in failure." As if this definition weren't enough, the car got the prize from *Life* magazine's contest listing the 10 best and 10 worst cars ever made. Edsel was right at the top of the list of the 10 worst cars.

"I was tickled to death *Life* named us the worst," said Perry. "I wouldn't want to be eighth or ninth on the list."

Actually, Perry feels the Edsel got a bad rap. "It was a good car planned five years ahead (unfortunately) for a market that was not there yet. It was a powerful gas guzzler

(9–15 miles per gallon), a true muscle car of its day. The aim was good, and the bullet right, but the problem was, the target (the public) moved."

Perry is proud of his 14-Edsel collection. He suggests collectors look for "all Edsel convertibles, which are collectible and have great potential in increasing value. In 1958, two Edsel convertibles were built. The Citation was the deluxe of the Edsels in many minds. This huge, beautiful monster was loaded. Only 930 were built. Double that many of the smaller Pacer model were made; and yet many think this convertible even more desirable than the Citation.

"The 1959 Corsair convertibles were all Ford mechanically (as opposed to the '58 Citation, which was on a Mercury frame) and command a good following." Rarest of all were the 1960 Edsel convertibles. Only 76 were made, and "these are the Edsels collectors talk about when high prices are mentioned."

Edsel literature and advertising is collectible, as the Edsel was one of the most researched and promoted cars in history. "Prices are reasonable for common items, and for extremely rare items prices may range upward from several hundred dollars. Model cars that were giveaways in 1958 are now finding ready markets for $60 and up depending on the condition."

Many related items are available and collectible, such as dealer books, key chains, view master reels, wax cans, banners, floor mats, TV ads, and promotional films. Perry said, "It is amazing that so much material exists since the car was discontinued so suddenly without notice. Dealers were so disillusioned and hurt by the failure of the car that they were glad to wipe the slate clean of the word Edsel and anything associated with it."

The Edsel was just a big, powerful, gas-guzzling monster that the American public was supposed to hail as the ultimate in modern machinery in the late '50s, when the bywords of Americans were "much, more and most." Something went wrong with either the design or the philosophy, or with the mechanics, because the Edsel flopped as no other car in the history of automaking has done, before or since.

The car was named in honor of Henry Ford's only son, Edsel, who was a nice, affable fellow who never could measure up to his father's demands. Henry Ford had wanted his son's name to go down in history, and it certainly did—way down.

To join the Edsel Owners Club, write to Perry Piper, President, West Liberty, IL 62475, and he will be happy to include you in the biggest losers' club there is. The one requirement to membership in the club: you have to own at least one example of the "worst car in the world."

Price Range

Edsel Cars

☐ **Edsel Ranger,** 1958, 8 cyl., 2-door hardtop 3000.00 4500.00

☐ **Edsel Citation,** 1958, 8 cyl., 4-door hardtop 2325.00 5000.00

☐ **Edsel Citation,** 1958, 8 cyl., 2-door hardtop 2400.00 4750.00

☐ **Edsel Citation,** 1958, 8-cyl., convertible 3300.00 14750.00

☐ **Edsel Ranger,** 1959, 8 cyl., 2-door hardtop 3500.00 8000.00

☐ **Edsel Corsair,** 1959, 8 cyl., convertible 5000.00 12950.00

☐ **Edsel Corsair,** 1959, 8 cyl., 2-door hardtop 2200.00 4000.00

☐ **Edsel Ranger,** 1960, 8 cyl., 2-door hardtop 2650.00 5500.00

☐ **Edsel Ranger,** 1960, 8 cyl., convertible 3000.00 7600.00

Price Range

Edsel Literature

☐ "This is the Edsel," large 12½ x 15 ED7101 showroom folder 30.00

☐ "This is the Edsel," smaller version ED7102 .... 12.00

☐ "This is the Edsel," fold-out showing all models ED7103 .... 8.00

☐ Product Information Service Letter, Canadian, one of series 4.00

☐ Salesmans' Film Strip, meeting plan with record, one of 8 .... 35.00

☐ An Announcement by Henry Ford II about new car, 8½ x 11 .... 12.00

☐ Edsel Pointers, Sept. 1957 (only issue) magazine 24.00

☐ Soft Trim Catalogue, shows interiors and paint in pictures 45.00

☐ Planning a New Automobile, by Emery Judge, 8½ x 11 .... 30.00

☐ Edsel Specifications Form 5707, 3 x 6   14.00

☐ "Once in a Lifetime Invitation to Grand Showing, Sept. 4, 1957 .... 11.00

☐ Viewmaster, with viewer and 5 reels on the Edsel 230.00

☐ Automatic Transmission Manual Form 5705 .... 24.00

☐ Edsel Scotchlite Road Signs Catalogue   26.00

☐ Press Packet for 1958 Edsel, complete   95.00

	Price Range

☐ **Salesman's Card with Citation,** in color ... 7.00

☐ **Air Conditioner Manual Form 5706** .. 24.00

☐ **Edsel Announcement Materials,** 18" x 18", many pages rare 275.00

☐ **Salesman Data Book,** spiral bound, 7¾ x 9¼ 200.00

☐ **Edsel Color and Upholstery Selections Soft Trim Book** 240.00

☐ **Master Parts Catalogue Ed7062.** Large, many sections 120.00

☐ **Salesman Desk Pad,** 17½" x 22" 8.00

☐ **Book Published by Chrysler for Them to Compare Edsel,** rare 80.00

Additional Cars

☐ **Ford Customline,** 1952, 8 cyl., club coupe 2000.00   4500.00

☐ **Ford Crestline,** 1952, 8 cyl., victoria ... 2600.00   5000.00

☐ **Ford Crestline,** 1954, 8 cyl., sedan 3500.00   8400.00

☐ **Ford Country Squire,** 1955, 8 cyl., station wagon 2600.00   5000.00

☐ **Ford Fairlane,** 1955, 8 cyl., victoria ... 2600.00   7600.00

☐ **Ford Fairlane,** 1956, 8 cyl., 2-door station wagon 3900.00   9000.00

☐ **Ford Thunderbird,** 1957, 8 cyl., roadster 14600.00   35400.00

☐ **Ford Thunderbird,** 1961, 8 cyl., hardtop 1600.00   5600.00

☐ **Ford Galaxie 500,** 1963, 8 cyl., hardtop 2100.00   4100.00

Price Range

☐ **Ford Mustang,** 1965, 8 cyl., hardtop ..   3000.00   5400.00

☐ **Ford Mustang GT,** 1966, 8 cyl., hardtop   6500.00 10500.00

☐ **Ford Thunderbird,** 1967, 8 cyl., hardtop   3600.00   8200.00

☐ **Ford Mustang Talladega (Torino),**
1969, 8 cyl., convertible 1600.00   5600.00

☐ **Lincoln Capri,** 1954, convertible 11500.00 12500.00

☐ **Lincoln Cosmopolitan,** 1950, 4-door
sedan 5000.00   6000.00

☐ **Mercedes-Benz 190SL,** 1959, both hard
and rag tops 19000.00 20000.00

☐ **Studebaker Champion,** 6 cyl., light
coupe 3000.00   7000.00

☐ **Studebaker Commander,** 1954, (V) 8
cyl., coupe 3000.00   6800.00

☐ **Studebaker President,** 1955, (V) 8 cyl.
259, coupe 3500.00   7200.00

☐ **Studebaker Golden Hawk,** 1958, (V) 8
cyl. 289, coupe 7800.00 12000.00

☐ **Studebaker Avanti,** 1963, (V) 8 cyl.,
coupe 7900.00 17000.00

☐ **Studebaker Daytona,** 1964, (V) 8 cyl.,
hardtop 2600.00   5200.00

Mail Order Autos

Bill McBride has 100,000-plus ads for all cars and trucks, American and foreign, from the turn of the century to the present, located on the second floor of his Hartford, Connecticut, rare book shop, which is known as the Jumping Frog. "We are always sending shipments out on approval with a price list," he told us. "People return what they don't want with a check for what they keep. We don't often get stiffed, but sometimes it takes us a couple years to get our stuff back. There's a basic honesty in this area and we're not at a terrible risk." McBride tries to send out as many ads as possible; however, sometimes a request can be very specific, say for a '62 Buick Electra Convertible. "Then we only have one ad to send anyway." Frequently, though, he'll get customers who will buy 100 at a time.

McBride Auto Ads is the name he uses for his mail-order business. He advertises mostly in *Hemmings Motor News.* The auto ads on the second floor are readily available to anyone who walks in and wants to browse.

McBride describes the auto ad collector as primarily an auto buff. They are the sort "who likes to try to get every picture of the '55 Pontiac, or are interested in specific mod-

Ford ad

els, or need reference information for restoration of paint color, trim, that sort of thing," he explained. Sometimes the requests are rather unusual, but McBride tries to fill it. "I saw an ad placed under the Antique Cars For Sale classifieds in the *Hartford Courant* several years ago asking for any and all information on 1902 Pope–Hartford mobiles, which is a descendant of the Pope Bicycles. The person was in Texas and said they wanted any information available on the Pope. They told us we were the only people from the Hartford area who sent anything. We had a couple of small black-and-white ads that gave him a couple of bits of information which he didn't have at all before."

There were a number of cars made in Connecticut at one time, with about 2,200 different makes and brands made in the United States alone. "It's pretty hard to find a state east of the Mississippi that didn't have half a dozen or more cars made in it. Out west, it's more limited because the auto was brand new at the turn of the century and the territory from the Mississippi to the west coast wasn't as well populated as the Industrial East."

Auto ad collecting is an inexpensive hobby for those who may not be able to afford the car itself. "They certainly can afford to buy an ad for a dollar or two dollars or three dollars, and there's a certain fun in trying to get, for example, every different '56 Chevy ad. And some ads are harder to find than others. They're in publications that aren't readily available or aren't popular." It can sometimes take years to locate a particular ad, so, as is the case with collecting anything, part of the fun is in the search.

The first Corvette came out in '53 and advertising for the car began almost immediately. The advertising was quite extensive through '68, but dropped to only one or two ads per year from '69 to the present. "There's a tremendous and ongoing interest in Corvette advertising," McBride says.

Corvette advertising appears in two general areas. "For the general public it's in *Sports Illustrated* and the *New Yorker*, from the 1950s to '68," says McBride. "Beyond that it gets very scattered. The second area is in car buff magazines like *Car and Driver, Road and Track, Motor Trend* and *Hot Rod*—the publications for the enthusiast." In the middle '50s, when *Sport* magazine was giving away a Corvette to the Most Valuable Player in the World Series, there were always a couple of Corvette ads in the magazine to tie-in with the promotion.

McBride says that all but one of the cars manufactured in the post-war years were "warmed over '42s." "The only exception was the Studebaker, which was introduced as a 1947 model. It was a completely different design outside, but the mechanics were still quite similar to the pre-war." A few '46 Studebakers had been produced but were never advertised. "They looked like '42s basically, but the '47 was really the first post-war Studebaker." In fact, McBride adds, their line was "First by far with a post-war car." Right after the war, a new car could almost be put up for auction. "You could never buy it for what the price sticker read," McBride emphasizes. As a matter of fact, they weren't even in the show room. "You would order it and wait until it came in and hope that you would receive it."

Photographs were not regularly used in automobile advertising until the '60s. Illustration was always the preferred method—a painting or drawing of the car—primarily because it gave the manufacturer and advertising agency an opportunity to exaggerate by making the car look bigger than it was and the people smaller. The last maker to use illustration was Pontiac, who used it up until '71–'72, then abandoned it. The earliest color photograph for an auto ad appeared in 1909 for a Pierce-Arrow. "It was a full-color photograph done by the Lumiere color process, introduced only the year before," says McBride. "In less than a year the color process was used to illustrate a Pierce-Arrow ad. Pierce had always used illustration, and after that (one) photo they went back to illustration until the '30s." Near the end of the Pierce Company's existence, they did use photos again, from 1934–1936.

"When talking about the post-war era, photography in advertising had been used more than you think," says McBride. "If you look at something like fashion advertising, it was used all the time, for *Vogue* and *Vanity Fair*. But after the '30s, it was almost always used for food and hard goods." This is because food products can be made to look more appetizing in a photograph than in a drawing.

There were attempts to sell economy cars, as we can see by going back to the Austin Bantam, which had a rooster as its symbol. The Bantam was an English car manufactured in America. It was about the size of a Volkswagen Beetle and could hold four people. "It was sold as a second car rather than a prime means of transportation," McBride explains. "The Ford Model A, and its immediate ancestor, the Model T, were sold as a basic, economical, functional piece of transportation. Later, some ads for the Model A, placed in *Vogue* and other publications, sold it as a stylish and very upbeat car to drive, when the limousine just wouldn't do." In 1952 the Henry J was brought out by Kaiser-Frazer, with Henry J. Kaiser as the head of Kaiser-Frazer. The Kaiser utilized celebrities like Burns and Allen, Art Linkletter, and Irene Dunn to help promote their product with the advertising. "I don't put a premium on car ads that feature a celebrity—people do want them and they are of special interest, but not to automobile collectors," says McBride. To movie star fans, however, celebrities represent an interesting sidestep into the hobby of movie memorabilia collecting. The idea of celebrities, or "well-known" persons, endorsing a company's product goes back to the 1920s at least. "There were explorers endorsing the cars—people taking them on expeditions to Africa," muses Bill. The "talkies" provided the celebrity with a profile, and more public visibility than in the '20s, when movies were silent. In the mid 1930s DeSoto utilized such celebrities as Bing Crosby, Jack Dempsey, Lowell Thomas, Walt Disney, Clark Gable and Gary Cooper, among others. However, there were some semi-celebrities endorsing the cars in the 1920s as well.

"Quite early in the 1950s you start to get the TV people," says McBride. "In '58 and '59 you had Ed Sullivan for Mercury, in '59, Helen Hayes for Lincoln; Bing Crosby came back to endorse the '59 Oldsmobile and others lent their names to various makes." Just two years before selling Oldsmobile in 1939, Bing was the happy face for the 1938 DeSoto, and the year before DeSoto he sold for the 1937 Dodge. "Bing knew where the money was," laughed McBride.

When McBride first started his business, he received more requests for '55–'57 Chevys and Model A Fords than much of anything else. Today, he doesn't know what kind of request he is going to get. "There isn't really any way to categorize it; I get requests from 'I'd like to collect every Studebaker ad that ever was printed' to 'I need an ad for a 1941 Ford dump truck.' It's not particularly heavily balanced [in collector interest] in any one direction, with the exception of Corvette, and that is because it is America's only sports car. It has a sustaining interest and the ads command a premium." McBride gets twice the price for a Corvette ad than he does for any other. The ads are harder to get, have appeared in few publications, and there is a great demand for them. "There is no particular peak on the charts for any particular ad except Corvette at this time," he says.

The '50s automobile designs were influenced by a number of occurrences during that decade, most especially the rise of the jet plane. "That's what gave us the fins," says McBride. Many of the cars used the F86 Sabre jets in their ads in an effort to relate the autos to the jet planes. Almost immediately thereafter came space travel, which was to prove very influential in all of the decades following. "It had a heavy influence on the design of the cars, and of course the design of the ads, which was an offshoot of the car itself. The car generally dictates what the ad is going to be. Of course, you don't really try to relate a jet plane with a Nash Rambler. It just doesn't work," he laughed.

McBride's Jumping Frog bookstore and mail-order auto ads are located at 161 South Whitney, Hartford, Connecticut (06105) for anyone who is interested in pursuing the hobby of auto ad collecting.

Campbell's Soup

Collectibles That Are M'm! M'm! Good!

"M'm! M'm! Good! M'm! M'm! Good! That's what Campbell soups are—M'm! M'm! Good!"

Everyone who watched TV in the '50s and '60s knows the happy singers of this commercial jingle—the famous Campbell Kids!

In talking with Geraldine Wine, enthusiastic collector of Campbell soups and Campbell Kids collectibles and founder of the International G. G. Drayton Association, much has been learned about this fascinating area of collecting, which stretches over the past 100 years.

Campbell's Boy "Kid"

Campbell's Girl "Kid"

Ms. Wine, who is quite knowledgeable about Grace Drayton and her collectibles—yet modest about her sizable collection—says she began collecting Drayton objects about 30 years ago, accumulating dolls and soup promotional items, such as banks and advertising pages. There were about 2000 different advertisements designed for Campbell soup from September 1905 through the late 1960s, and Miss Wine has about 1500 of these pages in her possession.

Ms. Wine's obsession with collecting began when she was a child back in the 1930s. "I used to sit and cut Grace Drayton's Dolly Dingle paper dolls out of the *Pictorial Review.* (There were, she says, 203 pages of Dolly Dingle cutouts in the *Review* from 1913 to 1933. "Today I have 202 of them. I never could find that last one!")

In the 1950s and '60s, Campbell Kids appeared on items such as quilts, sandpails, paper clips, and kitchen canisters. One of the more desirable items, the Fisher Price truck with wobbly Campbell Kid driver and vegetable cutouts, has a wide price range, Miss Wine explains. "I hesitate to estimate a price, because there is such a variety in prices on these items across the United States." She went on to explain that in the East, the Fisher Price truck might sell for $25, but that on the West Coast, it could go for as much as $125. (The prices that she has compiled for this book are estimates at best; they could vary greatly because they are dependent upon the regional availability of the collectible.)

Collectors of Campbell Kids memorabilia recall the '50s as the time of the "Big Birthday Celebration" ad campaign for the Campbell Kids. November issues of *Life* magazine from 1954, 1955 and 1956 ran numerous ads commemorating the Kids and recognizing their contribution to the American home scene.

Portrait of Grace Gebbie Drayton

Grace Gebbie became a commercial artist in 1893, at the tender age of 17. At 18 she sold her first magazine sketch and landed a contract to produce a newspaper comic strip called "Toodles and Pussy Pumpkins." Later, she produced children's books, magazine features, advertisements, and post cards. She drew the popular Dolly Dingle paper dolls and provided cover illustrations for the *Saturday Evening Post.* She began drawing the Campbell Kids in 1904, and continued to draw them for magazines, advertisements, posters and other future collectibles for the next 20 years. The Kids first appeared in a magazine advertisement in *Ladies Home Journal.* Gebbie was active until her death in 1936, and used various pen names over the years, including Margaret G. Hays, Grace Gebbie, Grace G. Wiederseim, Grace G. Drayton, and G. G. Drayton. A colorful personality, Grace Drayton claimed to have copied the features of herself as a child when she drew the famous Campbell Kids. The Kids' popularity declined in the Depression years, but, with television coming into the homes of many Americans in the early 1950s, they were revived and enjoyed great success with the public.

Today the '50s and '60s Kids live on in the form of everything from dolls and cooking sets to thermometers bearing their cherubic faces. Among the items in Geraldine's collection is a pair of 1910 Campbell Kids dolls, which, with a price tag of $100 to $125 each, are the most valuable items a Kids collector can hope to find. The "Can't Break 'Em" Kids came out in 1910, and Ms. Wine advises that "some of the earlier so-called Campbell Kid dolls are not real Campbell Kids. Beware of this discrepancy. Many people lump them together, but there is a difference. Grace Drayton did illustrate many children's books, but the children appearing in these books are not Campbell Kids."

The International G. G. Drayton Association is an organization separate from the Campbell Soup Company, Ms. Wine explains. "The Campbell Company about three years ago started to compile a list of memorabilia," enlisting the help of collectors and the International Grace Gebbie Drayton Association.

Geraldine founded the Association (commemorating Grace Gebbie Drayton, the artist who conceived the Campbell Kids early in the century) in 1978. "I'm the editor, president, vice president, treasurer, secretary, and all-around Girl Friday for the Association," she laughs. Its newsletter, the *Kids Illustrated Drayton Supplement* (*K.I.D.S.* for short), is available for $6 per year and provides recipients with information and photos, descriptions and offers for Campbell soups and Campbell Kids memorabilia five times per year. (To join, write to Geraldine Wine, 649 Bayview Drive, Akron, OH 44319.)

Geraldine remarks that there is no museum and no convention for the International G. G. Drayton Association at present, "although I'd love to get everyone together and show off our collectibles." The 130 current members of the Association will hopefully expand and be able to sponsor such an event in the future. "That's the only way to learn about new items and meet each other," says Ms. Wine.

Candy Bars

BACKGROUND: Back in 1894, Milton S. Hershey manufactured the first American chocolate bars. They were the Hershey Almond Bar and the Hershey Milk Chocolate Bar. The candy bar cost five cents in the 1950s and '60s, moving up to 10 cents in 1968. The main ingredients in a candy bar are chocolate, nougat, fudge, caramel, and marshmallow, although coconut and a variety of other nuts are included.

In the early days, the candy bar was individually wrapped—now, according to Ray Broekel in his *The Great American Candy Bar Book,* the National Confectioners Association claims it takes but a minute to wrap approximately 110 candy bars by machine, seal 180 bags of orange-flavored slices, wrap 600 pieces of hard candy, or wrap 750 pieces of toffee or caramel.

BOOKS: *The Great American Candy Bar Book,* Ray Broekel, Houghton Mifflin Company, 1982.

Peter Paul candy bar ad   Mars candy bar ad

Cigarettes

Time to "Light Up a Lucky"

"Smoke Gets in Your Eyes," recorded in 1959 by the immortal Platters, may be just right for a theme song for the smoking generation of the '50s and '60s. Everyone who was anyone smoked cigarettes. The world of the 1950s in particular was often viewed through a smokescreen. Many would "Walk a Mile for a Camel," and "Light My Lucky" was heard on every street corner and in every home.

The proof of the pudding was in every issue of *Life, Saturday Evening Post,* and other popular magazines of the period appearing on newsstands, where full-page ads showed the "pleasures" of smoking. And if you further doubted the wisdom of smoking, you could simply turn on the TV and

Lucky Strikes ad

be convinced by commercials exhorting the merits of Winston ("Winston Tastes Good, Like a Cigarette Should"), or inviting you to "Come Up to Marlboro Country."

Dick Elliott, long-time collector of cigarette memorabilia, and president of the Cigarette Pack Collectors Association, believes that "Cigarette pack collecting captures much of the 'art' of our popular culture." Trends, fads and notions of what the public liked and bought can be discovered from collecting cigarette memorabilia.

Regarding cigarette pack collecting as a hobby, Dick says, "There are still many packs and tins to be found at reasonable prices. Cigarette labels and advertising items continue to surface and often can be found for sale in the trade publications such as the *Antique Trader Weekly* and *Collectors News.* The period of the 1950s and 1960s was particularly rich with cigarette brands."

Dick has over 700 U. S. brands in his collection, along with about 3000 foreign labels. He says, "The U. S. brands date back to the 1880s, when cigarettes were sold in small 'slide shell' boxes with names like Dog's Head, Crosscut and Virginia Brights. From the '50s and '60s, some of the more collectible cigarette packs were Hale, a chlorophyl cigarette which was popular during the brief craze for the green additive. Waterford was a water filter cigarette based on tiny pockets of water which were released with a pinch. Brands extolling 'Stevenson for President' or 'I Like Ike' and given away during the 1952 campaign were manufactured by Tobacco Blending of Louisville. Little King pictured the famous cartoon character. Brand X was the '60s brand that 'insisted on comparison.' Vogue featured multi-colored cigarettes. Cookie Jar and Cake Box were regional favorites. Embassy sponsored some of the early TV programs in the '50s. Alligator enjoyed a brief popularity in the early 1950s and featured a puffing Alligator logo." Hit Parade is also often mentioned because people associate it with the popular TV show of the same era.

For new collectors, Dick advises, "Pick up the new brands. Often, brands last only a few months and are tomorrow's collectibles. For instance, the short-lived Real of 1983 was such a product. Find out about test market brands, and check out the flea markets and antique shops for old tins and boxes."

Dick remarks that the Cigarette Pack Collectors Association has about 200 members worldwide and is open to new memberships. Dues are $5 per year, which includes six issues of *Bandstand,* the Association's newsletter. "Ads in the newsletter are free to subscribers and non-subscribers," he adds. The address is Cigarette Pack Collectors Association, 61 Searle Street, Georgetown, MA 01833.

There will be a convention for the Cigarette Pack Collectors in late August of 1987 in Greensboro, North Carolina. An attraction to collectors interested in the tobacco industry is the Tobacco/Textile Museum, which is located in Danville, Virginia, and is open to the public.

The popularity of cigarette smoking has decreased with negative medical publicity and the ban on tobacco advertising on television, prompting many to "kick the habit." But back in the '50s and '60s, smoking was still "Kool," and tobacco products and their advertising reflected the times, public opinion and everyday life. Truly a collectible of "Old Gold" quality.

Price Range

Cigarette Packs

☐ **Alligator,** Larus & Bros., early 1950s ..	8.00	10.00
☐ **Cake Box,** Levitt & Pierce Tobacco Stores, private label, c. 1950s	5.00	8.00
☐ **Camel,** tins, flat fifty and round 100s or 50s, c. 1950	12.00	15.00

	Price Range	
☐ **Cavalier,** R. J. Reynolds, 100s, oval tin, c. 1960s	10.00	12.00
☐ **Colony,** American Tobacco, 1966	5.00	8.00
☐ **Cookie Jar,** R.R. Tobin, 1957	5.00	8.00
☐ **Embassy,** Lorillard, c. 1950s	5.00	8.00
☐ **Hale,** chlorophyl added, 1957	7.00	8.00
☐ **Hit Parade,** American Tobacco, 1956 . .	10.00	12.00
☐ **Holiday,** Laurus & Bros., pipe tobacco in a cigarette, c. 1950s	4.00	6.00
☐ **I Like Ike,** Tobacco Blending, c. 1950s	12.00	15.00
☐ **Regent,** Riggio Tobacco Co., boxed, c. 1950s	4.00	6.00
☐ **Sano,** US Tobacco, 1951	4.00	6.00
☐ **Spring,** Lorillard, c. 1950s	4.00	6.00
☐ **Stevenson For President,** Tobacco Blending, 1952	12.00	15.00
Skins, US Tobacco, early 1957	7.00	10.00
☐ **Vanity Fair,** pink or blue, American Tobacco, 1957	7.00	10.00
☐ **Virginia Rounds,** Benson & Hedges, dates back to 1940s but was popular in the 1950s	5.00	8.00
☐ **Vogue,** Stephano Bros., 1955	8.00	10.00
☐ **Waterford,** American Tobacco, water filter, c. 1960s	6.00	8.00

Coca-Cola

Coca-Cola Collectibles Are The Real Thing!

When the Coca Cola Company made what many consider the worst blunder in their history by changing the formula which had made them famous for the last 100 years, they also gained a lot of publicity for "The Real Thing."

"Our membership grew last year by 30 percent because of the publicity concerning Classic Coke and the new formula," said Randy Schaeffer, Publications Director for the Coca Cola Collectors Club International.

The club counts almost 5000 members among its ranks, hailing from 16 different countries. At the annual convention in 1986, over 2100 people descended upon the city of Atlanta (birthplace of Coca Cola in 1886) over the 4th of July week. "We hold the convention in a different place every year," Randy says. "In 1987, it will be in Cincinnati, during the first week of August. The following year we'll gather in Philadelphia." Members of the club also hold smaller, statewide conventions at more frequent intervals.

"Annual dues are $15, and for this sum members receive a monthly newsletter, which has articles about 'old stuff,' free classifieds, and information about what is happening in the world of Coke collecting," Schaeffer said.

His collection, shared by fellow collector William Bateman, is comprised of 20,000 items, and is believed to be the largest private collection of Coke collectibles in the world. Schaeffer says the collectible items from the popular period of the '50s and '60s includes metal trays, which are usually valued under $20. Eddie Fisher's TV show, "Coketime," ran for four years, from 1953 to 1957, and prompted many items which have increased in value through the years. Promotional items and giveaways from this show, including a cardboard cutout of Eddie, which is worth about $35, and a 45-rpm record, which may be worth from $5 to $10, are representative items.

Other items from these years include calendars, which the Coca Cola Company produced every year, and cardboard displays. A '50s calendar is worth from $20 to $30 today, and one dating from the '60s goes for about $10 less. "A big item to collect is cans," Schaeffer states. "In the late '50s and early '60s, there were different designs, by which you can effectively date the cans. From around 1959 to the early '60s, there was the large diamond can design, which is worth about $20 today. Then in the mid-'60s, the design was changed to a red and white checkerboard pattern, which is worth about $10." The metal serving trays, too, have changed off and on, such as the 1961 Pansy Garden tray and the Menu Girl tray from 1953, which brings about $20.

"The most valuable item in my collection would have to be the leaded glass Tiffany-type hanging shade," Schaeffer says. "It's rectangular, and I think it's the only one known. That type of shade hung in drugstores.

"The most valuable items from Coca Cola probably date primarily from before World War I. Coca Cola was not the earliest soft drink around, but it's been the most popular for quite a while. Hires bottled root beer in 1876, Dr. Pepper appeared in 1885, and Pepsi's been around since the 1890s." Coca Cola is in the middle, having first appeared in 1886. "I think the collectibles from Coca Cola represent a reflection of the times. Look at advertising from Coke products, and you've got a record of the last 100 years and the values those years represent in terms of advertising."

Randy started collecting Coke products about 15 years ago. He's proud of the quality and scope of his collection, and wants to stress the fact that "it's not just quantity."

How does Randy feel about Coke itself? "Yes, I drink Coke a lot. I like it. I prefer Classic, along with about every Coke drinker I can think of." Spoken like a true Coca Cola fan!

If you're a Coke fan and want to join the Coca Cola Collectors Club International, write to Publications Director Randy Schaeffer, Route 4, Box 2, Kutztown, PA 19530, for information about the club.

Price Range

Coca-Cola Collectibles

☐ **Ashtray,** aluminum, c. 1955 . . . .   3.00   6.00

☐ **Ashtray,** metal, 1963 . . . .   18.00   22.00

☐ **Cigarette Lighter,** musical, c. 1960 . . . .   30.00   40.00

☐ **Clock,** brass mantel type, c. 1954 . . . . .   95.00   150.00

☐ **Clock,** dome style, c. 1950 . . . .   180.00   200.00

Coca-Cola Santa

	Price Range	
☐ **Cardboard Cutout with Eddie Fisher,** 1953–57	30.00	40.00
☐ **Pansy Garden Tray,** 1961	5.00	15.00
☐ **Calendars,** 1950s, each	20.00	30.00
☐ **Calendars,** 1960s, each	10.00	20.00
☐ **Cans,** late 1950s, early 60s		
Large diamond can	15.00	25.00
Checkerboard can	5.00	15.00
☐ **Metal Trays,** 1953, menu girl on tray ..	15.00	25.00
☐ **Record,** 45 rpm, from Eddie Fisher's "Coketime" show, 1953–57	5.00	10.00

Edgar Bergen and Charlie McCarthy
Coca-Cola ad, 1950

Premiums

BACKGROUND: Premiums were often targeted toward children, beginning with the hey-day of radio adventure in the 1920s. A box top, a label or a red triangle—a request of proof of purchase—was usually required to send away for a cookbook, mug, drinking glass, or a badge from a favorite adventure hero like Buck Rogers or Tom Mix. Not only did the advertiser offering the premium sell more products, but public response was mirrored in the comparable popularity of a radio or TV show, like the "Cisco Kid" and "Howdy Doody."

Price Range

Premium Collectibles

☐ **"Captain Video,"** photo ring, 1950s, Powerhouse candy bar premium 50.00   60.00

☐ **"Cisco Kid,"** face mask, 1953 Tip-Top Bread premium 12.00   18.00

☐ **Gabby Hayes,** cannon ring, 1950s Quaker premium 40.00   50.00

☐ **Gabby Hayes,** ring, 1951 Quaker premium 15.00   25.00

☐ **"Howdy Doody,"** climber, 1951 Welch Grape Juice premium 35.00   45.00

☐ **"Howdy Doody,"** history album, 1950s Wonder Bread premium, 8 pp. 15.00   25.00

☐ **"Howdy Doody,"** mug, 1950s Ovaltine premium, rare 35.00   45.00

☐ **Lone Ranger,** photo, 1951 Cheerios premium, rare 25.00   35.00

	Price Range	
☐ **Lone Ranger,** life-size poster, 1950s Wheaties premium	65.00	85.00
☐ **Lone Ranger,** comic book, 1954 Cheerios premium	25.00	35.00
☐ **Mickey Mouse,** magic kit, 1955 Mars Candy premium, instructions for 20 tricks	35.00	45.00
☐ **Mickey Mouse,** puppet, 1955 Donald Duck Bread premium, cardboard punch-out assembles into moveable puppet	20.00	30.00
☐ **Roy Roger's,** coin, 1952 Post Cereal premium	10.00	15.00

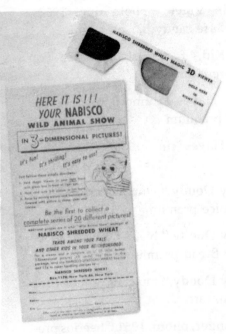

3-D memorabilia

Price Range

☐ **Sgt. Preston,** Ten-in-One Trail Kit,
1950s Quaker premium 75.00   100.00

☐ **Sgt. Preston,** totem pole, five different
1952 Quaker Oats premiums 20.00   25.00

What We Read

TYPES COVERED: Books (hardcover and paperback), magazines, newspapers.

Books

Hardcover Books

BACKGROUND: Science fiction and fantasy made great inroads during the decades of the '50s and '60s, with the emergence of authors such as Isaac Asimov and Ray Bradbury. The popularity of the genre prompted companies to rush "new" Edgar Rice Burroughs titles onto the market. In collecting hardcovers, it is always important to preserve the paper covers whenever possible. Because they often contain art and information not reproduced elsewhere in the book, and because of their ephemeral nature, dust jackets can be worth more than the volume they cover. Finally, it is important to note that the most desirable form of hardcover book is an autographed edition.

Titles, listed by author

	Price Range	
☐ **Asimov, Isaac,** *Currents Of Space,* New York, Doubleday, 1952, first edition ..	80.00	100.00
☐ **Ayrton, Michael,** *Maze Maker,* New York, Holt, Reinhart and Winston, 1967	8.00	11.00
☐ **Ayrton, Michael,** *Maze Maker,* autographed	10.00	14.00
☐ **Ballinger, Bill,** *The 49 Days Of Death,* Sherbourne, 1969, first edition	15.00	25.00
☐ **Ballinger, Bill,** *The 49 Days Of Death,* autographed	20.00	28.00
☐ **Barjavel, Rene,** *Ashes, Ashes,* New York, Doubleday, 1967	8.00	12.00
☐ **Barnes, Arthur K.,** *Interplanetary Hunter,* New York, Gnome Press, 1956	15.00	20.00

Price Range

☐ **Barnes, Arthur K.,** *Interplanetary Hunter,*
autographed 20.00   30.00

☐ **Barzman, Ben,** *Twinkle Twinkle Little Star,*
New York, Putnam, 1960 .... 8.00   12.00

☐ **Beeching, Jack,** *The Dacota Project,* New
York, Delacorte Press, 1968 .... 10.00   14.00

☐ **Blish, James,** *A Case Of Conscience,* New
York, Walker, 1969, first American edition in hardcover 50.00   70.00

☐ **Blish, James,** *I, Billy Shakespeare,* New
York, Doubleday, 1965, first edition .. 30.00   40.00

☐ **Burroughs, Edgar Rice,** *At The Earth's
Core,* Canaveral Publishing Co., 1962,
159 pages 9.00   15.00

☐ **Burroughs, Edgar Rice,** *John Carter of
Mars,* Canaveral Publishing Co., 1962,
159 pages 40.00   50.00

☐ **Burroughs, Edgar Rice,** *Tarzan and the
Jewels of Opar,* Grosset & Dunlap, 1950,
350 pages 3.00   5.00

☐ **Burroughs, Edgar Rice,** *Tarzan and the
Ant Men,* Grosset & Dunlap, 1950, 346
pages 3.00   5.00

☐ **Campbell, John W.,** *The Black Star Passes,*
Philadelphia, Fantasy Press, 1953, first
edition, limited to 500 signed and numbered copies 100.00   120.00

☐ **Campbell, John W.,** *Islands Of Space,* Philadelphia, Fantasy Press, undated, 1956,
first trade edition 40.00   50.00

Price Range

☐ **Campbell, John W.,** *The Moon Is Hell!,* Philadelphia, Fantasy Press, 1951, first edition, limited to 500 signed and numbered copies, in publisher's box 90.00   10.00

☐ **Disch, Thomas M.,** *Camp Concentration,* New York, Doubleday, 1969, first American edition 35.00   40.00

☐ **Ellison, Harlan,** *Dangerous Visions,* New York, Doubleday, 1967, first edition, stamped "Publisher's Complimentary Copy" 120.00   130.00

☐ **Gaskell, Jane,** *Strange Evil,* London, Hutchinson, undated, 1957, first edition 25.00   35.00

☐ **Gilbert, Stephen,** *Ratman's Notebooks,* London, Michael Joseph, undated, 1968, first edition 20.00   26.00

☐ **Harrison, Harry,** *Bill The Galactic Hero,* New York, Doubleday, 1965 .... 80.00   90.00

☐ **Jacobi, Carl,** *Portraits In Moonlight,* Wisconsin, Arkham House, 1965, first edition, limited to 1,987 copies 15.00   25.00

☐ **Lesser, Milton,** *Earthbound,* New York, Holt, Rinehart and Winston, 1956, second edition 10.00   12.00

☐ **Maddux, Rachel,** *The Green Kingdom,* New York, Simon and Schuster, 1957, first edition 9.00   13.00

☐ **Matheson, Richard,** *Born Of Man and Woman,* Philadelphia, Chamberlain Press, 1954, first edition of author's first book 100.00   110.00

Price Range

☐ **McNeil, Stanley,** *Something Breathing,* London, Villiers Publications, 1965, first edition, 500 copies printed 80.00   100.00

☐ **Mead, Harold,** *The Bright Phoenix,* New York, Ballantine, undated, 1956, first American edition 25.00   35.00

☐ **Nolan, William F.,** *The Ray Bradbury Review,* San Diego, William F. Nolan, undated, 1952, bound in soft covers, 63 pages 35.00   45.00

☐ **Norday, Michael,** *Dark Magic,* Modern Press, 1956 .... 15.00   25.00

☐ **Sohl, Jerry,** *The Altered Ego,* New York, Rinehart, 1954, first edition 20.00   30.00

☐ **Spinrad, Norman,** *The Men In The Jungle,* New York, Doubleday, 1967, first edition 40.00   60.00

☐ **Taine, John,** *The Crystal Horde,* Philadelphia, Fantasy Press, 1952, first edition, limited to 300 numbered and signed copies 60.00   100.00

☐ **Turner, James,** *Unlikely Ghosts,* Taplinger, 1969 .... 10.00   14.00

☐ **Vance, Jack,** *Big Planet,* New York, Avalon Books, undated, 1957, first edition 60.00   100.00

☐ **Walter, W. Grey,** *Further Outlook,* Duckworth, 1956, first edition 6.00   10.00

☐ **Wandrei, Donald,** *The Eye And The Finger,* Wisconsin, Arkham House, 1955, first edition, limited to 1,617 copies 95.00   105.00

Paperback Books

BACKGROUND: Science fiction and mysteries continue to be of fascination to readers and collectors of paperback books. Mysteries have been the leader in this field for many years; of course, they were the first paperbacks published and thus span the lifetime of paperback books. Agatha Christie books generated films like *Murder On the Orient Express,* which led to widespread interest in many of her lesser-known works.

Closely related to the motion picture paperback is the television paperback. Television paperbacks number far less, and are totally nonexistent for many of the day's popular programs. Often a TV paperback contains a history of the show or biographies of a show's performers.

Mass-market paperbacks belong to the 20th century, although their roots date much further back. The first mass-market paperbacks were the Pocket Books, selling for a mere 25 cents each in 1939.

Until the 1960s, the usual arrangement for paperback publishers was to buy softcover rights to hardcover books. There were very few "original" paperbacks. From the 1960s onward, paperback houses switched from issuing reprints to including new works in their own lines. Today, there are many more original works being published in paperback form.

	Price Range	
Titles, listed by author		
☐ **Abbot, Anthony,** *Murder Of The Clergyman's Mistress,* Popular 286, 1950	4.00	8.00
☐ **Adams, Cleve F.,** *Contraband,* Signet 902, 1951	2.00	3.00
☐ **Adams, Cleve F.,** *Contraband,* Signet 1298, 1956, third edition	3.00	4.00

Price Range

☐ **Adams, Cleve F.,** *Private Eye,* Signet D2588, 1964, second edition 1.50   2.25

☐ **Aldrich, Ann,** *We Walk Alone,* Gold Medal 509, 1956, second edition 5.00   7.00

☐ **Allan, Jack,** *Good Time Girl,* Newstand Library U148, 1960 . . . .   1.50   2.00

☐ **Ambler, Eric,** *A Coffin For Dimitrios,* Dell 1303, 1964, second edition 1.25   1.75

☐ **Anderson, Paul,** *After Doomsday,* Ballantine 579, 1962 . . . .   2.50   3.50

☐ **Archer, Alma,** *Your Power as a Woman,* Western Printing, 1957 . . . .   6.00   8.00

☐ **Asimov, Isaac,** *Caves Of Steel,* Pyramid F-784, 1962 . . . .   2.00   3.00

☐ **Ballinger, Bill S.,** *The Body In The Bed,* Signet G2569, 1964, fifth edition 1.50   2.50

☐ **Bertrange, Sister,** *A Woman Named Louise,* Macmillan, 1956 . . . .   5.00   7.00

☐ **Bezzerides, A.I.,** *Tough Guy,* Lion 153, 1953 . . . .   4.00   6.00

☐ **Boyd, Frank,** *Johnny Staccato,* Gold Medal 980, 1960 . . . .   2.00   3.00

☐ **Bracken, Steve,** *Baby Moll,* Crest 206, 1958 . . . .   3.00   4.00

☐ **Bradbury, Ray,** *The Illustrated Man,* Bantam 991, 1952 . . . .   5.00   7.00

☐ **Bradbury, Ray,** *Martian Chronicles,* Bantam 886, 1951 . . . .   9.00   12.00

Price Range

☐ **Braine, John,** *Room At The Top,* Signet
1569 (painted cover picturing Laurence
Harvey) 5.00   7.00

☐ **Heyerdahl, Thor,** *Aku-Aku,* Pocket
Books, GC758, 1958 . . . .   1.50   2.50

☐ **Lawrence, D. H.,** *Lady Chatterley's Lover,*
Pyramid PR25, 1959 . . . .   2.00   3.00

☐ **McCabe, John,** *Mr. Laurel & Mr. Hardy,*
Signet Q3366, 1968 . . . .   2.00   4.00

☐ **Pasternak, Boris,** *Doctor Zhivago,* Signet
T1802, 1960 . . . .   1.50   3.50

☐ **Spillane, Mickey,** *Bloody Sunrise,* Signet
D2718, 1965 . . . .   2.00   4.00

☐ **Uris, Leon,** *Exodus,* Bantam, S1995, 1959,
eighth edition 2.00   4.00

☐ **Wallace, Lew,** *Ben-Hur,* Dell F79, first
edition, 1959 . . . .   2.50   3.50

☐ **Yerby, Frank,** *An Odor Of Sanctity,* Dell
0134, 1967 . . . .   1.50   2.50

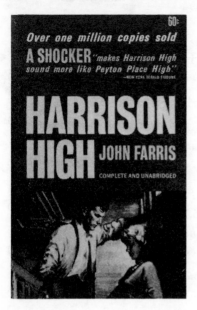

Harrison High, John Farris,
Dell 3448, sixth edition,
$2.00–$3.00

Catalina, Somerset Maugham,
Lancer Books 73447, fourth edition,
1965, $2.00–$4.00

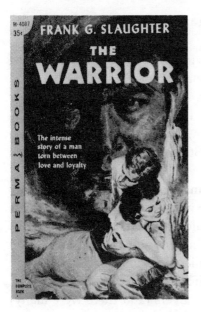

The Warrior, Frank G. Slaughter, Perma Books M4087, second edition, 1957, $1.50–$2.50

With Lawrence in Arabia, Lowell Thomas, Popular SP116, 1961, $2.00–$4.00

Magazines

BACKGROUND: No magazine was more popular during the 1950s and '60s than *Life* magazine, which just celebrated its 50th anniversary (it was first published in November 1938). From the depths of the Great Depression to the heights of the space program, America kept abreast of the happenings in the United States and abroad through its pages.

Interest in collecting *Life* magazines has increased greatly over the past ten years. If *Life* were sought only by collectors building sets, the values would be much more uniform. But values differ greatly depending on who appears on a given cover. There are Kennedy collectors, for example, who seek only those covers featuring JFK and members of his family. Movie buffs save only those covers (and there were many) depicting a film star.

The '50s saw a few great magazines vanish from the scene, as periodicals such as *Collier's* fell victim to the emergence of television. Meanwhile, sales of *TV Guide* and other television and movie magazines soared. The most desirable magazines of the period are those with Marilyn Monroe on the cover.

Price Range

Collier's

☐ **February 17, 1951** (Herbert Hoover—"The Personal Memoirs of Herbert Hoover," on cover) 11.00   13.00

☐ **April 14, 1951** ("What Truman Would Do to Congress" by Jonathan Daniels)   2.00   4.00

☐ **May 5, 1951** ("Secret 'Mr. Big' of Florida" by Lester Velie) 2.00   4.00

	Price Range	
☐ **January 4, 1957** (Princess Grace of Monaco on cover)	3.00	5.00

Dare

☐ **November 1952** (first issue)	4.00	6.00
☐ **January 1953**	2.00	3.00
☐ **March 1953**	2.00	3.00
☐ **April 1953**	2.00	3.00
☐ **May 1953**	2.00	3.00

Esquire

☐ **October, 1944**	10.00	20.00
☐ **September, 1951** (Color print of Marilyn Monroe)	45.00	55.00
☐ **February, 1952** (Mauro Scali painting)	10.00	20.00
☐ **June, 1952** (Pete Lawley painting)	10.00	20.00
☐ **October, 1952** (Pete Lawley painting)	10.00	20.00
☐ **November, 1952** (Eddie Chan painting)	10.00	20.00
☐ **July, 1953** (Peggy Carr)	10.00	20.00
☐ **January, 1954** (holiday issue)	20.00	30.00
☐ **July, 1954** (Sylvana Mangano)	15.00	25.00
☐ **March, 1955** (Mike Ludlow painting)	10.00	20.00
☐ **September, 1955** (Kim Novak)	10.00	20.00

Life

(Note that either the person or the subject of each cover story of *Life* is printed after the publication date for identification purposes. This section covers the years 1950 to 1964, a period in which good-condition copies now exceed the one-dollar mark.)

	Price Range	

1950

☐ **January 2, 1950** ("American Life and Times 1900–1950, Special Issue")	11.00	13.00
☐ **January 9, 1950** (Norma De Landa) ...	3.00	5.00
☐ **January 16, 1950** (Three-year-old Skater)	3.00	5.00
☐ **January 23, 1950** (Woman Wearing "Man-Tailored Suit")	3.00	5.00
☐ **January 30, 1950** (Childbirth Without Fear)	3.00	5.00
☐ **February 6, 1950** (Eva Gabor)	4.00	6.00
☐ **February 13, 1950** (Indonesian Woman)	3.00	5.00
☐ **February 20, 1950** (Atomic Explosion)	5.00	7.00
☐ **February 27, 1950** (Gregory Peck)	4.00	6.00
☐ **March 6, 1950** (Marsha Hunt)	3.00	5.00
☐ **March 13, 1950** (A Guided Tour of Spring Fashions)	3.00	5.00
☐ **March 20, 1950** (Artist Edward John Stevens Jr.)	3.00	5.00
☐ **March 27, 1950** (Anne Bromley)	3.00	5.00
☐ **April 3, 1950** (Iris Mann and David Cole)	3.00	5.00

Price Range

☐ **April 10, 1950** (Young Horsewoman) . .   3.00   5.00

☐ **April 17, 1950** (General Dwight Eisen-
hower) 8.00   10.00

☐ **April 24, 1950** (Woman Wearing Check-
ered Blouse) 3.00   5.00

☐ **May 1, 1950** (Ruth Roman) 3.00   5.00

☐ **May 8, 1950** (Jackie Robinson) 9.00   11.00

☐ **May 22, 1950** (Duke and Duchess of
Windsor) 7.00   9.00

☐ **May 29, 1950** (Mrs. William O'Dwyer)   3.00   5.00

☐ **June 5, 1950** (Stasia Kos) 3.00   5.00

☐ **June 12, 1950** (Bill Boyd) 18.00   20.00

☐ **June 19, 1950** (Children's Sand Styles)   3.00   5.00

☐ **June 26, 1950** (Cecile Aubry) 3.00   5.00

☐ **July 3, 1950** (Thomas Sully Painting of
George Washington at Trenton) 3.00   5.00

☐ **July 10, 1950** (Miroslava) 3.00   5.00

☐ **July 17, 1950** (U.S. Jet Pilot After Shoot-
ing Down a YAK) 5.00   7.00

☐ **July 24, 1950** (Boy Scout) 5.00   7.00

☐ **August 7, 1950** (Peggy Dow) 3.00   5.00

☐ **August 28, 1950** (General Douglas Mac-
Arthur) 7.00   9.00

☐ **September 18, 1950** (Enzio Pinza) 4.00   6.00

☐ **September 25, 1950** (Swedish Red Cross
Girl) 2.00   4.00

	Price Range	
☐ **October 2, 1950** (Stuart Symington) . . .	2.00	4.00
☐ **October 16, 1950** ("U.S. Schools, Special Issue")	2.00	4.00
☐ **December 4, 1950** (Berlin Girl)	2.00	4.00
☐ **December 11, 1950** (Lilly Palmer and Rex Harrison)	4.00	6.00
☐ **December 18, 1950** (George C. Marshall)	4.00	6.00
☐ **December 25, 1950** (Artist John Koch)	2.00	4.00

1951

☐ **January 1, 1951** (War Production Boss Charles E. Wilson)	2.00	4.00
☐ **January 8, 1951** (Janice Rule)	2.00	4.00
☐ **January 15, 1951** (Grand Marshal of Rose Parade)	2.00	4.00
☐ **January 29, 1951** (Betsy Von Furstenberg)	2.00	4.00
☐ **February 5, 1951** (Police Commissioner Tom Murphy)	2.00	4.00
☐ **February 12, 1951** (Woman Wearing Veil Hat)	2.00	4.00
☐ **February 19, 1951** ("The Adoption of Linda Joy")	2.00	4.00
☐ **February 26, 1951** (Debbie Reynolds)	5.00	7.00
☐ **March 5, 1951** (Christian Dior Fashions)	2.00	4.00
☐ **March 12, 1951** (Paul Douglas)	2.00	4.00
☐ **March 19, 1951** (Navy Couple)	2.00	4.00

	Price Range	
☐ **April 9, 1951** (General Omar Bradley)	4.00	6.00
☐ **April 16, 1951** (Esther Williams)	3.00	5.00
☐ **June 11, 1951** (Vivian Blaine of "Guys and Dolls")	3.00	5.00
☐ **June 18, 1951** (Iran's Royal Crown) ...	2.00	4.00
☐ **June 25, 1951** (Janet Leigh)	3.00	5.00
☐ **July 30, 1951** (Gary Crosby)	4.00	6.00
☐ **August 13, 1951** (Dean Martin and Jerry Lewis)	4.00	6.00
☐ **September 5, 1951** (Ginger Rogers) ...	4.00	6.00
☐ **October 1, 1951** (Princess Elizabeth) ..	4.00	6.00
☐ **October 8, 1951** ("The Lazy Life of a Slow Loris")	4.00	6.00
☐ **October 15, 1951** (Zsa Zsa Gabor)	4.00	6.00
☐ **November 5, 1951** (Ginger Rogers) ...	4.00	6.00
☐ **November 19, 1951** (Anthony Eden) ..	2.00	4.00
☐ **December 10, 1951** (President Harry Truman)	8.00	10.00
☐ **December 17, 1951** (Laurence Olivier and Vivien Leigh)	7.00	9.00

1952

☐ **January 21, 1952** (Dwight D. Eisenhower)	8.00	10.00
☐ **March 31, 1952** (Li'l Abner)	7.00	9.00
☐ **April 7, 1952** (Marilyn Monroe)	27.50	32.50

	Price Range	
☐ **April 28, 1952** (Dwight and Mamie Eisenhower)	8.00	10.00
☐ **May 5, 1952** (Diana Lynn)	2.00	4.00
☐ **June 23, 1952** (Mail-Order Fashions) ..	2.00	4.00
☐ **July 7, 1952** (Arlene Dahl)	4.00	6.00
☐ **August 4, 1952** (Adlai Stevenson)	5.00	7.00
☐ **August 18, 1952** (Marlene Dietrich) ...	5.00	7.00
☐ **September 15, 1952** (Rita Gam)	2.00	4.00
☐ **October 20, 1952** (Mamie Eisenhower)	5.00	7.00
☐ **November 3, 1952** (United Nations) ..	2.00	4.00
☐ **November 17, 1952** (Dwight and Mamie Eisenhower)	6.00	8.00
☐ **December 29, 1952** (Salzburg Marionettes)	2.00	4.00

1953

☐ **January 12, 1953** (Resort Clothes)	2.00	4.00
☐ **January 26, 1953** (Fashions)	2.00	4.00
☐ **March 9, 1953** (Vanessa Brown)	2.00	4.00
☐ **April 6, 1953** (Lucille Ball)	9.00	11.00
☐ **April 20, 1953** (Marlon Brando)	8.00	10.00
☐ **April 27, 1953** (Queen Elizabeth)	8.00	10.00
☐ **May 25, 1953** (Marilyn Monroe and Jane Russell)	25.00	30.00
☐ **June 8, 1953** (Roy Campanella of Brooklyn Dodgers)	19.00	21.00

	Price Range	
☐ **July 6, 1953** (Terry Moore)	8.00	10.00
☐ **July 20, 1953** (John F. and Jacqueline Kennedy)	22.50	27.50
☐ **August 31, 1953** (Donna Reed)	9.00	11.00
☐ **September 7, 1953** (Dinosaurs)	6.00	8.00
☐ **September 14, 1953** (Casey Stengel) ..	5.00	7.00
☐ **September 21, 1953** (Juanita Smith) ...	2.00	4.00
☐ **November 2, 1953** (Winston Churchill)	4.00	6.00
☐ **December 14, 1953** (Richard Nixon) ..	6.00	8.00

1954

☐ **January 18, 1954** (Dwight Eisenhower and Richard Nixon)	7.00	9.00
☐ **February 1, 1954** (Bathing Suits)	2.00	4.00
☐ **March 1, 1954** (Rita Moreno)	2.00	4.00
☐ **April 26, 1954** (Grace Kelly)	9.00	11.00
☐ **May 17, 1954** (Dawn Addams)	2.00	4.00
☐ **May 24, 1954** (Kaye Ballard)	2.00	4.00
☐ **May 31, 1954** (William Holden)	3.00	5.00
☐ **July 12, 1954** (Pier Angeli)	2.00	4.00
☐ **August 23, 1954** (Prince Philip)	4.00	6.00
☐ **September 13, 1954** (Judy Garland) ...	9.00	11.00
☐ **November 1, 1954** (Dorothy Dandridge)	2.00	4.00
☐ **November 22, 1954** (Gina Lolabrigida)	4.00	6.00
☐ **November 22, 1954** (Judy Holliday) ...	4.00	6.00

Price Range

☐ **December 27, 1954** (Pieter Bruegel Painting) 2.00   4.00

1955

☐ **January 10, 1955** (Greta Garbo) 6.00   8.00

☐ **January 31, 1955** (Spencer Tracy) 6.00   8.00

☐ **February 14, 1955** (Princess Margaret)   4.00   6.00

☐ **February 28, 1955** (Shelley Winters) . .   2.00   4.00

☐ **March 21, 1955** (Sheree North) 2.00   4.00

☐ **April 11, 1955** (Grace Kelly) 8.00   10.00

☐ **April 25, 1955** (Anthony Eden) 2.00   4.00

☐ **May 23, 1955** (Leslie Caron) 4.00   6.00

☐ **June 6, 1955** (Henry Fonda) 4.00   6.00

☐ **July 11, 1955** (Susan Strasberg) 2.00   4.00

☐ **July 18, 1955** (Audrey Hepburn) 3.00   5.00

☐ **July 25, 1955** (Cathy Crosby) 3.00   5.00

☐ **August 8, 1955** (Ben Hogan) 3.00   5.00

☐ **August 15, 1955** (General Douglas Mac-Arthur) 4.00   6.00

☐ **August 22, 1955** (Sophia Loren) 3.00   5.00

☐ **September 12, 1955** (Joan Collins) 3.00   5.00

☐ **September 26, 1955** (Harry S. and Bess Truman) 8.00   10.00

☐ **October 3, 1955** (Rock Hudson) 10.00   12.00

☐ **October 10, 1955** (Princess Margaret)   3.00   5.00

Price Range

☐ **November 14, 1955** (Dwight Eisenhower) 7.00 9.00

☐ **November 28, 1955** (Carol Channing) 3.00 5.00

1956

☐ **January 16, 1956** (Anita Ekberg) 2.00 4.00

☐ **February 6, 1956** (Shirley Jones) 4.00 6.00

☐ **February 13, 1956** (Harry Truman and Douglas MacArthur) 7.00 9.00

☐ **February 20, 1956** (Claire Bloom) 2.00 4.00

☐ **March 5, 1956** (Kim Novak) 3.00 5.00

☐ **March 12, 1956** (Dwight Eisenhower) 7.00 9.00

☐ **March 26, 1956** (Julie Andrews) 3.00 5.00

☐ **April 9, 1956** (Grace Kelly) 7.00 9.00

☐ **April 23, 1956** (Jayne Mansfield) 6.00 8.00

☐ **May 28, 1956** (Yul Brynner) 5.00 7.00

☐ **June 11, 1956** (Carroll Baker) 2.00 4.00

☐ **June 25, 1956** (Mickey Mantle) 14.00 16.00

☐ **July 16, 1956** (Gary Cooper) 7.00 9.00

☐ **August 20, 1956** (Audrey Hepburn) ... 4.00 6.00

☐ **August 27, 1956** (Adlai Stevenson and Eleanor Roosevelt) 3.00 5.00

☐ **September 24, 1956** (Janet Blair) 3.00 5.00

☐ **October 15, 1956** (Elizabeth Taylor) ... 4.00 6.00

☐ **November 5, 1956** (President Dwight Eisenhower) 6.00 8.00

	Price Range	
☐ **November 12, 1956** (Rosalind Russell)	3.00	5.00
☐ **November 26, 1956** (Ingrid Bergman)	5.00	7.00

1957

☐ **January 7, 1957** (Richard Nixon)	7.00	9.00
☐ **February 4, 1957** (Audrey Hepburn) ..	4.00	6.00
☐ **February 18, 1957** (Julie London)	3.00	5.00
☐ **March 4, 1957** (Queen Elizabeth and Prince Philip)	3.00	5.00
☐ **March 11, 1957** (John F. Kennedy)	14.00	16.00
☐ **March 18, 1957** (Bea Lillie)	3.00	5.00
☐ **March 25, 1957** (Princess Caroline of Monaco as Infant)	4.00	6.00
☐ **April 15, 1957** (Ernie Kovacs)	4.00	6.00
☐ **May 6, 1957** (Sophia Loren)	4.00	6.00
☐ **May 13, 1957** (Bert Lahr)	4.00	6.00
☐ **June 24, 1957** (Juan Carlos of Spain) ..	4.00	6.00
☐ **July 1, 1957** (Billy Graham)	2.00	4.00
☐ **August 12, 1957** (May Britt)	2.00	4.00
☐ **September 30, 1957** (Rex Harrison) ...	2.00	4.00
☐ **October 28, 1957** (Queen Elizabeth) ...	2.00	4.00
☐ **December 2, 1957** (Nikita Khushchev)	2.00	4.00
☐ **December 9, 1957** (Richard Nixon and James Hagerty)	4.00	6.00

1958

☐ **January 6, 1958** (Astronaut)	8.00	10.00

	Price Range	
☐ **January 20, 1958** (Lyndon Johnson) . . .	4.00	6.00
☐ **February 3, 1958** (Shirley Temple)	8.00	10.00
☐ **February 10, 1958** (Ralph Bellamy) . . .	2.00	4.00
☐ **March 10, 1958** (Yul Brynner)	4.00	6.00
☐ **March 17, 1958** (McGuire Sisters)	2.00	4.00
☐ **March 24, 1958** (Moscow and Chicago Students)	2.00	4.00
☐ **April 7, 1958** (Ray Robinson vs. Carmine Basilio)	2.00	4.00
☐ **April 14, 1958** (Gwen Verdon)	2.00	4.00
☐ **April 21, 1958** (John F. and Jacqueline Kennedy)	14.00	16.00
☐ **April 28, 1958** (Willie Mays)	11.00	13.00
☐ **May 26, 1958** (Richard Nixon)	6.00	8.00
☐ **June 2, 1958** (Charles De Gaulle)	2.00	4.00
☐ **June 30, 1958** (Dwight Eisenhower and Sherman Adams)	4.00	6.00
☐ **September 15, 1958** (Bing Crosby's Sons)	2.00	4.00
☐ **September 22, 1958** (George Burns and Gracie Allen)	2.00	4.00
☐ **November 17, 1958** (Mr. and Mrs. Nelson Rockefeller)	2.00	4.00
☐ **December 1, 1958** (Ricky Nelson)	11.00	13.00

1959

☐ **January 12, 1959** (Hubert Humphrey)	2.00	4.00

	Price Range	
☐ **February 2, 1959** (Pat Boone)	2.00	4.00
☐ **February 9, 1959** (Shirley MacLaine) ..	2.00	4.00
☐ **February 23, 1959** (Gwen Verdon)	2.00	4.00
☐ **March 9, 1959** (Jack Paar)	2.00	4.00
☐ **March 30, 1959** (Debbie Reynolds) ...	2.00	4.00
☐ **April 20, 1959** (Marilyn Monroe)	19.00	21.00
☐ **May 18, 1959** (Jimmy Hoffa)	2.00	4.00
☐ **June 8, 1959** (Audrey Hepburn)	2.00	4.00
☐ **June 29, 1959** (Zsa Zsa Gabor)	2.00	4.00
☐ **July 20, 1959** (Ingemar Johansson)	2.00	4.00
☐ **July 27, 1959** (Great White Fleet)	2.00	4.00
☐ **August 3, 1959** (Kingston Trio)	2.00	4.00
☐ **August 10, 1959** (Russian Women) ...	2.00	4.00
☐ **August 17, 1959** (May Britt)	2.00	4.00
☐ **August 24, 1959** (Jacqueline Kennedy)	11.00	13.00
☐ **August 31, 1959** (Rip Van Winkle) ...	2.00	4.00
☐ **September 7, 1959** (Bat Masterson) ...	2.00	4.00
☐ **September 14, 1959** (Astronauts)	2.00	4.00
☐ **September 21, 1959** (Astronauts' Wives)	2.00	4.00
☐ **September 28, 1959** (Ducks)	2.00	4.00
☐ **October 5, 1959** (Nikita Khruschev) ...	2.00	4.00
☐ **October 19, 1959** (Demonstrating in Peking)	2.00	4.00

	Price Range	
☐ **November 2, 1959** (Jackie Gleason) ...	2.00	4.00
☐ **November 9, 1959** (Marilyn Monroe)	18.00	20.00
☐ **November 23, 1959** (Mary Martin) ...	2.00	4.00
☐ **November 30, 1959** (Postage Stamps)	2.00	4.00
☐ **December 21, 1959** (Dwight Eisenhower)	4.00	6.00
☐ **December 28, 1959** ("Good Life")	2.00	4.00
1960		
☐ **January 11, 1960** (Dina Merrill)	2.00	4.00
☐ **January 25, 1960** (Colonial Folklore) ..	2.00	4.00
☐ **February 1, 1960** (Dinah Shore)	2.00	4.00
☐ **February 8, 1960** (U.S. Ski Team)	2.00	4.00
☐ **February 15, 1960** (Submarine Trieste)	2.00	4.00
☐ **February 22, 1960** (Henry and Jane Fonda)	2.00	4.00
☐ **February 29, 1960** (Winter Olympic Skier)	2.00	4.00
☐ **March 7, 1960** (Hypnosis)	2.00	4.00
☐ **March 14, 1960** (Princess Margaret and Lord Snowdon)	2.00	4.00
☐ **March 28, 1960** (John F. Kennedy and Harry S. Truman)	4.00	6.00
☐ **April 4, 1960** (Marlon Brando)	4.00	6.00
☐ **April 11, 1960** (Silvana Mangano)	2.00	4.00
☐ **May 9, 1960** (Actress Yvette Mimieux)	2.00	4.00

Price Range

☐ **May 16, 1960** (Royal Wedding of Princess Margaret and Lord Snowdon) 2.00   4.00

☐ **May 23, 1960** (Minuteman Statue) 1.50   3.50

☐ **May 30, 1960** (Nikita Krushchev) 1.50   3.50

☐ **June 6, 1960** (Lee Remick) 1.50   3.50

☐ **June 13, 1960** (Hayley Mills) 1.50   3.50

☐ **June 20, 1960** (Los Angeles Freeway) ..   1.50   3.50

☐ **June 27, 1960** (Walrus) 1.50   3.50

☐ **July 11, 1960** (Nelson Rockefeller) 1.50   3.50

☐ **July 18, 1960** (Ina Balin) 1.50   3.50

☐ **July 25, 1960** (Demonstration for John F. Kennedy) 1.50   3.50

☐ **August 1, 1960** (Fun Safari) 1.50   3.50

☐ **August 8, 1960** (Richard Nixon) 3.00   5.00

☐ **August 15, 1960** (Marilyn Monroe and Yves Montand) 8.00   10.00

☐ **August 22, 1960** (Olympic Swimmers)   1.50   3.50

☐ **August 29, 1960** (Record Breaking Olympic Jump) 3.00   5.00

☐ **September 5, 1960** (Ernest Hemingway)   3.00   5.00

☐ **September 12, 1960** (USA Gymnasts)   3.00   5.00

☐ **September 19, 1960** (Grandma Moses)   3.00   5.00

☐ **October 3, 1960** (Eisenhower Addressing the United Nations) 3.00   5.00

☐ **October 10, 1960** (Doris Day) 1.00   3.00

	Price Range	
☐ **October 24, 1960** (Nancy Kwan)	1.00	3.00
☐ **October 31, 1960** (Halloween)	2.00	4.00
☐ **November 7, 1960** (Earth as Viewed From a Satellite)	1.00	3.00
☐ **November 14, 1960** (Sophia Loren) ...	2.00	4.00
☐ **November 21, 1960** (John F. and Jacqueline Kennedy)	4.00	6.00
☐ **November 28, 1960** (Carroll Baker) ...	2.00	4.00
☐ **December 5, 1960** (Baltimore Colts Football Kickoff)	2.00	4.00
☐ **December 12, 1960** (Jill Haworth and Sal Mineo)	2.00	4.00
☐ **December 19, 1960** (John and Jacqueline Kennedy and John Jr.)	5.00	7.00
☐ **December 26, 1960** ("25 Years of Life—Special Double Issue")	19.00	21.00

1961

☐ **January 6, 1961** (The Civil War)	2.00	4.00
☐ **January 13, 1961** (Clark Gable)	4.00	6.00
☐ **January 20, 1961** (Surgeon)	1.00	3.00
☐ **January 27, 1961** (The Kennedy Inauguration)	5.00	7.00
☐ **February 3, 1961** (Queen Elizabeth in India)	1.00	3.00
☐ **February 10, 1961** (Chimpanzee in Space)	1.00	3.00
☐ **February 17, 1961** (Shirley MacLaine)	1.00	3.00

	Price Range	
☐ **February 24, 1961** (Dag Hammarskjold)	1.00	3.00
☐ **March 3, 1961** (John Glenn, Gus Grissom and Alan Shepard)	4.00	6.00
☐ **March 10, 1961** (Bing Crosby and Maurice Chevalier)	2.00	4.00
☐ **March 17, 1961** (Sheila Finn)	1.00	3.00
☐ **March 24, 1961** (Jack Paar and Ed Sullivan)	1.00	3.00
☐ **March 31, 1961** (Cherub)	1.00	3.00
☐ **April 7, 1961** (Sea Fishing)	1.00	3.00
☐ **April 14, 1961** (Mrs. Clark Gable)	1.00	3.00
☐ **April 21, 1961** (Soviet Cosmonaut Yuri Gagarin)	2.00	4.00
☐ **April 28, 1961** (Elizabeth Taylor)	2.00	4.00
☐ **May 5, 1961** (Anna Maria Alberghetti)	2.00	4.00
☐ **May 12, 1961** (Astronaut Alan Shepard)	2.00	4.00
☐ **May 19, 1961** (Astronaut Alan Shepard)	2.00	4.00
☐ **May 26, 1961** (Kennedys Visiting Canada)	2.00	4.00
☐ **June 2, 1961** (Fidel Castro)	2.00	4.00
☐ **June 9, 1961** (John F. Kennedy Visiting Paris)	2.00	4.00
☐ **June 16, 1961** (June Weddings)	2.00	4.00
☐ **June 23, 1961** (Princess Grace of Monaco)	2.00	4.00
☐ **June 30, 1961** (Leslie Caron)	2.00	4.00

	Price Range	
☐ **July 7, 1961** (Dwight Eisenhower)	2.00	4.00
☐ **July 14, 1961** (Ernest Hemingway)	2.00	4.00
☐ **July 21, 1961** (Flavio rescued)	2.00	4.00
☐ **July 28, 1961** (Brigitte Bardot)	2.00	4.00
☐ **August 4, 1961** (John F. Kennedy)`	3.00	5.00
☐ **August 11, 1961** (Sophia Loren)	2.00	4.00
☐ **August 18, 1961** (Mickey Mantle and Roger Maris)	2.00	4.00
☐ **September 8, 1961** (American Tank) ..	1.00	3.00
☐ **September 15, 1961** (Civilian Fallout Suit)	1.00	3.00
☐ **September 22, 1961** (Hurricane Carla)	1.00	3.00
☐ **September 29, 1961** (Death of Dag Hammarskjold)	1.00	3.00
☐ **October 6, 1961** (Elizabeth Taylor as Cleopatra)	1.00	3.00
☐ **October 13, 1961** (African Tribal Warrior)	1.00	3.00
☐ **October 20, 1961** (Communist Leaders)	1.00	3.00
☐ **October 27, 1961** (Guerrilla Warfare) ..	1.00	3.00
☐ **November 3, 1961** (Girl Kissing G.I. Farewell)	1.00	3.00
☐ **November 10, 1961** (Nikita Krushchev)	1.00	3.00
☐ **November 17, 1961** (Minnesota Vikings Football Team)	1.00	3.00
☐ **November 24, 1961** (John Kennedy Jr.)	2.00	4.00

	Price Range	
☐ **December 1, 1961** (Italian Fashions) . . .	1.00	3.00
☐ **December 8, 1961** (Plum Pudding)	1.00	3.00
☐ **December 15, 1961** (Chartres Cathedral)	1.00	3.00
☐ **December 22, 1961,** ("Our Splendid Outdoors; Special Issue")	1.00	3.00

1962

☐ **January 5, 1962** (Lucille Ball)	2.00	4.00
☐ **January 12, 1962** (Bomb Shelter)	2.00	4.00
☐ **January 19, 1962** (Ice Sailing)	2.00	4.00
☐ **January 26, 1962** (Robert Kennedy) . . .	3.00	5.00
☐ **February 2, 1962** (John Glenn)	2.00	4.00
☐ **February 9, 1962** (Seattle World's Fair)	2.00	4.00
☐ **February 16, 1962** (Rock Hudson)	4.00	6.00
☐ **February 23, 1962** (Shirley MacLaine)	2.00	4.00
☐ **March 2, 1962** (John Glenn)	2.00	4.00
☐ **March 9, 1962** (Tickertape parade for John Glenn)	2.00	4.00
☐ **March 16, 1962** (Richard Nixon)	2.00	4.00
☐ **March 23, 1962** (Desert Living)	2.00	4.00
☐ **March 30, 1962** (Robert Frost)	2.00	4.00
☐ **April 13, 1962** (Elizabeth Taylor and Richard Burton)	2.00	4.00
☐ **April 20, 1962** (Audrey Hepburn)	2.00	4.00
☐ **April 27, 1962** (Astronauts' Moon Suit)	2.00	4.00
☐ **May 4, 1962** (Seattle World's Fair)	2.00	4.00

	Price Range	
☐ **May 11, 1962** (Bob Hope)	3.00	5.00
☐ **May 18, 1962** (Astronaut Scott Carpenter)	2.00	4.00
☐ **May 25, 1962** (Juan Carlos)	1.00	3.00
☐ **June 1, 1962** (Rene Carpenter, Wife of Astronaut Scott Carpenter)	1.00	3.00
☐ **June 8, 1962** (Stock Market Flurry) . . .	2.00	4.00
☐ **June 15, 1962** (Natalie Wood)	2.00	4.00
☐ **June 22, 1962** (Marilyn Monroe)	13.00	15.00
☐ **June 29, 1962** (Ted Kennedy)	2.00	4.00
☐ **July 6, 1962** (Aerial Balloon)	1.00	3.00
☐ **July 13, 1962** (John F. Kennedy Visiting Mexico)	2.00	4.00
☐ **July 20, 1962** (Hydrogen Bomb Exploding)	1.00	3.00
☐ **July 27, 1962** (Elsa Martinelli)	1.00	3.00
☐ **August 3, 1962** (Astronaut Robert White)	1.00	3.00
☐ **August 10, 1962** (Janet Leigh)	1.00	3.00
☐ **August 17, 1962** (Marilyn Monroe) . . .	7.00	9.00
☐ **August 24, 1962** (Russian Space Capsules)	1.00	3.00
☐ **August 31, 1962** (Mail Robbery)	1.00	3.00
☐ **September 7, 1962** (Caroline Kennedy)	4.00	6.00
☐ **September 14, 1962** (Special Issue on "Take-Over Generation")	1.00	3.00

Price Range

☐ **September 21, 1962** (Victims of Iranian Earthquake) 1.00   3.00

☐ **September 28, 1962** (Los Angeles Dodgers Pitcher Don Drysdale) 7.00   9.00

☐ **October 5, 1962** (Jackie Gleason) 1.00   3.00

☐ **October 12, 1962** (Pope John XXIII) ... 1.00   3.00

☐ **October 19, 1962** (Yosemite) 1.00   3.00

☐ **November 2, 1962** (Cuban Missile Crisis) 4.00   6.00

☐ **November 9, 1962** (Secretary General U. Thant) 1.00   3.00

☐ **November 16, 1962** (India/China War) 1.00   3.00

☐ **November 30, 1962** (Sid Caesar) 1.00   3.00

☐ **December 7, 1962** (Boy Running) 1.00   3.00

☐ **December 14, 1962** (Marlon Brando) .. 3.00   5.00

☐ **December 21, 1962** (Year-End Double Issue Devoted to the Sea) 2.00   4.00

1963

☐ **January 4, 1963** (Greek Miracle) 1.00   3.00

☐ **January 11, 1963** (Ann-Margaret) 1.00   3.00

☐ **January 18, 1963** (Trojan Horse) 1.00   3.00

☐ **January 25, 1963** (Vietnamese Prisoners of War) 1.00   3.00

☐ **February 1, 1963** (Alfred Hitchcock's Motion Picture *The Birds*) 4.00   6.00

☐ **February 8, 1963** (Grecian Sculpture) .. 1.00   3.00

	Price Range	
☐ **February 15, 1963** (Abraham Lincoln's Casket)	1.00	3.00
☐ **February 22, 1963** (Kessler Twins)	1.00	3.00
☐ **March 1, 1963** (Snakes)	1.00	3.00
☐ **March 15, 1963** (Fidel Castro)	1.00	3.00
☐ **March 22, 1963** (Polaris Submarine) ...	1.00	3.00
☐ **March 29, 1963** (Crowd in Costa Rica)	1.00	3.00
☐ **April 5, 1963** (Greek Wars)	1.00	3.00
☐ **April 12, 1963** (Yukon Ordeal)	1.00	3.00
☐ **April 19, 1963** (Elizabeth Taylor and Richard Burton)	4.00	6.00
☐ **April 26, 1963** (Jacqueline Kennedy at Age Ten)	1.00	3.00
☐ **May 3, 1963** (Alexander The Great) ...	1.00	3.00
☐ **May 17, 1963** (Nelson Rockefeller and Happy Rockefeller)	1.00	3.00
☐ **May 24, 1963** (Astronaut Gordon Cooper)	1.00	3.00
☐ **May 31, 1963** (Mr. and Mrs. Gordon Cooper)	1.00	3.00
☐ **June 7, 1963** (Pope John XXIII)	1.00	3.00
☐ **June 14, 1963** (St. Peter's Basilica in Vatican City)	1.00	3.00
☐ **June 21, 1963** (Shirley MacLaine)	1.00	3.00
☐ **June 28, 1963** (Funeral of Civil Rights Advocate Medgar Evers)	1.00	3.00

	Price Range	
☐ **July 5, 1963** (Pope Paul VI)	1.00	3.00
☐ **July 12, 1963** (Steve McQueen)	1.00	3.00
☐ **July 19, 1963** (Greek Art)	1.00	3.00
☐ **July 26, 1963** (Tuesday Weld)	1.00	3.00
☐ **August 2, 1963** (Baseball Pitcher Sandy Koufax)	6.00	8.00
☐ **August 9, 1963** (Nikita Krushchev and Averill Harriman)	1.00	3.00
☐ **August 16, 1963** (Kennedy's Baby Vigil)	3.00	5.00
☐ **August 23, 1963** (Frank Sinatra and Frank Sinatra Jr.)	3.00	5.00
☐ **August 30, 1963** (Elsa Martinelli)	1.00	3.00
☐ **September 6, 1963** (Civil Rights Leaders Bayard Rustin and Philip Randolph) . .	1.00	3.00
☐ **September 13, 1963** (Russian Woman)	1.00	3.00
☐ **September 20, 1963** (Mount Everest) . .	1.00	3.00
☐ **September 27, 1963** (Team of Newly Selected Astronauts)	1.00	3.00
☐ **October 4, 1963** (DNA Molecule)	1.00	3.00
☐ **October 11, 1963** (Mme. Nhu, Vietnam's First Lady)	1.00	3.00
☐ **October 18, 1963** (Scene from "Anastasia")	1.00	3.00
☐ **October 25, 1963** (Yvette Mimieux) . . .	1.00	3.00
☐ **November 1, 1963** (Senator Barry Goldwater)	1.00	3.00

Price Range

☐ **November 8, 1963** (Bobby Baker) 1.00   3.00

☐ **November 15, 1963** (Vietnam Coup) . . 1.00   3.00

☐ **November 22, 1963** (Elizabeth Ashley) 4.00   6.00

☐ **November 29, 1963** (Assassination of John F. Kennedy) 19.00   21.00

☐ **December 6, 1963** (Kennedy Family) . . 8.00   10.00

☐ **December 13, 1963** (Lyndon Johnson) 6.00   8.00

☐ **December 13, 1963** (Same date as regular issue, but this was a special issue sold only on stands, not sent to subscribers, "John F. Kennedy Memorial Edition," biography of Kennedy with summary of all news surrounding assassination and funeral.) 9.00   11.00

1964

☐ **January 3, 1964** (Laconia Fire) 1.00   3.00

☐ **January 10, 1964** (General Douglas MacArthur) 1.00   3.00

☐ **January 17, 1964** (Pilgrimage of Pope Paul VI) 1.00   3.00

☐ **January 24, 1964** (Rioting in Panama) 1.00   3.00

☐ **January 31, 1964** (Geraldine Chaplin) 1.00   3.00

☐ **February 7, 1964** (War in Tanganika) 1.00   3.00

☐ **February 14, 1964** (Winter Olympics) 2.00   4.00

☐ **February 21, 1964** (Lee Harvey Oswald) 6.00   8.00

Price Range

☐ **February 28, 1964** (War in Cyprus) ...   1.00   3.00

☐ **March 6, 1964** (Muhammad Ali) 3.00   5.00

☐ **March 13, 1964** (Western front of World War I) 1.00   3.00

☐ **March 20, 1964** (American Ambassador Henry Cabot Lodge Visiting Vietnam)   1.00   3.00

☐ **March 27, 1964** (Charles De Gaulle Visiting Mexico) 1.00   3.00

☐ **April 3, 1964** (Carol Channing as "Dolly") 1.00   3.00

☐ **April 10, 1964** (Earthquake in Alaska)   1.00   3.00

☐ **April 17, 1964** (General MacArthur's Hat) 1.00   3.00

☐ **April 24, 1964** (Richard Burton as "Hamlet") 4.00   6.00

☐ **May 1, 1964** (New York World's Fair)   6.00   8.00

☐ **May 8, 1964** (Lyndon Johnson and Prospective Running Mates) 5.00   7.00

☐ **May 15, 1964** (Luci Baines Johnson) ...   1.00   3.00

☐ **May 22, 1964** (Barbra Streisand) 1.00   3.00

☐ **May 29, 1964** (Jacqueline Kennedy) ...   1.00   3.00

☐ **June 5, 1964** (Cremation of Indian Leader Nehru) 1.00   3.00

☐ **June 19, 1964** (Presidential Hopeful William Scranton With His Family) ..   1.00   3.00

☐ **July 3, 1964** (Robert Kennedy and His Children) 4.00   6.00

Price Range

☐ **July 10, 1964** (Lee Harvey Oswald's Diary) 5.00   7.00

☐ **July 17, 1964** (Carroll Baker) 1.00   3.00

☐ **July 24, 1964** (Republican National Convention) 1.00   3.00

☐ **July 31, 1964** (Summer Olympics) 1.00   3.00

☐ **August 7, 1964** (Marilyn Monroe) 4.00   6.00

☐ **August 14, 1964** (Lyndon Johnson) ...   4.00   6.00

☐ **August 21, 1964** (Lyndon Johnson) ...   4.00   6.00

☐ **August 28, 1964** (The Beatles) 20.00   25.00

☐ **September 4, 1964** (Lyndon Johnson)   4.00   6.00

☐ **September 11, 1964** (Japan) 1.00   3.00

☐ **September 18, 1964** (Sophia Loren) ...   1.00   3.00

☐ **September 25, 1964** (American Space Race) 4.00   6.00

☐ **October 2, 1964** (Warren Report on the Assassination of John F. Kennedy) ...   4.00   6.00

☐ **October 9, 1964** (Olympic Swimmer) ..   1.00   3.00

☐ **October 16, 1964** (Berlin Tunnel) 1.00   3.00

☐ **October 23, 1964** (New Soviet Leader Leonid Brezhnev) 1.00   3.00

☐ **October 30, 1964** (American Olympic Medal Winning Swimmer Don Schollander) 1.00   3.00

☐ **November 6, 1964** (Scene from the Motion Picture "Goldfinger") 4.00   6.00

Price Range

☐ **November 13, 1964** (Lyndon Johnson and His Running Mate Hubert Humphrey) 6.00   8.00

☐ **November 20, 1964** (Moscow Parade)   1.00   3.00

☐ **November 27, 1964** (Vietnam War) ...   1.00   3.00

☐ **December 4, 1964** (Dr. Paul Carlson) ..   1.00   3.00

☐ **December 11, 1964** (New York Radio City Music Hall Rockettes) 1.00   3.00

☐ **December 18, 1964** (Elizabeth Taylor)   1.00   3.00

Saturday Evening Post

☐ **May 19, 1956** (Norman Rockwell cover; Marilyn Monroe by Pete Martin) 20.00   30.00

☐ **October 6, 1956** (Adlai Stevenson cover by Norman Rockwell; Kim Novak) ...   20.00   30.00

☐ **October 13, 1956** (Eisenhower cover by Norman Rockwell; Rocky Marciano) ..   15.00   20.00

☐ **December 29, 1956** (Norman Rockwell cover) 25.00   35.00

☐ **April 20, 1957** ("Milwaukee Will Win the Pennant" by Warren Spahn) 10.00   20.00

☐ **May 25, 1957** (Norman Rockwell cover; Groucho Marx by Pete Martin) 10.00   20.00

☐ **June 29, 1957** (Norman Rockwell cover; "I Was Always Hungry" by Kirk Douglas) 10.00   20.00

☐ **June 28, 1958** (Norman Rockwell cover)   15.00   25.00

Price Range

☐ **November 8, 1958** (Norman Rockwell cover) 10.00   20.00

☐ **October 24, 1959** (Norman Rockwell cover) 10.00   20.00

☐ **February 13, 1960** (Norman Rockwell cover; Rockwell's own story with re-pros) 35.00   45.00

☐ **September 17, 1960** (Norman Rockwell cover; Pittsburg Bucs) 10.00   20.00

☐ **January 13, 1962** (Norman Rockwell cover; Shirley Jones by Pete Martin) .. 10.00   20.00

☐ **January 19, 1963** (Norman Rockwell cover of Nehru) 10.00   20.00

☐ **March 2, 1963** (Norman Rockwell cover of Jack Benny) 10.00   20.00

☐ **May 25, 1963** (Norman Rockwell cover of Nasser) 10.00   20.00

☐ **July 17, 1965** (Sean Connery cover and article) 10.00   15.00

☐ **July 30, 1966** (Bob Dylan cover and arti-cle) 5.00   15.00

☐ **August 27, 1966** (Beatles cover and arti-cle) 20.00   30.00

TV Guide

1950

☐ **August 5–12, 1950** (volume 3, #31, Fred Allen and Jack Haley on cover) 37.00   42.00

Price Range

☐ **August 12–18, 1950** (volume 3, #32, Grace Kelly on cover) 50.00   60.00

☐ **September 2–8, 1950** (volume 3, #35, Howdy Doody on cover) 60.00   70.00

☐ **September 16–22, 1950** (volume 3, #37, Jimmy Durante, Kate Smith, Groucho Marx, Frank Sinatra, Jack Benny and Fred Allen on cover) 32.00   37.00

☐ **September 30–October 6, 1950** (volume 3, #39, football scene on cover) 30.00   35.00

☐ **October 14–20, 1950** (volume 3, #41, Miss TV of 1950 on cover) 35.00   40.00

☐ **November 11–17, 1950** (volume 3, #45, Dean Martin and Jerry Lewis on cover)   35.00   40.00

☐ **November 25–December 1, 1950** [volume 3, #47, Howdy Doody, Rootie Tootie (later to be Rootie Kazootie) on cover] 60.00   70.00

☐ **December 9–15, 1950** (volume 3, #49, Walter Winchell on cover) 30.00   35.00

☐ **December 30, 1950–January 5, 1951** (volume 3, #52, model named Marie Dube on cover) 30.00   35.00

1951

☐ **January 20–26, 1951** (volume 4, #3, Sheriff Bob Dixon on cover) 22.50   27.50

☐ **January 27–February 2, 1951** (volume 4, Jerry Lester on cover) 15.00   17.00

Price Range

☐ **February 3–8, 1951** (volume 4, #5, cast
of "Leave It To The Girls" on cover) 15.00 17.00

☐ **February 17–23, 1951** (volume 4, #7,
Lilli Palmer on cover) 20.00 25.00

☐ **March 3–9, 1951** (volume 4, #9, Jack
Carter on cover) 25.00 30.00

☐ **March 10–16, 1951** (volume 4, #10, Sid
Caesar on cover) 27.50 32.50

☐ **March 24–30, 1951** (volume 4, #12, Arthur Godfrey on cover) 22.50 27.50

☐ **April 14–20, 1951** (volume 4, #15, Joe
DiMaggio and eight other famous ball
players on cover) 15.00 17.00

☐ **May 12–18, 1951** (volume 4, #19, Perry
Como on cover) 22.50 27.50

☐ **May 19–25, 1951** (volume 4, #20, Ken
Murray on cover) 25.00 30.00

☐ **May 26–June 1, 1951** (volume 4, #21,
Frank Sinatra on cover) 30.00 35.00

☐ **June 9–15, 1951** (volume 4, #23,
Groucho Marx on cover) 35.00 40.00

☐ **June 16–22, 1951** (volume 4, #24, Milton Berle on cover) 22.50 27.50

☐ **July 14–20, 1951** (volume 4, #28, unknown infant on cover) 17.50 19.50

☐ **July 28–August 3** (volume 4, #30,
Buster Crabbe on cover) 30.00 35.00

☐ **August 24–30, 1951** (volume 4, #34,
Jerry Lester on cover) 27.50 32.50

Price Range

☐ **August 31–September 6, 1951** (volume 4, #35, Howdy Doody and other TV kid show characters on cover) 45.00   50.00

☐ **September 21–27** (volume 4, #38, Arthur Godfrey on cover) 20.00   25.00

☐ **October 5–11, 1951** (volume 4, #40, Jimmy Durante on cover) 15.00   17.00

☐ **October 26–November 1, 1951** (volume 4, #43, Bert Parks and Betty Ann Grove on cover)......................... 27.50   32.50

☐ **November 9–15, 1951** (volume 4, #45, Jackie Gleason on cover) 22.50   27.50

☐ **November 30–December 6, 1951** (volume 4, #48, unknown caveman and woman on cover) 10.00   12.00

☐ **December 7–13, 1951** (volume 4, #49, Jerry Lester and Agathon on cover) ... 17.50   19.50

☐ **December 14–20, 1951** (volume 4, #50, Cathy Hild on cover) 15.00   17.00

1952

☐ **January 4–10, 1952** (volume 5, #1, Sid Caesar, Ed Sullivan, Arthur Godfrey, Milton Berle, Perry Como and Groucho Marx on cover) 40.00   45.00

☐ **January 25–31, 1952** (volume 5, #4, Lucille Ball and Desi Arnez on cover) ... 20.00   25.00

☐ **February 15–21, 1952** (volume 5, #7, Harry Truman, Ike Eisenhower, Estes Kefauver and Robert Taft on cover) .. 20.00   25.00

Price Range

☐ **March 14–20, 1952** (volume 5, #11, Martin and Lewis on cover) 55.00   65.00

☐ **April 18–24, 1952** (volume 5, #16, Jimmy Durante on cover) 17.50   19.50

☐ **May 16–22, 1952** (volume 5, #20, Gene Autry on cover) 40.00   45.00

☐ **June 20–26, 1952** (volume 5, #25, Pictures of previous *TV Guide* covers on cover) 25.00   30.00

☐ **June 27–July 3, 1952** (volume 5, #26, Paul Winchell and Jerry Mahoney on cover) 15.00   17.00

☐ **July 4–10, 1952** (volume 5, #27, Bob Hope on cover) 15.00   17.00

☐ **July 25–31, 1952** (volume 5, #30, Sandra Spence of Phantomime Quiz on cover) 35.00   40.00

☐ **August 1–7, 1952** [volume 5, #31, Don Russell and Lee Joyce (of Cavalcade of Stars) on cover] 10.00   12.00

☐ **August 15–21, 1952** (volume 5, #33, cast of "What's My Line" on cover) . .   14.00   16.00

☐ **August 22–28, 1952** (volume 5, #34, Perry Como and Dinah Shore on cover)   22.50   27.50

☐ **September 12–18, 1952** (volume 5, #37, Milton Berle and Lucille Ball on cover)   17.50   19.50

☐ **October 3–9, 1952** (volume 5, #40, Marie Wilson on cover) 15.00   17.00

Price Range

☐ **October 10–16, 1952** (volume 5, #41, L'il Abner characters and Al Capp on cover) 50.00   60.00

☐ **October 17–23, 1952** (volume 5, #42, Arthur Godfrey on cover) 27.50   32.50

☐ **November 21–27, 1952** (volume 5, #47, Howdy Doody and Rootie Kazootie on cover) 27.50   32.50

☐ **November 28–December 4, 1952** (volume 5, #48, Eddie Fisher, Perry Como, Julius LaRosa and Patti Page on cover)   22.50   27.50

☐ **December 12–18, 1952** (volume 5, #50, Arthur Godfrey and Haleloke on cover)   25.00   30.00

☐ **December 26, 1952–January 1, 1953** (volume 5, #52, Jack Russell, Judy Johnson, Bill Hayes and Marguerite Piazza on cover) 10.00   12.00

1953

☐ **January 2–8, 1953** (volume 6, #1, Jackie Gleason on cover) 35.00   40.00

☐ **January 23–29, 1953** (volume 6, #4, Marilyn Monroe on cover) 35.00   40.00

☐ **February 6–12, 1953** (volume 6, #6, Roxanne on cover) 20.00   25.00

☐ **February 13–19, 1953** (volume 6, #7, Kukla, Fran and Ollie on cover) 25.00   30.00

☐ **March 6–12, 1953** (volume 6, #10, Jimmy Durante on cover) 25.00   30.00

Price Range

☐ **March 13–19, 1953** (volume 6, #11, Ja-
nette Davis on cover) 15.00   17.00

☐ **March 20–26, 1953** (volume 6, #12,
Lucy's neighbors the Mertz's on cover)   17.50   19.50

☐ **March 27–April 2, 1953** (volume 6, #13,
Charlton Heston, John Newland, John
Forsythe and John Baragrey on cover)   25.00   30.00
(This is the last regional edition of *TV
Guide.* The next issue was for nationwide
distribution and the numbering system
was started again from #1.)

☐ **April 3–9, 1953** (issue #1, photo of Lucille Ball's baby on cover, with small
photo of Lucy in upper right corner,
headline "Lucy's $50,000,000 Baby."
This referred to the fact that many episodes of "I Love Lucy" in late 1952 and
early 1953 were built around Lucy's
pregnancy, and the fact that the baby
("Little Ricky") became an instant TV
star. Though the issue is labeled #1, it
was actually not the first issue of *TV
Guide,* as regional issues had been published previously; it was the first coast-
to-coast issue, and the first with a glossy
cover) 145.00   170.00

☐ **April 10–16, 1953** (issue #2, Jack Webb
on cover) 50.00   60.00

☐ **April 17–23, 1953** (issue #3, caricatures
of Lucille Ball, Arthur Godfrey, Milton
Berle, Sid Caesar and Imogene Coca on
cover) 20.00   25.00

Price Range

☐ **April 24–30, 1953** (issue #4, Ralph Edwards on cover) 22.50   27.50

☐ **May 1–7, 1953** (issue #5, Eve Arden on cover) 36.00   41.00

☐ **May 8–14, 1953** (issue #6, Arthur Godfrey on cover) 25.00   30.00

☐ **May 22–28, 1953** (issue #8, Red Buttons on cover) 20.00   25.00

☐ **June 12–18, 1953** (issue #11, Eddie Fisher on cover) 15.00   17.00

☐ **June 19–25, 1953** (issue #12, Ed Sullivan on cover) 10.00   12.00

☐ **July 3–9, 1953** (issue #14, Perry Como on cover) 8.00   10.00

☐ **July 17–23, 1953** (issue #16, Lucille Ball and Desi Arnez on cover) 25.00   30.00

☐ **July 24–30, 1953** (issue #17, caricature of Groucho Marx on cover) 25.00   30.00

☐ **August 14–20, 1953** (issue #20, Patti Page on cover) 15.00   17.00

☐ **August 21–27, 1953** (issue #21, Mary Hartline and Claude Kirchner of Super Circus on cover) 25.00   30.00

☐ **August 28–September 3, 1953** (issue #22, Jane and Audrey Meadows on cover) 12.50   14.50

☐ **October 2–8, 1953** (issue #27, Red Skelton on cover) 17.00   19.00

Price Range

☐ **October 16–22, 1953** (issue #29, TV beauty contestants on cover) 10.00   12.00

☐ **October 23–29, 1953** (issue #30, Arthur Godfrey on cover) 14.00   16.00

☐ **October 30–November 5, 1953** (issue #31, Beulah Witch, Kukla and Ollie on cover) 15.00   17.00

☐ **November 6–12, 1953** (issue #32, Warren Hull on cover) 15.00   17.00

☐ **November 20–26, 1953** (issue #34, Dorothy McGuire and Julius LaRosa on cover) 25.00   30.00

☐ **November 27–December 3, 1953** (issue #35, Lugene Sanders on cover) 10.00   12.00

☐ **December 4–10, 1953** (issue #36, Loretta Young on cover) 10.00   12.00

☐ **December 25–31, 1953** (issue #39, Perry Como, Patti Page and Eddie Fisher on cover) 10.00   12.00

1954

☐ **March 19–25, 1954** (issue #51, Groucho Marx on cover) 36.00   41.00

☐ **May 14–20, 1954** (issue #59, Frank Sinatra on cover with headline, "Can Frank Sinatra Make Good in TV?") . .   32.00   37.00

☐ **June 25–July 1, 1954** (issue #65, Howdy Doody and Bob Smith on cover) 45.00   50.00

☐ **August 14–20, 1954** (issue #72, Martin and Lewis on cover) 22.50   27.50

Price Range

☐ **October 23–29, 1954** (issue #82, Walt
Disney, Mickey Mouse, Donald Duck,
Pluto, Goofy and Dopey on cover) ...   35.00   40.00

☐ **December 24–31, 1954** (issue #91, Nelson family on cover (before Ricky Nel-
son launched pop music career) 45.00   50.00

1955

☐ **January 15–21, 1955** (issue #94, Gary
Moore on cover, and an article on
Johnny Carson) 16.00   18.00

☐ **March 5–11, 1955** [issue #101, Liberace
on cover (he was doing a daily late-
afternoon show)] 15.00   17.00

☐ **October 22–28, 1955** (issue #134,
George Gobel on cover) 9.00   11.00

☐ **December 17–23, 1955** (issue #142,
Robert Montgomery on cover) 14.00   16.00

1956

☐ **January 21–27, 1956** (issue #147, Lawrence Welk on cover) 7.00   9.00

☐ **April 14–20, 1956** (issue #159, Grace
Kelly wedding issue) 22.00   27.00

☐ **April 28–May 4, 1956** (issue #161, Red
Skelton on cover) 5.00   7.00

☐ **August 11–17, 1956** [issue #176, Democratic National Convention issue
(Adlai Stevenson was to oppose Presi-
dent Eisenhower)] 7.00   9.00

TV Guide, February 12–18, 1955

TV Guide, February 19–25, 1955

Price Range

☐ **September 8–14, 1956** (issue #180, Elvis Presley on cover, first *TV Guide* cover of Elvis; he had just hit the big time via appearances on the Jackie Gleason show) 80.00   90.00

☐ **December 1–7, 1956** (issue #192, caricature of George Burns on cover) 22.00   27.00

1957

☐ **January 19–25, 1957** (issue #199, Jerry Lewis on cover) 9.00   11.00

☐ **February 23–March 1, 1957** [issue #204, Charles van Doren on cover (he was a national sensation after winning a fortune on Jack Barry's "21" quiz program)] 9.00   11.00

☐ **May 11–17, 1957** (issue #215, James Arness on cover, article on Rod Serling of "Twilight Zone") 32.00   37.00

☐ **August 31–September 6, 1957** (issue #231, Clint Walker on cover) 32.00   37.00

☐ **November 23–29, 1957** [issue #243, Mary Martin on cover (Larry Hagman's mother)] 7.00   9.00

1958

☐ **February 8–14, 1958** (issue #254, Tab Hunter on cover) 14.00   16.00

☐ **April 5–11, 1958** (issue #262, Gale Storm on cover) 8.00   10.00

☐ **April 19–25, 1958** (issue #264, Polly Bergen on cover) 11.00   12.00

Price Range

☐ **October 4–10, 1958** (issue #288, Dick Clark on cover) 22.00   27.00

☐ **November 8–14, 1958** (issue #293, Loretta Young on cover) 7.00   9.00

☐ **November 22–28, 1958** (issue #295, Ronald Reagan on cover (he was host of a show called "Death Valley Days") .. 60.00   70.00

1959

☐ **January 10–16, 1959** (issue #302, Milton Berle on cover) 14.00   16.00

☐ **February 7–13, 1959** (issue #306, Chuck Conners on cover) 27.00   32.00

☐ **March 21–27, 1959** (issue #312, Ann Southern on cover) 17.00   19.00

☐ **June 27–July 3, 1959** (issue #326, Lloyd Bridges on cover, with article on the death of George Reeves (who had played "Superman" on TV) 32.00   37.00

☐ **November 7–13, 1959** (issue #345, Jack Benny on cover) 10.00   12.00

☐ **December 12–18, 1959** (issue #350, Danny Thomas on cover) 7.00   9.00

1960

☐ **January 9–15, 1960** (issue #354, Jane Wyatt on cover) 17.00   19.00

☐ **February 27–March 4, 1960** (issue #361, Robert Stack on cover) 14.00   16.00

☐ **May 7–13, 1960** (issue #371, Elvis Presley on cover) 40.00   50.00

Price Range

☐ **June 11–17, 1960** (issue #376, cast of "Bachelor Father" on cover) 14.00   16.00

☐ **August 13–19, 1960** (issue #385, Nick Adams on cover) 14.00   16.00

☐ **October 15–21, 1960** (issue #394, Carol Burnett on cover) 17.00   19.00

1961

☐ **January 28–February 3, 1961** [issue #409, Ron Howard on cover (as young boy—pre-"Happy Days")] 17.00   19.00

☐ **May 27–June 3, 1961** (issue #426, Ronald Reagan on cover) 27.00   32.00

☐ **July 1–7, 1961** (issue #431, The Flintstones on cover) 22.00   27.00

☐ **October 7–13, 1961** (issue #445, Walter Cronkite on cover) 7.00   9.00

☐ **December 16–22, 1961** (issue #455, Richard Chamberlain on cover) 6.00   8.00

1962

☐ **January 6–12, 1962** (issue #458, Vince Edwards on cover) 6.00   8.00

☐ **March 10–16, 1962** [issue #467, Jack Paar on cover (he hosted "The Tonight Show" before Johnny Carson)] 6.00   8.00

☐ **April 21–27, 1962** (issue #473, Connie Stevens on cover) 6.00   8.00

☐ **November 10–16, 1962** (issue #502, Beverly Hillbillies on cover) 7.00   9.00

Price Range

1963

☐ **January 12–18, 1963** (issue #511, Arnold Palmer on cover) 6.00 8.00

☐ **February 9–15, 1963** (issue #515, Ernest Borgnine on cover) 6.00 8.00

☐ **February 16–22, 1963** (issue #516, Princess Grace of Monaco on cover) 10.00 12.00

☐ **June 8–14, 1963** (issue #532, Johnny Carson on cover) 9.00 11.00

☐ **October 5–11, 1963** (issue #549, Phil Silvers on cover) 6.00 8.00

☐ **October 19–25, 1963** (issue #551, Judy Garland on cover) 9.00 11.00

☐ **November 30–December 6, 1963** (issue #557, George C. Scott on cover) 6.00 8.00

1964

☐ **February 1–7, 1964** (issue #566, Danny Kaye on cover) 6.00 8.00

☐ **April 18–24, 1964** (issue #577, James Franciscus on cover, coverage of Beatles on Ed Sullivan Show) 10.00 12.00

☐ **September 5–11, 1964** (issue #597, Lucille Ball on cover) 8.00 10.00

☐ **October 17–23, 1964** (issue #603, Lassie on cover) 5.00 7.00

☐ **December 12–18, 1964** (issue #611, Julie Newmar on cover) 5.00 7.00

	Price Range	

1965

☐ **January 2–8, 1965** (issue #614, The Munsters on cover) 7.00   9.00

☐ **March 6–12, 1965** (issue #623, David Janssen on cover) 5.00   7.00

☐ **September 11–17, 1965** [issue #650, Fall Preview Issue (these are always a premium item for collectors)] 20.00   25.00

☐ **October 16–22, 1965** (issue #655, Red Skelton on cover) 5.00   7.00

☐ **November 13–19, 1965** (issue #659, Joey Heatherton on cover) 5.00   7.00

☐ **December 11–17, 1965** (issue #663, F Troop on cover) 5.00   7.00

1966

☐ **January 1–7, 1966** (issue #666, Carol Channing on cover) 5.00   7.00

☐ **January 15–21, 1966** (issue #668, Bill Cosby on cover, article on Ronald Reagan) 15.00   17.00

☐ **February 5–11, 1966** [issue #671, Larry Hagman on cover (he was starring in "I Dream of Jeannie")] 8.00   10.00

☐ **March 26–April 1, 1966** [issue #678, Adam West ("Batman") on cover] 10.00   12.00

☐ **May 7–13, 1966** (issue #684, Lyndon Johnson on cover) 9.00   11.00

☐ **May 14–20, 1966** (issue #685, Frank Sinatra on cover) 5.00   7.00

TV Guide, Aug. 27, 1966

	Price Range	
☐ **September 10–16, 1966** (issue #702, Fall Preview Issue)	18.00	20.00
☐ **October 29–November 4, 1966** (issue #709, Bruce Lee on cover)	10.00	12.00
1967		
☐ **January 21–27, 1967** (issue #721, Diana Rigg on cover)	8.00	10.00
☐ **March 4–10, 1967** (issue #727, Leonard Nimoy and William Shatner on cover, this issue ranks as a "Star Trek" collector's item)	25.00	30.00
☐ **May 13–19, 1967** (issue #737, Elizabeth Montgomery on cover)	5.00	7.00
☐ **August 12–18, 1967** (issue #750, Mike Douglas on cover)	5.00	7.00

Price Range

☐ **November 18–24, 1967** (issue #764, Leonard Nimoy and William Shatner on cover; this issue ranks as a "Star Trek" collector's item) 25.00   30.00

1968

☐ **January 6–12, 1968** (issue #771, Robert Conrad on cover) 4.00   6.00

☐ **June 29–July 5, 1968** (issue #796, Robert Wagner on cover) 4.00   6.00

☐ **August 31–September 6, 1968** (issue #805, caricature of Johnny Carson on cover) 6.00   8.00

☐ **October 19–25, 1968** (issue #812, Jim Nabors on cover).................. 4.00   6.00

TV Guide, July 20, 1968

TV Guide, March 30, 1968

TV Guide, Aug. 24, 1968

Price Range

☐ **November 30–December 6, 1968** (issue
#818, Ann-Margret on cover) 4.00   6.00

1969

☐ **April 5–11, 1969** (issue #836, Smothers
Brothers on cover) 5.00   7.00

☐ **June 14–20, 1969** (issue #846, Glen
Campbell on cover) 4.00   6.00

☐ **December 6–12, 1969** (issue #871,
Doris Day on cover) 4.00   6.00

TV Guide, Nov. 2, 1968

Newspapers

BACKGROUND: No published product is more frequently saved in times of major national and international developments than the newspaper. Headlines reporting on the assassination of President Kennedy and the first moon landing are among the most saved items of all time. Consequently, papers reporting on the death of JFK, for example, are fairly common. The most desirable are those from Dallas, which are today capable of netting over $50. The moral: seek newspapers from the cities in which major events took place.

	Price Range	
☐ **The Blade,** Toledo, July 21, 1969, "Americans Walk On Moon With World As Witness" overlarge photos of Armstrong's first steps on the moon, first section of 16 pp., some light brown	8.00	12.00
☐ **The Daily Journal-Gazette,** April 19, 1951, "MacArthur Tells Nation His Story," "Says Military Chiefs Share View On Asia," with front-page photos	3.00	5.00
☐ **Ledger-Star,** November 25, 1963, 56 pp., "John Fitzgerald Kennedy 1917–1963," black-boardered photo, front-page article, large piece torn from lower right front page, of interest is a 2nd section feature on the Lincoln assassination, in which is illustrated an April 15, 1865 New York Herald, which is in fact a reprint	4.00	6.00
☐ **The "Portland Sunday Telegram" Parade Supplement,** in color, dated March 11, 1962, Elvis Presley on cover	8.00	10.00

Price Range

☐ **The Sacramento Bee,** November 23, 1963, Kennedy assassination 6.00   8.00

☐ **Virginian-Pilot,** November 24, 1963, 104 pp., "A Leader Is Fallen But A Nation Still Stands," "President At Work Amid U.S. Sorrow," front page photos of JFK's flag-draped coffin, LBJ, Oswald, full coverage within 8.00   12.00

☐ **Wyoming State Tribune,** April 12, 1957, news of the day, sports, comics, etc., on masthead is a sticker proclaiming that this paper is "Compliments of the Streamliner" city of San Francisco train   4.00   8.00

Who We Voted For

In the slogan-crazy '50s, a three-word message epitomized the era: "I Like Ike." The political scene of the '50s, despite the strong undercurrent of the Cold War Years, appeared almost tranquil. Everyone's favorite grandfather-figure, the "Old General," Dwight Eisenhower, was in the White House—the seemingly perfect conclusion to the postwar years.

The political scene was to change markedly during the '60s with the election of John F. Kennedy as President. The "New Frontier" was

Premiere Presentation of The
EISENHOWER COLLEGE COLLECTION
DINNER MATS

A collection of fine art prints from the paintings
of the 34th President of the United States.

Eisenhower placemats

launched, and before it was over we were promised the moon. (Kennedy personally went on record in 1963 that man would land on the moon and return safely to the earth before the decade was out.)

But Kennedy's own assassination on November 22, 1963 brought to an early end his New Frontier, and the administration of his successor, Lyndon Baines Johnson, was rife with domestic and international strife. At the center of the turmoil was the controversial war in Vietnam. The decade ended with the beginning of the Nixon years. Nixon promised to return normalcy to the country and had a "secret plan" to end the war in Vietnam, a plan he called "Vietnamization." Most Americans believed he could do it. He was still a few years from his own personal Waterloo, Watergate.

Political Memorabilia

TYPES COVERED: Political newspaper headlines, letters, magazine covers, autographed photographs, assorted campaign memorabilia.

In Pursuit of the Presidency

Raleigh DeGeer Amyx is like most people. He has a business, and he has a hobby. However, the function of his business (an autograph service) is to pay for his hobby. "My hobby," said Raleigh, "is my passion. It's my museum of presidential memorabilia."

Raleigh's museum, located in Vienna, Virginia, near Washington, D.C., is unusual in many ways. In the first place, he charges no admission at the door. Secondly, the

(photo by Cornelius J. Dwyer)

Raleigh DeGeer Amyx with JFK's eyeglasses

museum is in his own home. Finally, the museum contains personal and unique memorabilia from all of the Presidents of the United States, beginning with George Washington and continuing through the present administration.

It all started back in 1981, when Raleigh was recovering from throat cancer and decided to get involved in something he had always loved—collecting items from all the Presidents and putting them together. The result is a museum which is unique in America. It's called Presidential U.S.A., and it's situated close to the nation's capital, about 15 miles from the Smithsonian Institution. Raleigh began, he said, with almost nothing, and now has over 600 items in his museum, including Harry Truman's famous Stetson hat and a survey conducted by 17-year-old George Washington.

Raleigh has amassed his collection over the past few years by approaching former members of the White House staff and people who have been close enough to the Presidents to have received items from them. Many times the recipients, mostly elderly and retired, don't know what else to do with such things. "It's hard to put a price on some of these items, which may be priceless as sentimental keepsakes," Raleigh remarked. "Many times a person will accept a donation to his or her favorite charity rather than direct payment." Raleigh assures the donors of his honorable intentions, and promises them that the important items in his museum will someday be given to the American people. "I don't know just how to go about doing that yet," he admitted. Right now, however, he gives tours through his museum, free of charge, preferably on an appointment basis, since, "the museum is in my home."

The Amyx museum has a more extensive collection of presidential items than the Smithsonian, although Raleigh said matter-of-factly that he can't come close to the extensive First Lady Collection that the Smithsonian boasts. His security system, however, rivals that of the Smithsonian, since "People entrust me with their most valued possessions, and I feel it's my duty to protect them to the fullest."

(photo by Don Rutledge/Camera Press)

Original oil painting by Eisenhower

Items have been entrusted to Raleigh DeGeer Amyx by former Secret Service agents, White House doormen, laundresses, maids, cooks, butlers, and chauffeurs. "These people may grow old realizing that they have no one to give these mementos to who might really care for them, and so they pass them on to me," Raleigh explained. "I feel that I am very lucky. I am doing exactly what I want to in my life. If at the same time I am able to do a service for the American people, that's fine with me."

The largest amount of memorabilia in Raleigh's collection from the '50s-'60s era comes from the presidency of Dwight D. Eisenhower. Usually, the items of most value once belonged to John F. Kennedy. These items are hard to come by, since "Kennedy died at a young age—47—and many members of his staff are still living, and still holding on to their mementos. Some of them, in fact, still work at the White House."

This is true of the Presidents from the '60s to the present. Items from the '60s, especially, are scarce.

Eisenhower's gold Rolex watch

(photo by Don Rutledge/Camera Press)

"You can tell much of a president's personality from the things he had and gave away to people," Raleigh said. "People collected golfballs that Eisenhower sliced on the White House lawn. Harry Truman, on the other hand, liked to walk. He never walked anywhere without a hat. To one man who asked him for something to remember him by when he was leaving the White House in 1952, Truman proffered his hat. 'I hope you don't mind that my name is inside,' he said. And he'd give things to people from his pockets—matchboxes and pins that read, 'I swiped this from Harry Truman.'"

Another item of great interest in Raleigh's museum is John F. Kennedy's last pair of prescription glasses. "They are chewed at the tips," Raleigh observed, "because he had a habit of chewing on the stems when he was deep in thought."

Richard Nixon, on the other hand, collects elephants. "I have this pewter elephant which was his," Raleigh said. "I think it's symbolic of the things he held dear, being the symbol both of strength and of the Republican party."

Presidential U.S.A. includes Raleigh DeGeer Amyx's autograph business as well. "The autographs," Raleigh stressed, "are chiefly to pay for the museum." If you want to begin collecting autographs, Raleigh suggests, "Go to the library and check out every book on the subject. Learn all you can, and then when you get an autograph, take it to an expert to verify its authenticity."

For autographs of U.S. presidents, Raleigh is willing to divulge some hints to the prospective collector. "Many presidents use a secretary or an autopen—a signature machine—to sign their names. Many secretaries are very good at this—so good, in fact, that it's difficult to tell the difference between their signature and the real thing."

If you have an autograph of Dwight Eisenhower's, written while he was at the White House, Raleigh explained, there is about a 95 percent chance that it's the real thing. "Eisenhower never used an autopen at the White House, and he didn't allow other people to sign his name for him at that time."

However, with the autographs of Kennedy, LBJ, and Nixon, it's a different story. "If you have an autograph of any of these presidents," Raleigh says, "chances are less than half that it's an authentic signature. These presidents commonly used an autopen."

Is autograph-collecting the sort of thing an ordinary person can afford as a hobby? "Yes," Raleigh says, "if you stick to cut signatures." Cut signatures are those cut or clipped from a document. Collecting cut signatures as well as writing to movie stars or personalities for their autographs is a good way to start an autograph collecting hobby.

Fame and fortune, however, can be misleading, Raleigh explains. "For instance, the autograph of Jimmy Stewart is worth far less than that of Cary Grant. This does not reflect on the worth or acting ability of one actor over the other. The case is simply that Jimmy Stewart is a very nice guy who signs his name for anybody who asks him for it. Cary Grant, however, valued his privacy in the extreme, and very seldom autographed anything for anyone, which makes his signature scarce. Jimmy Stewart's signed photograph, therefore, may be worth only $20 or so, while I just bought an autographed picture of Cary Grant for $200."

Another important factor in collecting autographs, Raleigh explains, is the item on which the signature appears. A photograph with a signature on it may be worth a nominal amount of money, while an important or unique letter or other document bearing the same signature may be worth a great deal more.

Raleigh DeGeer Amyx is a unique man in the world of collecting. Modest yet forthright, he best sums up his own philosophy about his museum. "It's true that I am very proud of my museum and the fine quality it represents, but I want to stress the quality because I want the museum to be passed on to the American people someday. I also know I'm very lucky, because people entrust me with their most prized possessions. I try to be worthy of that trust."

Price Range

Eisenhower, Dwight D.

☐ **Invitation, Inaugural Invitation for Dwight D. Eisenhower and Richard M. Nixon,** in original envelope with freefrank of Senator Styles Bridges, 1953, first term 20.00   30.00

☐ **Letter, Dwight Eisenhower,** signed personal letter to his brother, 1950 ...... 250.00   270.00

☐ **Newspaper Headlines, Results of Presidential Elections**
1952, Eisenhower/Stevenson 3.00   6.00
1956, Eisenhower/Stevenson 2.00   4.00

☐ **Sticker, "I Like Ike,"** 3 x 3½", 1952 or 1956 .... 5.00   10.00

Price Range

Goldwater, Barry

☐ **Soda Carton, "Goldwater—The Right
Drink For The Conservative Taste,"**
cardboard carton that once held six cans
of soda, soda cans missing, 1964 . . . . .   16.00   24.00

Johnson, Lyndon

☐ **Button, 1964, Johnson/Goldwater** . . .   2.00   4.00

Kennedy Collectibles: Souvenirs of The New Frontier

"Ask not what can your country do for you. Ask what
you can do for your country."

John F. Kennedy's immortal words struck deep into the
hearts of many Americans. One of them is Bonnie Gardner,
president of the Kennedy Political Items Collectors, a 200-
member organization dedicated to the preservation of memorabilia from the Kennedy family.

In 1960, Americans put their faith in the youngest president ever elected to office. (The 43-year-old Kennedy was
undercut in age only by 42-year-old Theodore Roosevelt,
who had gained the presidency after President McKinley
was assassinated in 1901.)

John Fitzgerald Kennedy was born in 1917 destined to
become this country's 35th president. He graduated from
Harvard in 1940, gained fame as a PT boat commander from
1941 to 1945, and was awarded the Navy and Marine Corps
Medal. He wrote *Profiles in Courage,* a book for which he received the Pulitzer Prize. From 1947 to 1953 he served as a
Congressman from Massachusetts, after which he was
elected to the Senate. He went on to win the Presidency in
1960, defeating Republican Richard Nixon. He was also the
first Catholic president of our country.

Kennedy's most important accomplishment as President was his handling of the Cuban Missile Crisis in 1962. He also bucked the steel industry, backed the civil rights movement, established a mental health program, and expanded medical care for the elderly. He supported the space program and was one of the most popular presidents this nation has ever had. With his wide smile and wavy hair, he was an attractive, original figure who was extremely popular with the young.

Why the continued interest in the Kennedys today, 24 years after JFK's death, and nearly 20 years since his brother Bobby's assassination?

"Basically, the '60s with JFK was fresh and exciting," says Bonnie, who is a junior high school principal in California. "He made us feel so alive! The feeling was, 'We're the greatest country in the world!' And you've got to admit, the Kennedys are such an interesting family, just from the human interest they provide, no matter what your political views are."

The Kennedy Political Items Collectors are a chapter of the larger American Political Items Collectors, which is 2000–3000 members strong. To join the 10-year-old Kennedy chapter, members must first join the APIC, a nonprofit organization dedicated to the study and preservation of materials relating to political campaigns of the U.S. The APIC was organized in 1945, and includes political items from the entire field of American politics, from presidential campaigns to gubernatorial contests, mayoral races to those of local candidates, and from campaign memorabilia to mementos of private lives. Membership dues are $16 per year, and members receive the *APIC Keynoter,* a quarterly journal of historical and research articles and hobby news, plus the *APIC Newsletter,* an annual roster-handbook, and the opportunity to attend meetings and conventions nationwide.

To join the KPIC, dues are an additional $7.50 per year, which make a member eligible to receive a bi-monthly newsletter, the *Hyannisporter,* which includes latest news on

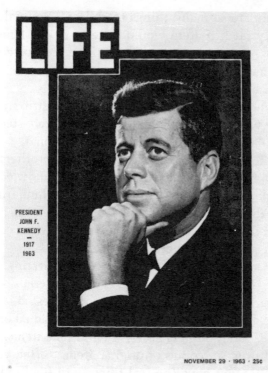

PRESIDENT
JOHN F.
KENNEDY
—
1917
1963

NOVEMBER 29 · 1963 · 25¢

Life magazine covering JFK assassination

the yearly auction of Kennedy materials, a broad variety of items on all the Kennedys, classified ads, and much more. For more information, write to Secretary/Treasurer John Henigan, 1124 Arthur Avenue, Racine, Wisconsin 53405.

As far as conventions go, there is a national APIC convention every two years in Louisville, Kentucky; usually in August. There is no museum, but the Smithsonian has a large number of Kennedy items, and the Kennedy Library in Boston is open to the public. During 1987, an exhibition will be held May 29–30.

"There are so many things to collect," Bonnie Gardner says. "My favorite item would have to be the handcarved Kennedy meerschaum pipe. Then there are posters, pamphlets, matchbooks, stamps, plates, newspapers, and of course, the buttons."

The most common items are buttons distributed while Kennedy was in office in 1962. Then, there were steel workers' so-called "SOB" buttons (dispute buttons).

"I collect items from all three Kennedy brothers," Bonnie says. "I collect for my own pleasure and knowledge. The most important thing is that you learn something from your hobby. And political items collecting is a learning experience! Just think of all the history you absorb when you begin to collect political memorabilia."

To start a hobby of political items collecting, Bonnie suggests: "Study the hobby. Read APIC materials. Find out all you can about the era you are most interested in." After you have done your research, contact the national organization, APIC, and join a chapter. "Avoid fake items, such as phony buttons, or copies of original items. Often you can't tell whether you have the real thing until it's too late."

Some of the most expensive buttons around came from the 1960 campaign, in which the printer goofed and put Kennedy's picture under Nixon's name, and vice versa. These buttons sold at auction for $150 and $200 each.

There was a deluge of memorabilia produced after the assassination of John F. Kennedy, and all sorts of memorial items appeared on the American scene. There were medals, two postage stamps, a 13-cent and a five-cent, and a First Day issue on his birthdate in 1964. There were cloth tapestries, banners and large silk handkerchiefs.

John F. Kennedy put the spirit of Camelot into our country for a short time during the early '60s. With people like Bonnie Gardner and the Kennedy Political Items Collectors around, his spirit will live on in the memories of Americans for a long time to come.

Price Range

Letter

☐ **Typed letter signed December 27, 1960,**
a month before inauguration 250.00   300.00

Magazines

Modern Screen

☐ **December, 1964** (JFK & Jackie cover) .. 20.00   30.00

☐ **October, 1967** (Jackie Kennedy cover) 10.00   20.00

Movie Stars Parade

(Becomes *Movie Stars* in 1960s.)

☐ **October, 1964** (Jackie Kennedy cover) 10.00   20.00

Newspaper Headlines

(Result of Presidential Election)

☐ **1960, Kennedy/Nixon** 8.00   12.00

John Kennedy cards

Price Range

Robert Kennedy Memorabilia

☐ **Photo,** promotional photo, with facsimile signature, distributed during his campaign in California, primary election of 1968, brief biographical sketch on reverse, 5½" x 8½", 1968 . . . .   40.00   50.00

Richard Nixon Memorabilia

☐ **Newspaper Headlines,** Results of Presidential Elections of 1968, Nixon/Humphrey 2.00   4.00

☐ **Photo, Richard Nixon,** 11 x 14 b & w photo, signed in 1969 . . . .   250.00   300.00

☐ **Sticker, "Let's Back Nixon,"** 4 x 6" paper sticker showing Nixon pointing his finger at Khrushchev, 1960 campaign 15.00   20.00

Nixon-Lodge pinback

Price Range

Ronald Reagan Memorabilia

☐ **Ronald Reagan,** portrait autographed to
John Ford, 1960s 300.00   400.00

Ronald Reagan during his movie days

Ronald Reagan V-8 ad

Our New Heroes

The late '50s and '60s brought us a new form of hero via the manned space program. The Mercury astronauts, upon the completion of their missions, were given the greatest hero welcomes since Lindberg. Overnight, John Glenn, Alan Shepard, and Scott Carpenter became household names as schools suspended regular classes to allow students to watch the takeoffs live over national television. Before the end of the decade, television would be carrying transmissions live from the moon.

DESCRIPTION: Manned spacecraft collectibles are enjoying a steady increase in interest. The future bodes well for this field of collectibles, as these first voyagers into space will be viewed as pioneers in the distant future. The most popular collectibles stem from the mission of Apollo 11, man's first landing on the moon.

Manned Spacecraft Collectibles

The seven Apollo astronauts

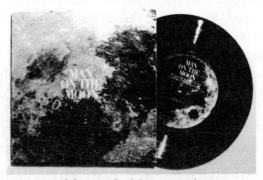

Man on the Moon record

Apollo First Day Cover

Postcard of John Glenn's home town

Photograph of Buzz Aldrin walking
on the moon

Booklet documenting the flight of
Astronaut Carpenter

Booklet documenting the flight of Astronaut Glenn

A March 25, 1965, edition of *Spaceport News*,
published by NASA

See You At The Fair

The era was marked by two successful world expositions, the New York World's Fair of 1964–65, and Expo '67, held in Montreal. While not as popular as the New York World's Fair of 1939–40 with collectors, items from these two fairs are gaining in interest with buffs. Memorabilia is still readily available and collectors are advising that now is the time to make your purchases.

World's Fair Collectibles

Expo '67 booklet

Souvenir map of Expo '67

Expo '67 record

New York World's Fair map

New York World's Fair ticket

Kid's World

DESCRIPTION: Toys, products and printed materials targeted toward children. The post-war baby boom prompted a greatly increased output of merchandising geared toward children during the 1950s and '60s. Lifelike dolls, outer space toys and themes, a steady abundance of Disney products (backed-up by Disney television programs and numerous successful Disney films of the '50s and '60s) were all a part of being a kid during these years.

TYPES COVERED: Books, comics and funnies, Disneyana, dolls, toys and games.

Children's Books

A Revolution in Juvenile Fiction

When we think of books for kids in the '50s and '60s, the first word that comes to mind is "variety."

This was the era which gave us many now-famous classics of literary or artistic works: Garth Williams and his unique, furry animals; *Paddington Bear* by Michael Bond; the *Chronicles of Narnia* by C. S. Lewis; and *Charlotte's Web* by E. B. White. Children's textbooks during the '50s, such as those featuring Dick, Jane and Sally, continue to monopolize children's reading books as they have for years.

In the '60s, however, books for children experienced something of a revolution. *Ramona Quimby,* by Beverly Cleary, made her dynamic appearance, at first as the annoying little sister of Beezus, then as a main character of many books in her own right. Ezra Jack Keats became the first artist to depict children of the slums and black children as main characters of children's books. His *A Snowy Day* won the

Maurice Sendak book

Caldecott Medal for the best picture book of the year in 1962, marked by bold, colorful, simple illustrations—a distinct break from tradition.

Russell and Lillian Hoban made badgers unforgetable characters when the independent and stubborn Frances came on the scene. Maurice Sendak's sensitive three-color illustrations for Else Minarik Holmenund's *Little Bear* books were among the most worthy developments of the '60s. But it was in 1963 that the illustrator made history with an entirely different book which caused a stir among librarians and patrons of the literary world with his book, *Where the Wild Things Are.* The book was awarded the Caldecott Medal for that year, but was banned from many library shelves and bookstores because of its "unnatural and disobedient nature." Max, the hero of the book, dared to rebel against his mother when she sent him to bed without his supper. He fantasized about a land where he could be king, in a time when most books urged children to be good and conform. In many ways, Sendak's book for children mirrored what was happening in the adult world during the tumultuous decade.

In the 1960s, a renewed interest in folklore started a boom in the folktale literature which lasted well into the next decade. Folklore progressed beyond the Brothers Grimm and Hans Christian Andersen for the first time, and tales from the Orient, Africa, India, and other faraway lands graced library shelves. People who grew up associating Snow White and Sleeping Beauty with the Disney characters read realistic interpretations of these tales which eliminated the "cuteness" of the Disney versions and adhered to the original Grimm tellings. This trend has continued through the '70s and '80s.

As the '60s continued, children's books reflected a wide range of social issues: the women's movement, the civil rights movement, poverty, the ecology. Women were portrayed for the first time in something other than a domestic role, and blacks and other ethnic groups became main char-

A Kiss for Little Bear

acters in books, instead of background characters. The so-called "problem" stories were born, dealing with heretofore hush-hush subjects such as death, divorce, alcoholism, and bigotry. Finally, Dick, Jane and Sally disappeared from elementary school classrooms and were replaced by other children who were more in step with the times.

Juvenile fiction of the '50s and '60s, which for the most part has yet to stabilize on the collecting marketplace, is a safe bet on emerging as one of the period's great "sleepers"—subtle souvenirs of a period of major social change.

Price Range

Children's Books Collectibles

☐ *Angel* **coloring book,** Saalfield #2485, features artwork by Mel Casson, dated 1956 . . . .   9.00   13.00

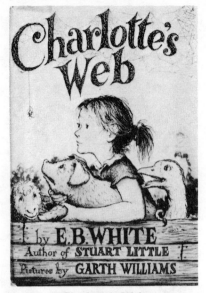

Charlotte's Web

	Price Range	
☐ *Hoppalong Cassidy Western Magazine,* Vol. 1, No. 2, colored cover, published by Best Books, 162 pp., Winter 1951	60.00	70.00
☐ *Hoppalong Cassidy with Cole Bros. Circus,* souvenir program, color cover, 32 pp., 1950	25.00	35.00
☐ *Hoppalong Cassidy* coloring book, Abbott Publishing Co., 10″ x 15″, unused, 1950	18.00	22.00
☐ *Little Lulu,* 1960, Whitman paper doll book, #1999, cut	30.00	40.00
☐ *Patti Doll Book,* 1961, Samuel Lowe, cut	2.00	4.00

	Price Range	
☐ *Prom Home Permanent,* 1952, Samuel Lowe, paper-doll book, uncut	10.00	18.00
☐ *School Friends,* 1955–60, Merrill book, #1556, three dolls—Linda, Bobbie and Diane, dresses and cowgirl suit, uncut	12.00	18.00
☐ *Shirley Temple,* 1958, Saalfield book #5110, statuette doll, assorted dresses, folder, cut	40.00	50.00
☐ *Sports Time,* 1952, Whitman book #2090, blonde doll in white slip, uncut	10.00	18.00
☐ *Star Time,* c. 1960s book #1317, reprint of book from 1950s, six dolls, parts of Butterfly Ballet and Ice Carnival, assorted costumes, uncut	12.00	18.00

Shirley Temple book, 1958

Price Range

☐ *Story Princess, T.V. Arlene Dalton,*
1957, Saalfield book #2761, Civil War
era costumes, uncut 45.00   55.00

☐ *Sugar and Spice,* 1966, Saalfield, paper
doll book, uncut 2.00   4.00

☐ *Sugar Plum Pals,* 1966, Saalfield book   2.00   8.00

☐ *Susan Book,* 1950, Merrill book, #3446,
three dolls, assorted clothes, cut 8.00   12.00

☐ *Umbrella Girls,* 1956, Merrill book,
paper dolls, uncut 25.00   35.00

Little Golden Books are Popular Again!

"Once upon a time, four kittens were born in a corner
of a barn.

'I wonder what kind of cats they'll grow up to be,'
thought the mother cat. . . ."

Simple stuff? Yes. Popular? You bet, especially if you
were a kid during the '50s and '60s. The opening lines to
"Four Little Kittens," written by Kathleen M. Daly and illustrated by Adriane Mazza Saviozzi in 1957, typified the
soft, gentle storylines which made Little Golden Books beloved to young readers in the '50s and '60s. This is the same
appeal which today is responsible for a steady increase in
their status as collectibles.

Steve Santi, bitten by the nostalgia bug of Little Golden
Books from their inception in 1942, started collecting them
about six years ago. "I started buying them at flea markets
and got carried away," he recalls.

Steve today collects Golden Books numerically. "My favorites are the books from the mid-'50s to mid-'60s." The
Golden Books collected from this era range in price from one
or two dollars to ten dollars, which nevertheless represents
at least a tenfold increase in their value over the years. The

earlier titles have seen greater appreciation in value, as Steve points out, as evidenced by the fact that the first Little Golden Book from 1942, a Disney title, already costs $45. (The prices in the accompanying price list, he stresses, are for first editions. Other editions would start at 25 percent less, for first editions. "Remember," Steve adds, "these are for mint books—no tears, pencil, ink marks, or broken spines.")

Steve has written a *Little Golden Book Guide,* which includes interesting background information on the books, hints and prices. His guide is available for seven dollars by writing to: Steve Santi, 19626 Ricardo Avenue, Hayward, CA 94541. The book covers all Little Golden Books printed from 1942 to 1986, listed in numerical order, with author, illustrator, and copyright included. Steve says that there is no collectors' club for LGB collectors, but he hopes to get a newsletter going in the coming year.

Steve advises the beginning collector to check flea markets and garage sales for Little Golden Books. "The books are getting harder to find, but are still available." He feels that this source can be expected to diminish in coming years as more collectors discover the books.

Regarding condition, Steve says that "Pencil marks can be erased, but ink and crayon cannot. A tear may be okay, but a missing or partly torn page is not." Concerning repairs, Steve admonishes, "Never use tape on a book!" To keep your books in top shape, he suggests Mylar bags, "They make them look nice and help to keep them that way."

Some examples of the rarer or more valuable books of the '50s and '60s are "Leave It To Beaver" books (chiefly due to the current popularity of Beaver), as well as other books based on TV programs of the day, such as Westerns (Annie Oakley, Roy Rogers), and children's shows (Howdy Doody, Rootie Kazootie). Disney titles also remain leaders with Little Golden Books, along with titles in conjunction with the Mickey Mouse Club beginning in the late '50s.

Fellow collector John Wharton prefers Disney titles and Little Golden Books with Garth Williams artwork, and adds that, because Giant Little Golden Books, Activity Books and spinoff puzzles found intact are very rare and among the most valuable children's books of the period, they also attract his attention.

Elaborating on condition, he says, "Little Golden Books should have their spines intact, minor tears or no tears, have the cover gloss present, and have a minimal amount of writing." Wharton stores his books in bags, away from direct sunlight and upright on a bookshelf.

Collector Kirk Stines said he has had luck in tracking down needed titles by "running ads in collector and antique newspapers."

Steve Santi was kind enough to provide us with the following history of the books, as summarized in his guide:

Simon and Schuster, Inc., published Little Golden Books until 1959, when Golden Press, Inc., took over. In 1965, Western Publishing acquired publication rights to the books and is still issuing them today.

By the middle of the 1950s, the influence of television was reflected in Little Golden Books. Children's TV shows and westerns were attention-grabbers in the books, until the early '60s, when Saturday morning cartoon shows took over as topics. From 1965 until the early '70s, Little Golden Books dropped TV subjects and went back to original stories as subject matter.

The price of Little Golden Books changed subtly for their first 30 years of publication, changing from the original price of 25 cents (1942 to 1962) to 29 cents. In 1968, the price was increased to 39 cents, followed by a 1974 increase to 49 cents, then 59 cents in 1977, 69 cents in 1979, 89 cents in 1982, and 99 cents in 1986.

Walt Disney Little Golden Books have been published since 1944, but it wasn't until 1947 that new stories were published quite regularly, and have been ever since.

By 1954, the publishers were boasting that more than 300,000,000 Golden Books had gone into the homes of children of all nations.

In 1955, Simon and Schuster started their activity series, which ran until 1961, and included books offering masks, puzzles, stencils, decals, tape, tissue and even Band Aids for young readers.

In 1958, Simon and Schuster brought out Giant Little Golden Books. Most of these contained three Little Golden Books of the same subject in one volume. Puzzles in boxes, which were made from pictures of the covers of Little Golden Books, were released in the early 1950s.

To determine the edition of a book, look on the last page in the lower right hand corner by the spine. The letter shown there designates the edition. If no letter is present, the front of the book will state the printing. Although Little Golden Books have not changed a great deal in their basic appearance over the past four and a half decades, there have been many alterations in style and packaging. Thinner paper, full color illustrations, a silver strip over the spine instead of gold, and the above-mentioned price adjustments are some of the changes which have come about over the years.

Rare and hard-to-find Little Golden Books include the following:

—*Brave Cowboy Bill,* published in 1950, #93 in the series. Cowboy Bill was a novelty book which included a jigsaw puzzle, and it is understandable that a copy of the book with all the puzzle pieces intact is quite a rare find.

—*Doctor Dan the Bandage Man,* #11, complete with six Band Aids.

—*How to Tell Time,* including a die-cut cover with clock face and movable metal hand, is another gold mine in the magical world of Little Golden Books.

Collector Kirk Stines' best advice to collectors of Little Golden Books is brief but valuable: "Enjoy them."

Little Golden Books Collectibles

(*Note:* Each title contains the original issue number, year of first printing, names of author and illustrator, and current value.)

Price

☐ **99,** *Howdy Doody's Circus,* 1950, Liz Dauber (illustrator), Don Gormley (author) 10.00

☐ **107,** *Kittens Surprise,* 1951, Feodor Rojankovsky and Richard Kelsey (illustrator), Nina (author)   4.00

☐ **120,** *Bugs Bunny and the Indians,* 1951, Warner Bros. (illustrator), Annie North Bedford (author) 2.50

☐ **124,** *Robert and His New Friends,* 1951, Corinne Malvern (illustrator), Nina Schneider (author) 3.50

☐ **132,** *Whistling Wizard,* 1953, Mel Crawford (illustrator), Alan Stern (author) 8.00

Little Golden Book, 1946

Price

☐ **133,** *The Rainy Day Play Book,* 1951, Corinne Malvern (illustrator), Rupert Pray (author) 3.50

☐ **142,** *Frosty the Snowman,* 1951, Corinne Malvern (illustrator), Annie North Bedford (author) 3.00

☐ **144,** *The Road to Oz,* 1951, Harry McNaught (illustrator), L. Frank Baum (author) 20.00

☐ **151,** *Emerald City of Oz,* 1952, Harry McNaught (illustrator), Peter Archer (author) 20.00

☐ **156,** *Sailor Dog,* 1953, Garth Williams (illustrator), Margaret Wise Brown (author) 6.00

☐ **157,** *Doctor Squash,* 1952, J.P. Miller (illustrator), Margaret Wise Brown (author) 5.00

☐ **159,** *The Tin Woodsman of Oz,* 1952, Harry McNaught (illustrator), L. Frank Baum; Peter Archer (author) 20.00

☐ **160,** *Danny Beaver's Secret,* 1953, Richard Scarry (illustrator), Pat Scarry (author) 4.00

☐ **166,** *Wiggles,* 1953, Eloise Wilkin (illustrator), Louise Woodcock (author) 7.00

☐ **168,** *My Teddy Bear,* 1953, Eloise Wilkin (illustrator), Patricia Scarry (author) 7.00

☐ **170,** *The Merry Shipwreck,* 1953, Tibor Gergely (illustrator), Georges Duplaix (author) 3.50

☐ **171,** *Howdy Doody's Lucky Trip,* 1953, Harry McNaught (illustrator), Edward Kean (author) 8.00

☐ **172,** *Howdy Doody in Funland,* 1953, Art Seiden (illustrator), Edward Kean (author) 8.00

☐ **179,** *Jack and the Beanstalk,* 1953, Gustaf Tenggren (illustrator), English Folk Tale 5.00

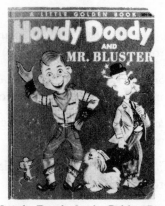

Howdy Doody Little Golden Book

Price

☐ **180,** *Airplanes,* 1953, Herbert and Lenora Combes (illustrator), Ruth Mabee Lachman (author) ...   3.00

☐ **193,** *Paper Doll Wedding,* 1954, Hilda Miloche and Wilma Kane (illustrator) 15.00

☐ **195,** *Roy Rogers and Cowboy Toby,* 1954, Mel Crawford (illustrator), Elizabeth Beecher (author) ...   10.00

☐ **196,** *Georgie Finds a Grandpa,* 1954, Eloise Wilkin (illustrator), Miriam Young (author) 5.00

☐ **203,** *Little Lulu and Her Magic Tricks,* 1954, Marjorie Henderson Buell (illustrator), Marjorie Henderson Buell (author) 20.00

☐ **220,** *A Pony For Tony,* 1955, William P. Gottleib (illustrator), William P. Gottlieb (author) 4.00

☐ **221,** *Annie Oakley,* 1955, Mel Crawford (illustrator), Ann McGovern (author) 7.50

☐ **222,** *Circus ABC,* 1955, J.P. Miller (illustrator), Kathryn and Byron Jackson (author) 4.00

Marilyn Monroe, the epitome of American beauty in the 1950s

Beatles collector Charles F. Rosenay

John Lennon's Rolls Royce sold for $2.9 million at a Sotheby's auction in New York City in 1985

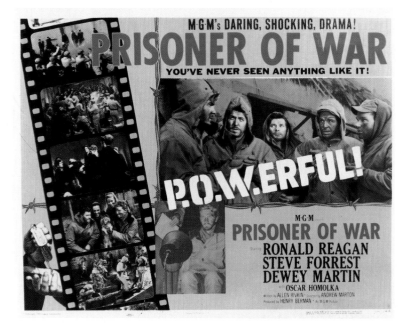

Movie poster from *Prisoner of War*, starring Ronald Reagan

James Dean collectibles from the Bill Hutchinson collection

Mr. Hutchinson's 1952 Chevy Deluxe at the James Dean gravesite in Fairmount, Indiana

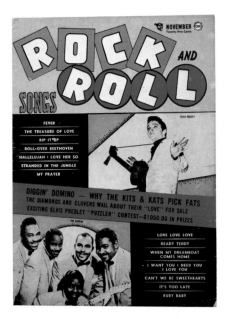
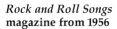

Rock and Roll Songs
magazine from 1956

**Hopalong Cassidy and
Roy Rogers comics
from the '50s**

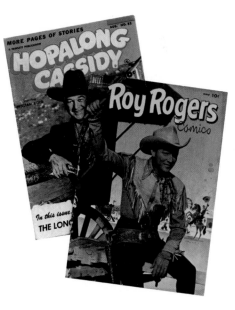

Howdy Doody card game

Howdy Doody's Christmas
Party record

Howdy Doody plastic figures

Coca-Cola Santa (1960), autographed by artist Haddon Sundblom

Snoopy model kit from Mattel, worth $10-$25

Peanuts nodders, worth between $15-$35

"I Like Ike" cigarette pack

"Stevenson for President"
cigarette pack

Cookie jar cigarette pack

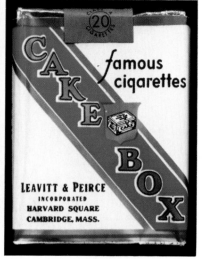

Cake box cigarette pack

Price

☐ **226,** *Rootie Kazootie Joins The Circus,* 1955, Mel Crawford (illustrator), Steve Carlin (author) 8.00

☐ **227,** *The Twins,* 1955, Eloise Wilkin (illustrator), Ruth and Harold Shane (author) 6.00

☐ **228,** *Snow White and Rose Red,* 1955, Gustaf Tenggren (illustrator), Fairy Tale 4.00

☐ **230,** *Gene Autry,* 1955, Mel Crawford (illustrator), Steffie Fletcher (author) 7.50

☐ **245,** *Out of My Window,* 1955, Plooy Jackson (illustrator), Alice Low (author) 3.50

☐ **246,** *Rin Tin Tin and Rusty,* 1955, Mel Crawford (illustrator), Monica Hill (author) 7.50

☐ **250,** *My Snuggly Bunny,* 1956, Eloise Wilkin (illustrator), Patsy Scarry (author) 3.00

☐ **253,** *Dale Evans & the Coyote,* 1956, E. Joseph Dreany (illustrator), Gladys Wyatt (author) 7.50

☐ **254,** *Buffalo Bill, Jr.,* 1956, Hamilton Greene (illustrator), Gladys Wyatt (author) 6.00

☐ **255,** *Lassie Shows the Way,* 1956, Lee Ames (illustrator), Monica Hill (author) 4.00

☐ **259,** *Roy Rogers and the Indian Sign,* 1956, Mel Crawford (illustrator), Gladys Wyatt (author) 10.00

☐ **261,** *Captain Kangaroo,* 1956, Art Seiden (illustrator), Kathleen N. Daly (author) 3.50

☐ **263,** *The Lone Ranger,* 1956, E. Joseph Dreany (illustrator), Steffi Fletcher (author) 7.50

☐ **275,** *Annie Oakley Sharpshooter,* 1956, E. Joseph Dreany (illustrator), Charles Spain Verral (author) 5.00

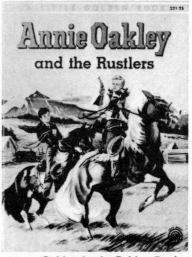

Annie Oakley Little Golden Book

Price

☐ **279,** *My Baby Brother,* 1956, Eloise Wilkin (illustrator), Patricia Scarry (author) 5.00

☐ **280,** *Paper Dolls,* 1951, Hilda Miloche and Wilma Kane (illustrator) 15.00

☐ **286,** *Fury,* 1957, Mel Crawford (illustrator), Kathleen Irwin (author) 6.00

☐ **287,** *Cleo,* 1957, Edward B. Graybill (illustrator), Irwin Shapiro (author) 6.00

☐ **294,** *Brave Eagle,* 1957, Si Vanderlaan (illustrator), Charles Spain Verral (author) 6.00

☐ **299,** *Broken Arrow,* 1957, Mel Crawford (illustrator), Charles Spain Verral (author) 6.00

☐ **303,** *Baby's Mother Goose,* 1958, Eloise Wilkin (illustrator), Folk Tale 3.00

Price

☐ **304,** *Rin Tin Tin & The Outlaw,* 1957, Mel Crawford (illustrator), Charles Spain Verral (author) 7.50

☐ **310,** *The Lone Ranger and The Talking Pony,* 1958, Frank Bolle (illustrator), Emily Brown (author)   10.00

☐ **312,** *Bugs Bunny,* 1949, Warner Bros. (illustrator), Warner Bros. (author) 3.00

☐ **313,** *Peter Rabbit,* 1958, Adriana Saviozzi (illustrator), Beatrix Potter (author) 3.00

☐ **314,** *Pussy Willow,* 1951, Leonard Weisgard (illustrator), Margaret Wise Brown (author) 3.00

☐ **315,** *The Life and Legend of Wyatt Earp,* 1958, Mel Crawford (illustrator), Monica Hill (author) . . .   10.00

☐ **318,** *Cheyene,* 1958, Al Schmidt (illustrator), Charles Spain Verral (author) 10.00

☐ **320,** *Gunsmoke,* 1958, E. Joseph Dreany (illustrator), Seymour Reit (author) 5.00

☐ **326,** *Wagon Train,* 1958, Frank Bolle (illustrator), Emily Broun (author) 7.50

☐ **336,** *Fury Takes The Jump,* 1958, Mel Crawford (illustrator), Seymour Reit (author) 6.00

☐ **342,** *Exploring Space,* 1958, Tibor Gergely (illustrator), Rose Wyler (author) 3.50

☐ **347,** *Leave It To Beaver,* 1959, Mel Crawford (illustrator), Lawrence Alson (author) 15.00

☐ **356,** *Steve Canyon,* 1959, Milton Caniff (illustrator), Milton Caniff (author) 10.00

☐ **357,** *Helicopters,* 1959, Mel Crawford (illustrator), Carl Memling (author) 4.00

Price

☐ **360,** *Party in Shariland,* 1958, Doris and Marion Henderson (illustrator), Ann McGovern (author) 8.00

☐ **367,** *The Lion's Paw,* 1959, Gustaf Tenggren (illustrator), Jane Werner Watson (author) 4.00

☐ **372,** *Woody Woodpecker, Steps to Drawing,* 1959, Harvey Eisenberg and Norman McCary (illustrator), Carl Buettner (author) 6.00

☐ **378,** *Ruff and Reddy,* 1959, Harvey Eisenburg ; Al White (illustrator), Ann McGovern (author) ... 5.00

☐ **386,** *Dennis the Menace,* 1959, Hawley Pratt (illustrator); Lee Holley (illustrator), Carl Memling (author) 6.00

☐ **395,** *Yogi Bear,* 1960, M. Kawaguchi (illustrator), S. Quentin Hyatt (author) 5.00

☐ **398,** *Quick Draw McGraw,* 1960 .... 5.00

☐ **399,** *Doctor Dan at the Circus,* 1960, Katherine Sampson (illustrator), Pauline Wilkins (author) 8.00

☐ **404,** *Baby Looks,* 1960, Eloise Wilkin (illustrator), Eloise Wilkin (author) 4.00

☐ **406,** *Huckleberry Hound and Friends,* 1960, Ben de Nunez and Bob Totten (illustrator), Pat Cherr (author) 5.00

☐ **408,** *Rocky and His Friends,* 1960, Ben de Nunez and Al White (illustrator), Lillian Soskin and —Gardner (author) 6.00

☐ **431,** *National Velvet,* 1961, Mel Crawford (illustrator), Kathryn Hitte (author) 5.00

☐ **432,** *Dennis the Menace Waits for Santa Claus,* 1961, Al Wisman (illustrator), Carl Memling (author) .. 6.00

Little Golden Book, 1957

Price

☐ **444,** *Hokey Wolf and Ding-A-Ling,* 1961, Frans Van Lamsweerde (illustrator), S. Quentin Hyatt (author) 5.00

☐ **449,** *Yanky Doodle and Chopper,* 1962, Al White and Hawley Pratt (illustrator), Pat Cherr (author) . .   5.00

☐ **450,** *The Flintstones,* 1961, Mel Crawford (illustrator), Mel Crawford (author) 5.00

☐ **453,** *Top Cat,* 1962, Hawley Pratt and Al White (illustrator), Carl Memling (author) 5.00

☐ **473,** *Nurse Nancy,* 1958, Corinne Malvern (illustrator), Kathryn Jackson (author) 5.00

☐ **477,** *Ruff and Reddy,* 1959, Harvey Eisenburg and Al White (illustrator), Ann McGovern (author) . . .   4.00

Price

☐ **483,** *Mr. Ed,* 1962, Mel Crawford (illustrator), Barbara Shook Hazen (author) 6.00

☐ **488,** *Gay Purr-ee,* 1962, Hawley Pratt, Harland Young, and Herb Fillmore (illustrator), Carl Memling (author) 7.50

☐ **492,** *Supercar,* 1962, Mel Crawford (illustrator), George Sherman (author) 10.00

☐ **500,** *The Jetsons,* 1962, Hawley Pratt and Al White (illustrator), Carl Memling (author) 10.00

☐ **514,** *Thumbelina,* 1953, Gustaf Tenggren (illustrator), Hans Christian Anderson (author) 2.00

☐ **522,** *Jamie Looks,* 1963, Eloise Wilkin (illustrator), Adelaide Holl (author) 4.00

☐ **537,** *Beanie Goes to Sea,* 1963, Hawley Pratt and Bill Lorencz (illustrator), Monica Hill (author) 6.00

☐ **542,** *Hey There It's Yogi Bear,* 1964, Hawley Pratt and Al White (illustrator), Carl Memling (author)   4.00

☐ **546,** *Fireball X-L5,* 1964, Hawley Pratt and Al White (illustrator), Barbara Shook Hazen (author) 10.00

☐ **549,** *Tarzan,* 1964, Mel Crawford (illustrator), Gina Ingoglia Weiner (author) 7.50

☐ **550,** *Good Humor Man,* 1964, Tibor Gergeley (illustrator), Kathleen N. Daly (author) 2.00

☐ **554,** *Charmin' Chatty,* 1964, Dagmar Wilson (illustrator), Barbara Shook Hazen (author) 4.00

☐ **556,** *Peter Potamus,* 1964, Hawley Pratt and Bill Lorencz (illustrator), Carl Memling (author) ...   5.00

Price

☐ **558,** *Hop, Little Kangaroo,* 1965, Feodor Rojankovsky (illustrator), Patricia Scarry (author)   2.00

☐ **564,** *New Brother, New Sister,* 1966, Joan Esley (illustrator), Jean Fiedler (author) 1.50

☐ **574,** *So Big,* 1968, Eloise Wilkin (illustrator), Eloise
Wilkin (author) 3.00

Disney Little Golden Books

☐ **D14,** *Donald Duck's Adventure,* 1950, Campbell
Grant (illustrator), Annie North Bedford (au-
thor) 10.00

☐ **D19,** *Alice in Wonderland Meets The White Rabbit,*
1951, Al Dempster (illustrator), Jane Werner (au-
thor) 10.00

☐ **D29,** *Mickey Mouse and His Space Ship,* 1952, Milton
Banta and John Ushler (illustrator), Jane Werner
(author) 10.00

☐ **D34,** *Donald Duck and the Witch,* 1953, Dick Kelsey
(illustrator), Annie North Bedford (author) 10.00

☐ **D41,** *Donald Duck's Safety Book,* 1954, Manuel Gon-
zales and George Wheeler (illustrator), Annie
North Bedford (author) 7.50

☐ **D51,** *Mother Goose,* 1952, Al Dempster (illustrator)   7.50

☐ **D75,** *Manni the Donkey,* 1959, Walt Disney Studio
(illustrator), Felix Salten (author) 7.50

☐ **D82,** *Shaggy Dog,* 1959, Rus Anderson (illustrator),
Charles Spain Verral (author) 7.50

☐ **D91,** *Pollyanna,* 1960, Karen Hedstrom (illustrator), Elizabeth Beecher (author) 7.50

Price

☐ **D98,** *Ludwid Von Drake,* 1961, Hawley Pratt and Herbert Statt (illustrator), Gina Ingoglia and George Sherman (author) 7.50

Little Golden Books—Activity

☐ **A1,** *Words,* 1955, Gertrude Elliot (illustrator), Selma Lola Chambers (author) 7.50

☐ **A15,** *Trim the Christmas Tree,* 1957, Doris and Marion Henderson (illustrator), Elsa Ruth Nast (author) 10.00

☐ **A26,** *Train Stamps,* 1958, E. Joseph Dreany (illustrator), Kathleen N. Daly (author) 5.00

☐ **A32,** *Ginger Doll* 10.00

☐ **A33,** *Sleeping Beauty,* 1959, Julius Svendsen, Frank Armitage, Walt Peregoy, C.W. Satterfield and Thelma Witmer (illustrator), Walt Disney Studios (author) 15.00

☐ **A52,** *Tammy,* 1963, Ada Salva (illustrator), Kathleen N. Daly (author) 10.00

Little Golden Books—Giants

☐ **5004,** *Walt Disney's Favorite Stories* 15.00

☐ **5005,** *Donald Duck Treasury* 15.00

☐ **5010,** *Wild Animals,* 1958, W. Suschitzky (illustrator) 6.00

☐ **5021,** *Captain Kangaroo,* 1959, Art Seiden and Edwin Schmidt (illustrator), Kathleen N. Daly and Barb Lindsay (author) 10.00

☐ **5024,** *Quiz Fun,* 1959, Tibor Gergeley (illustrator), Horace Elmo (author), Nancy Fielding Hullick (author) 6.00

Comics and The Funnies

BACKGROUND: In 1954, Dr. Fredric Wertham wrote a book called *Seduction of the Innocent,* giving examples of "harmful" comics in a scathing attack on the comics industry. Soon, the New York State Legislature Committee, after an investigation into the industry, decided that comics publishers were guilty, and the Comics Code Authority was born to enforce special guidelines. Some publishers, like Fawcett, were so convinced that the comics publishing business would go down the drain that they ceased publishing them. From 1955 to 1960, it was a rough time for the industry, with poor sales and no new titles or characters introduced. The birth of comics collecting in the early 1960s helped to turn the industry around and put it back on its feet, with well-known works from people like Stan Lee (Spiderman) at Marvel Comics.

The Sunday comics date as far back as 1896, when "The Yellow Kid," drawn by R. F. Outcault, appeared in the February 16 edition of *New York World.* The "Hogan's Alley" setting was always the same, as were the characters, including The Yellow Kid himself. In each issue, the Yellow Kid appeared wearing a nightdress with a different message on its front. Outcault also created Buster Brown.

A different kid with the same last name began emerging in the early '50s. Charlie Brown and the rest of the "Peanuts" gang took most of the '50s to develop into the characters we know today. And when they finally did, they unleashed the greatest avalanche of comic character merchandise since Mickey Mouse.

"He's Your Dog, Charlie Brown!"

When Linus, Lucy, Schroeder, Peppermint Patty and the rest of the Peanuts gang shout, "HE'S YOUR DOG, CHARLIE BROWN!," everyone knows exactly who they're talking about: that universally loved and admired beagle, Snoopy! Snoopy, the comic strip originally developed and written by Charles M. Schulz in 1950, has millions of fans worldwide.

The star canine of the world of Peanuts has undergone many changes since he was first portrayed by Schulz. He has evolved from a simple pet to a wonderfully complex personality, complete with secret lives and fantasies, the ability to think, and the uncanny ability to outsmart his human companions at every turn.

The development of Snoopy into a more "human" character began in 1958. It was about this time that he began to walk on his hind legs instead of all fours. Soon followers of the comic strip came to recognize Snoopy's ability to think and display human emotions (such as his unique, raucous laugh, and his planting of wet kisses on Lucy's disgruntled face).

Snoopy has millions of fans worldwide, and Freddi Margolin, an energetic woman who has an enormous collection of Snoopy memorabilia, certainly is one of the foremost. For years, Snoopy has been a big part of her life, and today she is the living personification of the perpetual youth which is so much a part of the Peanuts character.

"People always ask me when I'm going to grow up," Freddi laughs, as she describes her mania. "I tell them, 'never, I hope,'" she adds. Freddi, who appears to be in her 20's (but confessed that she has a grown daughter), has assembled a museum of Snoopy items in her home.

The secret of Snoopy's popularity, she says, is the hardest question to answer. But, as Freddi points out, Snoopy and the Peanuts gang make more people feel forever young. "Snoopy makes me feel better," she says. "He's my sanity—my world away from the 'real' world." The fact is, more adults than children collect Snoopy items. The Snoopy Fan Club has members who range in age from 18 to 81 who reside all over the country and operate like "one big family," Freddi explains. "I correspond with about 75 fan-club members on a regular basis," she adds. "We had a fantastic convention (in the summer of 1985) in Santa Rosa, California. It was the first one ever and it went over very well." Freddi says that the only disappointment was that Charles Schulz was not there. "He was on tour with the ice skating show," she explained. "Mr. Schulz is a shy, gentle, humble, delightful man, and those qualities reflect in his characters."

Freddi says she first started collecting Snoopy items when she was in grad school. "I took a lot of kidding about it," she admits. Her love for the irascible beagle continued as she began her career as a school teacher.

Today she continues amassing Snoopy collectibles wherever and whenever they turn up. She says that it was only after she had "accumulated so many things that I was filling up my house" that she realized she had become a collector.

Her crowning glory is her museum, of which she is understandably proud. Her husband designed and built it for her, and it contains "between five and six thousand items—everything from ceramics to stickers, stuffed toys to clothing."

Freddi has many Japanese-made Peanuts items in her collection as well. She says that many would-be collectors do not realize that Japan has a very big Snoopy market. "I'm going there next year," Freddi says happily. "There's a Snoopy piano there that I'm dying to get my hands on."

In separating the valuable from the common, Freddi warns collectors to steer away from Snoopy items which may be widely accessible, even though they may be 20 years or more old. "Some things which were made in the '60s are very available and therefore not worth much. At the same time, things which were made at a much later date may be very valuable simply because they're rare." Many advanced buffs can identify the production year of a Peanuts item on sight merely by having studied the artwork and how it has changed from year to year. After a while, one becomes familiar with the Peanuts family tree. Charlie Brown was copyrighted in 1950, Lucy in 1952, Woodstock in 1965, and

Peppermint Patty in 1971. Snoopy himself has a copyright of 1950, but he was registered again by United Features Syndicate in 1956 for his dancing pose. Snoopy of 1958 is easily recognizable as the same Snoopy of today, although his paunch and head have seen further modifications. The 1965 aviator pose with goggles and helmet, and the astronaut pose, also prompted further trademark registrations. For more information on the Snoopy club, send a self-addressed, stamped envelope to: Andrea Podley, Snoopy Collectors Club, P. O. Box 94, N. Hollywood, CA.

Peanuts and Snoopy Collectibles

	Price Range	
☐ **Ceramic Sitting Snoopy,** handpainted in Italy	40.00	60.00
☐ **Ceramic Standing Snoopy,** next to bowl planter with a sign "Snoopy," Determined	30.00	35.00
☐ **Charlie Brown and Snoopy,** clock, battery operated, Equity	25.00	30.00
☐ **Charlie Brown,** mug bubble bath, white and blue, blue lid, 1969, Avon	11.00	14.00
☐ **Charlie Brown,** bath mitt and soap, 1969, Avon	8.00	10.00
☐ **Cutting Board,** Snoopy imprint	10.00	25.00
☐ **Hungerford Dolls,** rubber		
Charlie Brown	5.00	15.00
Linus	5.00	15.00
Lucy	5.00	15.00
Pig Pen	40.00	60.00
Sally	30.00	50.00
Schroeder and His Piano	90.00	125.00
Snoopy	20.00	25.00
☐ **Ice Bucket,** "Snoopy" imprint	25.00	35.00

Price Range

☐ **Joe Cool,** large punching bag, Ideal ...   15.00   20.00

☐ **Love A La Peanut,** pop-up-book, Hall-
mark 20.00   25.00

☐ **Lucy,** bubble bath, 4 oz. (2.50), Avon,
1969 ....   6.00   8.00

☐ **Lucy,** mug liquid soap, white and yellow, yellow lid, 1969, Avon 11.00   14.00

☐ **Music Box,** wooden, "Who Else Do You
Know Whose Dog Has Just Been Pro-
moted To 'Head Beagle'?" 20.00   25.00

☐ **Nodders,** large older bobble heads
Charlie Brown 15.00   35.00
Linus 15.00   35.00
Lucy 15.00   35.00
Pig Pen 15.00   35.00
Schroeder 15.00   35.00
Snoopy 15.00   35.00

☐ **Peanuts,** kindergarten rhythm set,
Chein 25.00   60.00

☐ **Peanuts,** project book, Determined ...   10.00   15.00

☐ **Peanuts,** parade drum, Chein 25.00   50.00

☐ **Peanuts,** statue of "Peanuts" baseball
team, "How Can We Lose When We're
So Sincere?" 25.00   40.00

☐ **Peanuts,** talking bus, battery operated   65.00   150.00

☐ **Peanuts,** wooden piano, rare 50.00   75.00

☐ **Schroeder's,** piano, battery operated,
Child Guidance 15.00   25.00

Price Range

☐ **Schroeder,** at piano, wooden music box,
Anri 50.00   80.00

☐ **Snoopy See 'N Say,** talking toy, Mattel   15.00   25.00

☐ **Snoopy Radio,** with microphone 20.00   35.00

☐ **Snoopy,** sign mobile, Avalon 15.00   20.00

☐ **Snoopy the Critic,** battery operated toy   20.00   25.00

☐ **Snoopy's Beagle Bugle,** Child Guid-
ance, battery operated 25.00   40.00

☐ **Snoopy & His Motorcycle** (Snap Tite
Kit), monogram hobby kits by Mattel   10.00   25.00

☐ **Snoopy & His Bugatti Race Car** (Snap
Tite Kit), monogram hobby kits by
Mattel 10.00   25.00

☐ **Snoopy & His Flyin' Doghouse,** battery
operated, Mattel 25.00   35.00

☐ **Snoopy-Matic,** instant-load camera,
Helm Toy Co. 40.00   60.00

☐ **Snoopy,** on grass mound, radio, Deter-
mined 25.00   40.00

☐ **Snoopy,** remote control fire engine,
Aviva 60.00   75.00

☐ **Snoopy,** lying on top of big peanut, top
comes off, Determined 35.00   45.00

☐ **Snoopy,** soap dish and soap, 1968,
Avon, along with booklet, ...   7.00   10.00

☐ **Snoopy Doghouse,** non-tear shampoo,
Avon, 1969 . . . .   7.00   10.00

"A Distinguished Combat Hero"

	Price Range	
☐ **Snoopy the Flying Ace,** bubble bath, with goggles, 4 oz. (3.00), Avon, 1969	6.00	8.00
☐ **Snoopy,** surprise package, "Excalibur" or "Wild Country" after shave lotion, Avon, 1959	7.00	10.00
☐ **Snoopy,** mug, liquid soap, white with orange, orange lid, 1969, Avon	11.00	14.00
☐ **Snoopy,** ceramic bell, Schmid	35.00	40.00
☐ **Snoopy,** tea set, Chein	15.00	40.00
☐ **Snoopy,** 5-pc. dish set, c. 1965	5.00	8.00
☐ **Speak Up, Charlie Brown,** story book that talks, Mattel	25.00	35.00

"Holy Cow, Batman! We're Collectible!"

Sixties television spawned many crazes and trends. Yet none seemed to rise to such unprecedented heights (and dwindle just as rapidly) as the craze that developed out of a most unlikely character—a comic book hero named "Batman."

Batman originally appeared in a 1939 issue of *Detective Comics,* identified as the "weird figure of the Dark, the avenger of Evil." Created by two enterprising young men, Bill Finger and Bob Kane, their original conception would prove worlds apart from the pop hero who would zap his way through the ABC Television series beginning on January 12, 1966. Every Wednesday and Thursday night at 7:30, Batman and his sidekick Robin took on a wide assortment of villains who terrorized the fictitious Gotham City. Wednesday's episode would end with the Dynamic Duo (as they were called) deeply in the midst of some perilous situation. An announcer's voice (actually that of series' producer William Dozier) would ask, "Is this the end for Batman and Robin?" To find out, viewers were told to tune in the next night, "same Bat-time, same Bat-channel."

Although designed to be a parody, the show's actors contributed much to its concept. Batman was played by Adam West, who gave the role the image its producers were seeking. He spoke in a monotone voice, lecturing and admonishing all wrongdoers with the air of a concerned parent. Burt Ward, as the over-exuberant Boy Wonder Robin, could be counted on for his astute observations in times of trouble. Ward's execution of lines like "Holy ice cubes, Batman, it's getting cold in here!" usually signalled the latest dilemma. During the show's run, the duo were nearly frozen, melted, scalded and fed to the wild beasts, yet in the end, goodness prevailed. In fact, so intent were the show's creators that it appeal to everyone that an order was issued that there be no murders on the show. While other shows, such as "The Man From U.N.C.L.E.," faced stiff criticism from groups like the PTA for its exploitive violence, "Batman" was embraced by just about everybody. This good natured, often tongue-in-cheek wholesomeness resulted in the release of an amazing amount of memorabilia. It was estimated that sales of Batman items reached nearly 80 million dollars in the first year the show was on the air. No wonder everyone was learning to dance the Batusi!

What has happened to all that memorabilia? It's turning up in greater numbers every year, as Batman collectors continue to step out of the Batcave and into the spotlight some 20 years after the program ended production. The Batman collector's time has come, although for some people, like J. Randolph Cox, it never went away. "Batman was one of those things I did after school," he says. "I kept on buying comics through school and college. He was a hero to me that was believable. He relied on his wits and acrobatic abilities." Cox's infatuation with Batman led him to collect from the early days, when Batman was primarily a comic book hero, to the days he refers as "the '60s blitz."

Cox has an impressive comic book collection of upwards of 10,000 comics, not all Batman-related, as well as a Batman collection of Batmobiles, puzzles and plastic figures. He says that the '60s market was so jammed with Batman that an overview itself can be a maze of mass confusion to the amateur collector. "It's so difficult to isolate the different areas," he explains. This is particularly the case with the comic book conventions, where Batman-related items can be overwhelming.

The key to a sensible collection is knowledge, according to Cox, "Knowledge of the field is important; the more you know, the more you can get a fairly good sense of value." Cox recommends comics for the beginner, as they are still fairly accessible (except for the first-run issues in which Batman and Robin made their debuts. *Detective Comics* #27 and 38, respectively, can and do get up to $8000 on the market today). Cox also warns against "trying to collect everything at once."

This advice was echoed by Cox's fellow collectors. "At first I tried to keep up with it all," laughs collector Tom Fagan, "I think I lasted two weeks. In one toy catalog alone from the mid-'60s that I now have, they list over 1000 items, all Batman related toys." Fagan, whose earliest encounter was long ago after Sunday church in Wallingford, Vermont, has been an avid Batman devotee for decades. He is unable to estimate the size of his collection, but says, "There's not enough room for me and Batman in my house—eventually one of us has got to go, probably me."

Batman-collecting is a source of joy for Fagan, who has in his possession cherished original artwork by Bob Kane, as well as scores of '60s-produced items—items such as books, lamps, clocks, pins, even a Batman radio. Fagan is particularly interested in the early years of Batman, when Batman relied more on his own wits and merits than on the '60s brand of "camp" humor, a word Fagan tends to wince at. Nonetheless, the collector whose house appears to be overrun with memorabilia (including an equally impressive collection of memorabilia related to actor James Dean), continues to preserve the Batman legacy year in and year out. In fact, he has become a celebrity in his own right, marching faithfully for over 25 years in the annual Halloween parade in Rutland, Vermont, dressed as, you guessed it, the Caped Crusader.

"I never thought there was anything collectible in Batman," he marveled, while noting that Batman periscopes now sell for $25 in some markets, and a Batman helmet can fetch up to $50. He is quick to note the irony of his statement when he mentions a favorite item, a plastic Batplane. Purchased back in the '60s for less than a dollar, the collector says quickly "I wouldn't take $500 for it now."

With such a strong gathering of fans and the current revival, thanks partly to Frank Miller's first-class production, "The Dark Knight Returns," it seems amazing that no one major fan club exists in his name. Fagan's bible in Batman's heyday was the publication entitled *Batmania*. Produced by

B. J. White from 1964 to 1967, the fanzine was off to a slow start. "Then the television series hit," White recalls, "and I got more mail and subscriptions than I ever could have dreamed of." White's collection contains the highly-sought Batman wallpaper, which he insists could make a collector a small fortune should he have a roll intact, from which he could sell samples. He also prizes his models, and a set of drinking glasses originally obtained from a service station in the mid-'60s. Although there was a Batman item for everyone, White says that quality is important to him. "There were good and bad. There was such a variety of quality, from the Aurora Toy Company's plastic models—which were really neat with a lot of fine details—to some absolutely shoddy items."

Although White's publication *Batmania* changed hands, it has since ceased publication. "It really was time-consuming," he states, adding that people still often ask him to start it up again.

White, like many serious collectors, still searches for that one odd item to fill a gap in his collection, and what other one-of-a-kind item could there be but a prop from the show? "Common sense would tell you that a show that was that popular would also result in valuable props." One of the props White would love to get his hands on is "the red emergency phone that rang in Bruce Wayne's study." (Like Superman, aka Clark Kent, Batman had an alter ego, Bruce Wayne.)

In speaking with some of the many Batman collectors, one realizes that collecting Batman is not just done for the monetary value; for most, it is a labor of love. Wisconsin collector Joe Desris is adamant on that point. "A few people do it as more of an investment," he says. "For me, it's a nice bonus if what I have turns out to be worth money, but it's more for fun." Desris describes himself as an original fan of the '60s TV show. "The show was popular right away," he says. "Most collectors are fans of the series." He identifies a typical Batman collector as someone "in their 20's or 30's" who is trying to collect "to regain or retain his/her childhood."

Like Fagan and Cox, Desris is a formidable expert on Batman. He believes a lot of his present collection is due to his early collecting instincts. "The gum cards first came out in the spring of '66. I know that because it was toward the end of the school year," he recalls. Eventually there were five different card series produced. The first three were cartoon paintings which featured stories on the back; the fourth featured photographs from the show, and the fifth, entitled "The Riddler's Riddle," was composed of shots from the feature film made at the height of the TV show's popularity. Desris says that the "Riddle" card set took him a long time to complete, and therefore is the hardest to find.

Desris has a collection as varied as it is huge. "It would take a week to see it all," he laughs. "It's ridiculous." He explains that "a lot of toy companies had a license to market Batman products. Like Aurora, they were already geared up by 1964. By 1966, they just had to make up other plastic figures—Robin, Penguin, the Batmobile (a customized '57 Lincoln, the Batmobile was as popular with viewers as the actors themselves), the Batplane, and the Batboat.

Desris has what has to be one of the oddest Batman curios around in his collection, a coin-operated Batmobile ride that played the Batman theme when the money was deposited. He keeps the item in his office and it is a constant source of amusement to Desris. "My clients hear that I have the thing and bring their kids in to see it."

Desris is aware that it is easy to become obsessive when collecting, and he does draw a line occasionally. "There's a Batman pajama set now out on the market, and if you wanted to get silly I suppose you could collect EVERY size," he says. "I bought only the largest. However, I do have about 12–15 variations on Batman Halloween Costumes."

Price Range

Batman Collectibles

☐ **Robin in the Batcave with Batman Coloring Book,** Western Publishing Co./National Periodical Publications, 8" x 11", 1966 .... 40.00   60.00

☐ **I'm a Batman Crime Fighter,** National Periodical Publications, button, red/white/blue, 1⅛", 1966 .... 6.00   10.00

☐ **Batman Batmask Sunglasses,** 9-piece optiray, 1960s 10.00   12.00

☐ **Batman, Batmobile,** toy made by Soshin of Japan, mid-1960s 125.00   175.00

☐ **Batman,** script, 1966, Adam West, Burt Ward, 123 pp 75.00   85.00

☐ **Batman and Robin,** ceramic figural banks, c. 1966 .... 70.00   90.00

Life magazine, March 11, 1966, $20.00–$30.00

Price Range

☐ **Batman and Robin, From Alfred to Zowie!,** by Ruthanna Thomas, Golden Press, 1966, S953, book is die-cut in shape of Batman's head 2.00 4.00

☐ **Batman,** button, Batman and Robin Official Member, full color, 3½", mid 1960s 6.00 8.00

☐ **Batman,** button, lithographed tin, Batman in flight, TV inspired, 1966 . . . . . 7.00 9.00

☐ **Batman Meets Blockbuster** Coloring Book, published by Whitman under license from National Periodical Publications, original price 39 cents, 1956, 8" x 10¾" 4.00 6.00

☐ **Batman,** charm bracelet, with five figures (Batman, Robin, Penguin, The Rider, The Joker), on original store card, 1966 . . . . 10.00 14.00

Batmobile pinback, $6.00–$8.00

Batman cup

	Price Range	
☐ **Batman,** costume, with mask, gray outfit, large yellow monogram with black bat on chest, blue cape, black halfmask, c. 1960	30.00	40.00
☐ **Batman, Batplane,** toy, originally sold for 99 cents	40.00	50.00
☐ **Batman,** lunch box, 1966	8.00	12.00

Comic Books

☐ **Brave and the Bold,** D.C./National Periodical Publications, 1959		
Cave Carson, #40	10.00	16.00
Cave Carson, #41	10.00	16.00
Hawkman, #42, Kubert artwork	14.00	18.00
Origin of Hawkman, #43, Kubert artwork	20.00	30.00
Aqua Man, #51, Hawkman	15.00	25.00
Plastic Man, #95, Batman	2.00	4.00
☐ **Buck Rogers in the 25th Century,** Gold Key Comics, 1964, painted cover	10.00	20.00

Price Range

☐ **Dr. Strange,** #1, Marvel Comics Group, 1968, Dr. Strange and huge octopus creature, cover artwork by Brynner ...   15.00   25.00

☐ **Fantastic Four, Marvel Comic Group,** 1961
Origin of the Fantastic Four, #1, Kirby artwork 2000.00 2500.00
Skrulls From Outer Space, #2, ...   700.00 900.00
Mance Of The Miracle Man, #3 ....   300.00 350.00

☐ **Fantasy Masterpieces,** Marvel Comics Group, 1966
Beware, The Ghost Surrounds Me, #1   4.00   8.00
The Red Skull, #6 ....   2.00   4.00

☐ **Flying Saucers,** 1950, Avon Publisher, cover depicts extra-terrestrials emerging from saucer and descending upon city   140.00 150.00

☐ **Incredible Hulk,** Marvel Comics Group, 1962
Coming of The Hulk, #1 ....   1000.00 1300.00
Terror Of The Toad Men, #2 ....   300.00 380.00
Beauty And The Beast, Hordes of General Fang, $5 ....   130.00 160.00

☐ **Iron Man,** Marvel Comics Group, 1968
Alone Against AIM, #1 ....   70.00 100.00
Day Of The Demolisher, #2 ....   15.00   25.00
My Friend, My Foe, #3 ....   8.00   12.00

☐ **John Carter of Mars,** #375, Gold Key Comics, Dell Four Color, John Carter battling monster with four arms on cover, 1964 ....   55.00   65.00

☐ **Marvel Tales,** Marvel Comics Group, 1964

Katy Keene Spectacular, 1956

Katy Keene Charm, 1958

	Price Range	
Spiderman, #1	75.00	85.00
X-Men, #2	8.00	12.00
Face To Face with the Lizard, Human Torch, #3	7.00	12.00
Man Called Electro, #6	4.00	8.00
☐ **Metamorpho, The Element Man,** D.C. Comics, 1965	5.00	10.00
☐ **Strange Worlds,** Avon publisher, 1958, cover depicts man firing handgun at two-headed dinosaur-type monster as he attempts to rescue girl	100.00	130.00
☐ **Sub-Mariner,** Marvel Comics Group, 1968		
Origin Retold, #1	13.00	16.00
Cry Troton, #2	4.00	6.00
Burn Namor Burn, #14	2.00	6.00
☐ **Tales of Suspense,** Marvel Comics Group, 1963		
Birth of Iron Man, #39	280.00	320.00
Iron Man Vs. Gargantus, $40	100.00	130.00
Stronghold of Dr. Strange, $41	45.00	55.00
Sinister Scarecrow, #51	8.00	12.00

Life with Woody Woodpecker

Walter and Gracie Lantz are known the world over as the creator and voice, respectively, of Woody Woodpecker. Walter also created for the '50s and '60s generation of comic book readers Andy Panda and Chilly Willy.

The couple, now in their eighties, are good-natured, and have a middle-America air about them. Gracie did the on-screen voice of Woody Woodpecker for over 30 years. As the couple tells it, there is indeed a true-life story behind the creation of a woodpecker for the comic pages.

3-D comic books

The Lantzs used to have a woodpecker always banging on the roof of their cabin in the Sierras, which always made Walter furious. Walter decided to immortalize the woodpecker, and Woody debuted in an Andy Panda picture by wrecking the roof of Andy's house. The picture was made in 1941, and titled *Knock! Knock!*

It was Mel Blanc who first did the voice of Woody; but he went on to Warner Brothers to do the voice for a rabbit named "Bugs." After that, Walter worked with several other voice artists. At the same time, he decided the "ugly" Woody he had created needed to be modified to look cuter. After the redesign of Woody, it was agreed that a new voice was needed for him. Gracie had asked if she could audition, and Walter told her no, because Woody was a boy. Gracie went to a studio, made a recording, and put it in with the recordings under consideration for the new Woody voice. Without anyone's realizing who it was, her voice was selected.

Walt Lantz's career began in 1916, when he worked for Hearst as an office boy. At the age of 15, he was washing the brushes of Winsor McCay, famous for his comic strip "Little Nemo in Slumberland." Four years later, Walt left Hearst to work on "Mutt and Jeff."

Walt has donated his old cels to UCLA, hundreds of thousands of them, and seven truckloads of materials. Universal Studios opened a small Woody Woodpecker Museum in June 1982 which houses dolls, toys, games, old pictures, cels, and original drawings. It is part of the Universal Studios tour. There is also a theater with a 15-minute show called "The Evolution of Woody," made by Walt and Gracie. In November of 1982, a permanent exhibit of Woody Woodpecker materials was unveiled at the Smithsonian in Washington, D.C.

Woody Woodpecker Collectibles

Woody Woodpecker comic book

Andy Panda Big Little book

Walter Lantz's New Funnies

Disneyana

BACKGROUND: The term "Disneyana" refers to all those items made by or for Walt Disney Productions, the folks responsible for Snow White, Mickey Mouse, Donald Duck, and a host of other familiar characters.

Price Range

Disney Collectibles

☐ **Bagheera,** made by Steiff of Germany under license from Walt Disney Productions, character from the Disney film "The Jungle Book," plush, made in 1960s 45.00   65.00

☐ **Baloo,** copyright by Walt Disney Productions, character from the Disney film *The Jungle Book,* ceramic, dated 1965, 5½" 18.00   22.00

☐ **Bambi,** made by Marx under license from Walt Disney Productions, one of Marx "Disneykyn" figures, boxed, c.1961 .... 5.00   10.00

☐ **Captain Hook,** made by Marx under license from Walt Disney Productions, one of Marx Snap-Eeze figural toys, early 1960s, boxed 10.00   14.00

☐ **Disneyland,** ceramic bank figural of Happy from *Snow White,* 6", c.1960 ... 40.00   60.00

☐ **Geppetto,** made by Marx under license from Walt Disney Productions, plastic, one of Marx's Snap-Eeze figural toys, early 1960s, boxed 10.00   14.00

Price Range

☐ **Gyro Gearloose,** made in France under license from Walt Disney Productions, character in the Donald Duck comic strip, hard rubber, 1960s, 3" 20.00   25.00

☐ **Joe Carioca,** made by Marx under license from Walt Disney Productions, character in "Salutos Amigos," one of Marx's "Disnekyn" figures, boxed, c.1962 .... 6.00   8.00

☐ *Jungle Book, The,* Disney animated, 1967

1 sheet poster 100.00   150.00
14 x 36 .... 80.00   120.00
11 x 14 set of 9 .... 90.00   110.00
Presskit, 3 stills (1984R) 5.00   10.00
Presskit, 4 stills (1984R) 8.00   12.00

☐ **King Louie,** made by Steiff in Germany under license from Walt Disney Productions, character from the Disney film *The Jungle Book,* plush, made in 1960s   45.00   65.00

☐ *Lady And The Tramp,* Disney animated, 1955

1 sheet poster 1972R 25.00   35.00
1 sheet poster 1980R 10.00   20.00
22 x 28, 1980R 10.00   15.00

☐ **Ludwig Von Drake,** made by Marx under license from Walt Disney Productions, plastic, one of Marx Snap-Eeze figural toys, early 1960s, boxed .. 10.00   14.00

Price Range

☐ **Mad Hatter,** made by Marx under license from Walt Disney Productions, plastic, one of Marx Snap-Eeze figural toys, early 1960s, boxed 7.00   10.00

☐ **March Hare,** made by Marx under license from Walt Disney Productions, plastic, one of Marx's Snap-Eeze figural toys, early 1960's, boxed 10.00   14.00

☐ **Mickey Mouse, Donald Duck and Goofy,** Mattel, "Skediddlers" toys, set of three in original boxes, c.1960 .....   40.00   50.00

☐ **Minnie the Moo Sponge Puppet,** and 3-oz. soap (1.75), Avon, 1965 ....   16.00   20.00

☐ **Pinocchio,** made by Marx under license from Walt Disney Productions, plastic, one of Marx's Snap-Eeze figural toys, early 1960s, boxed 10.00   14.00

☐ **Pressbook,** *Computer Wore Tennis Shoes,* 1969, Disney 8.00   12.00

☐ **Pressbook,** *Dad, Can I Borrow the Car?,* 1969, Disney 4.00   6.00

☐ ***Pressbook,*** *Silver Fox,* 1962, Disney 4.00   6.00

☐ **Sleepy,** made by Marx under license from Walt Disney Productions, c.1961, boxed 5.00   10.00

☐ **Sneezy,** made by Marx under license from Walt Disney Productions, c.1961, boxed 5.00   10.00

Price Range

☐ **Thumper,** made by Marx under license
from Walt Disney Productions, one of
Marx's "Disnekyn" figures, c.1961,
boxed 5.00   10.00

Dolls

BACKGROUND: Dolls have been called the most emotion-inducing of collectibles and their appeal is such that they rank among the top four forms of collectibles in popularity. Dolls trace back to the ancient world, although the first dolls were not considered playthings at that early time. There is some question as to what they were used for. During the '50s and '60s, dolls became more and more lifelike, reaching a zenith with the emergence of the Barbie doll in 1959. Note: The dolls in this section are listed by manufacturer, as most collectors choose to specialize in this way.

BOOKS: *The Official Price Guide to Collector Dolls,* House of Collectibles, 1985.

Price Range

Doll Collectibles

Alexander Doll Company, Inc.

☐ **Cynthia,** hard plastic, rare black Alexander with Margaret face, 14", 18", 23", c.1952 .... 450.00   550.00

☐ **Ecuador Girl,** bent knees, dark pigtails, blue sleep eyes, coin earrings, straw hat, 8", c.1960s 200.00   400.00

☐ **Edith,** "The Lonely Doll," vinyl head, rubber body, blue sleep eyes, pouty mouth, party dress, c.1950 .... 200.00   300.00

☐ **Elise,** character, vinyl, jointed at elbows, knees, ankles, brown rooted hairs, blue sleep eyes, closed mouth, pink and white checked dress, white straw bonnet with flower trim, hose, high heels, 16", c.1957 .... 200.00   250.00

Price Range

☐ **Elise,** hard plastic head, vinyl, long brown hair, blue sleep eyes, dressed as a bridesmaid, long chintz gown, wide-brimmed hat, 16½", c.1957 . . . .   150.00   200.00

☐ **Israeli,** doll, knee bends, 8", c.1965 . . .   40.00   80.00

☐ **Kathy,** character, vinyl, blonde rooted hair, brown sleep eyes, pink dress, matching bonnet, pacifier on ribbon around neck, wrist tag, 17", c.1956 . . .   175.00   275.00

☐ **Kelly,** character, vinyl, blonde rooted hair, blue sleep eyes, closed mouth, pink dress with tiers of white lace, matching bonnet, original mint, no box, wrist tag, 15", c.1956 . . . .   150.00   250.00

☐ **Margot Ballerina,** plastic, blonde, blue eyes, Margaret face, turquoise costume, satin slippers, #1841, c.1955 . . . .   150.00   200.00

☐ **Marlo Thomas,** vinyl, sleep eyes, black hair, wears knee-length wool dress, strand of graduated pearls, textured stockings, boots, 16½", 1967 (A scarce doll, inspired by the TV show "That Girl," starring Marlo Thomas, it was produced only in 1967; although Marlo and the show were hits, the doll was not—apparently because Marlo's role on the show was too "grown up" to appeal to little girls.) 400.00   500.00

Price Range

☐ **Scarlett O'Hara,** doll, vinyl, sleep eyes, long black glossy hair, satin gown with trimming, satin bonnet, wears cameo on a chain at the neck, marked Alexander, 1961, 21" 200.00   300.00

☐ **Shirley Temple,** c.1950s, Gabriel #300, statuette doll, snap-on clothes, assorted real picture faces, numerous outfits, cut   20.00   30.00

☐ **Sleeping Beauty,** doll, Disney special edition, 1959, 9" 300.00   400.00

☐ **Sonja Henie,** composition body, blonde mohair wig, sleep eyes, short lavender skating dress, ice skates, 14", c.1950 ..   300.00   400.00

☐ **Southern Belle,** ribbon-trimmed white gown, with box, 11", c.1968 ....   300.00   500.00

☐ **Wendy Bride,** plastic, sleep blue eyes, blonde hair, white satin dress, rhinestones, veil, 21", c.1950s 250.00   350.00

That Doll Ginny

"Open your heart, open your mind, look for the best, and that's what you'll find!"

Those are the words of wide-eyed Ginny as she learns to be brave in new situations in *Ginny's First Secret,* a "Ginny" book written in 1958 by Lee Kingman and illustrated by Hazel Hoecker. Ginny's open, honest, and cheerful outlook captivated children in the '50s and '60s, and continues to bring them delight today. A Ginny doll from that era can bring a small fortune in the '80s, and the collecting of Ginny dolls is widespread and growing.

Ginny's First Secret

Ginny Doll newsletters

Miss Jandolin Marks, assistant of the Ginny Doll Club, a non-profit organization headed by Mrs. Jeanne Niswonger, gives spirited insight into the world of collecting Ginny dolls and accessories.

As it turns out, the loveable Ginny can be an expensive investment. Jandolin gave the prize for the most valuable Ginny to the black, hard-plastic Ginny, which is worth up to $1000 today. The Ginny Coronation Queen is currently worth about $800 (a comprehensive price list follows).

Marks attributes the appeal and popularity of the Ginny dolls to the fact that Ginny was "an attractive and attainable doll for people of all social levels," as opposed to the Madame Alexander dolls, for instance, which "were financially out of reach for some people."

Ginny had many outstanding qualities, making her irresistible to countless little girls of the '50s, the collector says. "Ginny was ahead of her time," Marks explains. "Independent, friendly, generous and fearless, she rode the wave of popularity in her heyday until Barbie dolls came along."

The story of Ginny detailed in the *Ginny Doll Club News* ("The Ginny Doll Story"), is an American success story.

Ginny, the All-American "good little girl," was born in Medford, Mass., in 1937. In the years that followed, she so won the hearts of children across the country with her button nose, sparkling eyes, and down-to-earth nature that a Ginny Doll Fan Club emerged in the 1950s when her popularity was at its zenith. Children loved Ginny because she looked like them.

Ginny was the first doll to have an elaborate wardrobe, and also the first to have her own "family," and custom-made furniture.

When Mrs. Jennie Graves of Vogue Dolls commissioned doll sculptor Herr Bernard Lipfert to design a small 8" toddler doll with the proportions of a real little girl, a head that swiveled, moveable arms and legs, blue eyes that glanced to the right and molded hair, Ginny was born. She was named after Mrs. Graves' oldest daughter, Virginia.

In 1945, the same Virginia Graves, now with Vogue Dolls, recognized her namesake's potential as a trendsetter. Determined that Ginny should look and be dressed like American children, she created a wardrobe that included active and formal wear, and costumes based on nursery rhymes and foreign lands, which were accurately and lovingly replicated. The Graves' commitment to fine workmanship and quality was reflected in each costume. Ginny eventually earned the title, "Fashion Leader in Doll Society."

The 1950s were years of tremendous success and transformation for Ginny. During those years her composition was changed, and she began to walk. She was joined by Sparkie, her wire-haired terrier, and several sisters and brothers. In 1956, the Ginny Doll Club was established.

Ginny dolls are available today, in vinyl, handcrafted porcelain, and a limited-edition collectors series. The best of the old and the new, Ginny continues to captivate children and doll collectors everywhere.

To explain Ginny's popularity, Jandolin remarks, "Ginny had more accessories and costumes than other dolls. Kids didn't get bored with Ginny." To preserve Ginny dolls, she advises, "Keep them high and dry. Avoid dampness and cockroaches, which like to eat the glue in composition (wood) dolls, and eat starch found in some clothes. Pack dolls in mothballs and seal boxes with heavy duty tape. Keep all dolls out of prolonged sunlight, as they will fade." She also advises collectors to avoid harsh cleaners, as some cleaners will leave streaks, remove color in cheeks, etc. Avoid using bleach when washing doll clothes as well.

Why are the hard plastic dolls of the '50s and '60s so desirable today? "In short," says Miss Marks, "they last!" The hard plastics used in the '40s and '50s were generally top quality, and "new plastic dolls can't hold a candle to the old ones. They hold color longer, and many 35-year-old dolls look brand new. Vinyl dolls often develop a tacky feeling or strange color with time." According to the Ginny doll expert, hard plastic dolls, including Ginny and Alexanders, "look better with age, developing a look and aura I dare any new manufacturer to duplicate." Also, "Ginny dolls appeal to many collectors who have limited space for their collections, because she is only eight inches tall."

For newcomers to the doll collecting field, Miss Marks advises, "Try not to buy sight-unseen unless you have a photo." She suggests that collectors join a club concentrating on dolls from a particular manufacturer, such as Alexander, Terri Lee, Barbie, Ginny, and so forth.

The Ginny Doll Club and its newsletter, headed by Jeanne Niswonger, are located at 305 W. Beacon, Lakeland, FL 33803. Membership in the club is available for $12 per year, or $20 for two years. Members receive a bi-annual journal, the *Ginny Doll Club News,* which features articles about Ginny dolls, pen pals, want ads, doll care and patterns. The club sponsors a Modern Doll Convention every year as well, and currently boasts 2000 members in its 15th year. Members also receive back issues of the *News* and a club pin. *That Doll Ginny,* a book filled with history of Ginny and hundreds of photos, is available from the Club for $16 postpaid. Marks would like requests for club membership or the book to include mention of this price guide.

As a last suggestion to collectors, Marks says, "Buy a doll because it appeals to you and you will become a doll collector for the right reason."

Ginny Dolls and Related Collectibles

	Price Range	
☐ **Bent Knee Walker,** very good condition, original	100.00	120.00
☐ **Black Ginny,** 1953	700.00	800.00
☐ **Ginny Coronation Queen,** 1950 version	800.00	850.00
☐ **Ginny Nun**	160.00	200.00
☐ **Crib Crowd**	380.00	420.00
☐ **Just Me**	600.00	700.00

Price Range

☐ **Nude,** strung 50.00   100.00

☐ **Painted Lash Walker,** original 100.00   150.00

☐ **Poodle Cut,** mint condition 300.00   350.00

☐ **Red Riding Hood,** pale lips 160.00   200.00

☐ **Toddles Dutch Boy** 650.00   660.00

Ginny Accessories

☐ **Ginny Trouseau** 480.00   520.00

☐ **Ginny Pin,** 1950s 45.00   55.00

☐ **Mib Pup,** with coat, leash, ear button
(Steiff tag missing) 180.00   200.00

☐ **Necklace** 60.00   70.00

☐ **Wardrobe** 45.00   55.00

Additional Doll Collectibles

Hasbro

☐ **G. I. Joe,** Action Marine, plastic, molded
hair, brown, brown eyes, painted,
marked 7700, G.I. Joe TM Copyright by
Hasbro Patent Pending, made in USA,
made in 1964, 11½" 45.00   50.00

☐ **G. I. Joe,** Action Marine, plastic, molded
hair, brown, brown eyes, painted,
marked 7500, G. I. Joe TM Copyright
1964 by Hasbro, pat. No. 3,277,602,
made in U.S.A., 11½" 20.00   25.00

Price Range

☐ **G. I. Joe,** Action Soldier, black, plastic,
molded black hair, brown eyes, painted,
marked 7900, G. I. Joe Copyright 1964
by Hasbro Patent Pending, made in
U.S.A., made in 1965, the first black G.
I. Joe, 11½", rare 50.00   100.00

☐ **G. I. Joe,** hard plastic, blonde molded
hair, marine dress uniform, c.1964 . . . .   40.00   60.00

Barbie: A Doll for the '60s

Barbie was born in 1959, the first mass-marketed doll
to look like a woman and not a child. Her popularity over
the years has increased, and collectors are avidly searching
for "that first Barbie—with the holes in the feet." The original Barbie was issued with holes in the feet to make it easier
for her to be placed on her stand. Ruth Cronk of City Island,
New York, has a collection of over 700 individual dolls, including that first Barbie and all of her friends which followed: Ken, Francie, Midge, Allan and Skipper. Ruth not
only owns a blonde Barbie number one, but has negotiated
for a very rare brunette Barbie number one. "There were
twice as many blondes as there were brunettes, so getting
one is the epitome of my collection," she said.

Changes in Barbie's fashions have advanced rapidly over
the past two-and-a-half decades. "The styles have mirrored
women's fashions," adds Ruth.

Her collection of Barbies began when Ruth started to
buy them at garage sales. She was going regularly, and about
that same time started to haunt the Salvation Army stores.
"I wanted to begin collecting, but I wasn't sure what," she
says. "I found a brand new, mint-in-box 'Perfectly Plaid'
Barbie set. When my husband asked me why I wanted to

buy it, I just told him I thought I'd like to collect Barbies."
Since that time, Ruth has pursued the tracing of the doll's
line back to its inception.

"Barbie was conceived by Ruth Handler and designed
by her husband Elliot," she notes. The Handlers had
launched Mattel, Inc., from their garage in California in the
1940s, and the idea for Barbie began when Ruth Handler no-
ticed how much her daughter enjoyed playing with paper
dolls depicting glamorous women. During a trip to Italy,
Handler saw a doll named Lily, which had much the same
shape that Barbie was to become.

Barbie changed from a ponytail to flip hairstyle when
the first bendable doll was issued; then, Barbie wigs were
added to the line. The "sleepy-eyed" Barbie was produced
only during 1964, and in 1967 the first black doll, Francie,
was marketed. She, like the "sleepy-eyed" Barbie, is very
difficult to obtain, as she was issued for just one year.

Ruth formed the Barbie Doll Collectors Club in 1978
with just 29 members. She began editing the *International Barbie Doll Collectors Gazette* on a monthly basis with the help of
club members. The club now has several hundred members,
and everyone celebrated Barbie's 21st birthday in the fall of
1980 with a convention. A 60-page book published for the
event is now part of the Barbie collection in the Smithsonian
Institution.

"You know," Ruth once said, "I realized how much a
part of our family Barbie had become the night I came into
the house after a meeting and heard my husband George say
to someone on the phone, 'Well, it may not be a number
one Barbie if it doesn't have holes in the feet.'"

Price Range

Barbie Dolls and Related Collectibles

☐ **Barbie,** bubble cut blonde, angel outfit,
    c. 1963 . . . .   50.00   70.00

Price Range

☐ **Barbie,** plastic molded and painted features, ponytail with bangs, slotted feet designed to fit in stand, loop earrings, marked 850, made in 1959, 11½ " 700.00   800.00

☐ **Barbie's Friend Christie,** black, plastic, molded and painted features, talker, brown hair (parted), wears knitted green shirt and red shorts, marked 1126, sold in 1968, 11½ " 100.00   150.00

☐ **Talking Barbie,** plastic, molded and painted features, wears ponytail, talker, dressed in shorts and knitted shirt, marked 1115, sold in 1968, 11½ " 150.00   200.00

☐ **Spanish Talking Barbie,** plastic, molded and painted features, wears ponytail, talker, dressed in shorts and knitted shirt, marked 8348, sold in 1968, the same as the standard talking Barbie, introduced that same year, differs only in that she speaks Spanish, intended for sale in Spanish-speaking areas of New York, California and Texas, 11½ " 100.00   150.00

☐ **Wig Wardrobe Barbie,** plastic, molded and painted features, sold with three interchangeable wigs, marked 0871, sold in 1964, 11½ " 150.00   200.00

Price Range

Additional Doll Collectibles

Remco

☐ **Little Orphan Annie,** printed cloth, mop hair, (red), wearing a shirt reading "Kiss'n Hug Me," sold originally with a tag reading 1967 Remco Ind., Inc., 16"   20.00   30.00

☐ **Snugglebun,** all vinyl, crier, green sleep eyes, blonde hair, red two-piece outfit, made in 1966, 15" 25.00   35.00

"Only You Can Prevent Forest Fires!"

Alfred Grimes is a tall, heavy set man, pleasant but authoritative—precisely the sort of man you would expect to find collecting Smokey Bear ("Only You Can Prevent Forest Fires") memorabilia. You see, Al and the famous bear have something in common—expounding fire safety. Al is a New Hampshire forest ranger, and is responsible for the safety of his district.

Al has been a member of the NH Forest Fire Service since 1972, and an avid collector of Smokey Bear memorabilia for the past 10 years. "Paper products—posters, signs, and such, are the hardest items to find," Al says, "since they're so perishable." Paper items go back a long way. "Smokey has been a symbol of the Forest Fire Service for 42 years now, and there's been a poster for every year. I've got almost all of them." The most valuable poster is perhaps the original from 1944, which may be worth anywhere from $10 to $25. Other items in Al Grimes' collection include dolls, plates, Christmas ornaments, figurines, jewelry, poster pins and bumper stickers—all bearing the likeness of Smokey. A great many items have been targeted toward children, as Smokey has long been a favorite with school children who first hear about him during Fire Prevention Week programs.

Smokey visiting children in the '60s

Where does Al find his Smokey items? "I check out flea markets and antique shops." But his best success has been through other Fire Service people. Fire Service employees or retired employees often have saved posters and other Smokey items in their attics or closets, and are often willing to part with them so they may join Al's ever-growing collection. Al has found many items that way, and probably saved many Smokey collectibles from oblivion, or the trash.

The first Smokey Bear stuffed toy was produced by Ideal in 1952. An application to become a Junior Forest Ranger was included with each toy, and children were encouraged to write to Smokey to receive Junior Forest Ranger Kits. Many Smokey Bear stuffed toys have followed since that time.

Newer Smokey items may be obtained from catalogs. For example, many collectibles were made especially for Smokey's 40th birthday in 1984, including some limited edition items, which Al said are growing in value continually.

Every state in the country participated in this celebration, which proved to be a big boost for the national Smokey Bear program.

"All Smokey Bear items are licensed by the U.S. Forest Service," Al explains. "It's a federal offense to produce or sell these things—or to wear a Smokey suit—without the permission of the Forest Service."

Al feels that the interest in Smokey is definitely experiencing an upward trend. "Only Coca Cola beats Smokey for recognizability worldwide," Al ventures. "And 95 percent of the people asked to complete the sentence, 'Only You . . .' could complete it correctly.

"Right now, my collection is just a hobby," Al says. Someday he hopes to share his treasures with others. "When I retire, I hope I'll have time to visit Forest Service shows on behalf of Smokey all around the country."

Smokey Bear the Forest Fire Symbol, and Smokey Bear the real bear, were not one and the same until the 1950 Capitan Forest Fire in New Mexico left a tattered and burned survivor, a small bear cub found by a ranger up in a blackened treetop. The Smokey Bear campaign, however, began long before, dating back to 1942, when forestry officials, afraid of Japanese attacks on the California shore and the possible forest fires which could have resulted, decided a campaign to increase public awareness was necessary. During 1942 and '43, wartime slogans were used. After Walt Disney's Bambi was introduced on a poster in 1944, proving very popular with the public, the Forest Service decided to choose an animal symbol. But since Bambi, however lovable, appeared too defenseless to actually help prevent forest fires, another animal was eventually chosen. In 1944, a bear, with an "appealing, knowledgeable expression, and perhaps wearing a campaign (or Boy Scout) hat that typifies the outdoors and the woods," was agreed upon. The bear was reportedly named Smokey after Smokey Joe Martin, Assistant Chief of the New York City Fire Department from 1919 to

1930. Smokey was first seen pouring water over a campfire on a 1944 poster. And overnight, Smokey Bear, the new national symbol for fire prevention, was born.

Smokey was to undergo several changes in the years that followed. The famous message, "Only YOU Can Prevent Forest Fires," was presented to the public in 1947.

In 1950, a New Mexico forest fire produced the real, living victim of carelessness in our national forests. "Smokey" was found by forest rangers, nursed back to health and sent to live at the National Zoo in Washington, D. C.

Over three million people visited Smokey yearly at the zoo. After his death about five years ago, the Fire Service decided that the Smokey campaign needed rejuvenation. A 40th birthday celebration was planned, and today Smokey can once again be seen on numerous posters, on television, and in catalogs distributed by the National Forest Service promoting the sales of toys and collectibles. In addition, Smokey, accompanied by Forest Service officials and usually arriving on a fire truck, continues to visit schools across the nation to spread the message of fire safety and prevention.

Smokey Bear patches

Further information about Smokey is available by writing to: Smokey Bear Program Manager, USDA Forest Service, P. O. Box 2417, Room 1001 RP-E, Washington, D.C. 20013.

Smokey Bear Collectibles

Posters

(*Note:* Cardboard posters are generally not worth as much as paper posters.)

	Price Range	
☐ **1944,** original Smokey poster in good condition	10.00	30.00
☐ **1945–1969,** in good condition	5.00	15.00

Smokey Bear poster

Price Range

☐ **Stand-up Posters with forest scenes and Smokey**

Large	10.00	14.00
Medium	4.00	6.00
Small	2.00	4.00
Street Car, wide posters	10.00	20.00

☐ **Stuffed Smokey,** blue and with Jr. Ranger badge for 1950s 20.00 30.00

☐ **Small Stuffed Smokey** 5.00 8.00

☐ **Large Stuffed Smokey,** with soft hat .. 25.00 35.00

☐ **Giant 30" Smokey** 80.00 100.00

Toys and Games

BACKGROUND: Lithography on the board games from the 1800s and turn of the century has proved a fascination for collectors since the phasing-out of art of lithography many years ago. Toys that hold collector fascination are mechanical gems like a "Hoppy on a Horse" produced for about four or five years during the '50s or an Olive Oyl with pop-up squeaker by Linemar Toys (a subsidiary of Marx).

BOOKS: *Character Toys and Collectibles,* David Longest, Collector Books, 1984; *The Knopf Collectors' Guides to American Antiques—Toys,* Blair Whitton, Alfred Knopf, 1984; *The Illustrated Encyclopedia of Metal Toys,* Gordon Gardiner and Alistair Morris, Harmony Books, 1984; *Modern Toys, American Toys 1930–1980,* Linda Baker, Collector Books, 1985.

[*Note:* For television program-related toys, see the Entertainment section. (Special thanks to collector/author Richard Friz for providing the toy listings which follow.)]

Price Range

Toy Collectibles

☐ **Amazing Magic Robot,** 4th Edition, Merritt Toys Ltd. (Great Britain), actually a game which includes a 3" lithographed tin robot, complete, 10" x 15" box, 1953 . . . .   60.00   70.00

☐ **Athlete,** Horsman, mechanical, plastic/vinyl, molded and painted hair, molded and painted features, stands on platform, operates by spring-driven motor, marked Horsman 1967, 5½" . .   6.00   8.00

☐ **Big Max Robot,** made by Remco, all plastic, battery powered, robot hoists loads by electromagnet, places them on

Price Range

belt which deposits them into truck, was featured in 1958 Sears Roebuck catalog 170.00   180.00

☐ **Bing Crosby's Call Me Lucky,** Parker Brothers, board game picturing Bing Crosby on cover, box measuring 10" x 20", c.1953 .... 25.00   35.00

☐ **Bootsie,** black, plastic/vinyl, rooted hair, black, sleep eyes, brown, marked 1125-4-Horsman made in 1969, 12" .. 30.00   40.00

☐ **Cadillac,** toy replica, TN, Japan 20.00   30.00

☐ **Chalk and Checkers,** The Ohio Art Company, #523, c.1960s, metal, slate, plastic, eraser, chalk 6.00   10.00

☐ **Checkers,** The Ohio Art Company, #97, c.1950s, tin, multicolored, Chinese and regular checkers, diameter 13" ... 8.00   12.00

☐ **Chrysler Imperial,** 16" toy, Isahi Toy Company, Japan 50.00   75.00

☐ **Donald Duck Car,** Italy, Paperino Politoys, 1960s, nephews Huey, Dewey and Louie in rumble seat 50.00   75.00

☐ **Donald Duck Wind-up Car,** 1955, Marx (figure originally was made of tin) ... 100.00   125.00

☐ **Doug Davis,** Major Matt Mason's Space Buddy, robot, Mattel, plastic, 1968, 6½", blisterpack 12.00   16.00

☐ **Firestone Van,** Dinky Toys, 1964 ..... 20.00   30.00

Price Range

☐ **Hopalong Canasta,** boxed game, includes deck of Hoppy cards, score sheets, rules and plastic card holder designed as a saddle, 1950 . . . .   35.00   45.00

☐ **Hoppy on a Horse,** 1950s, Marx 150.00   200.00

☐ **Horseshoe Set,** The Ohio Art Company, #531, c.1950s, metal, vinyl, black, red   8.00   10.00

☐ **Howdy Doody and Buffalo Bob,** piano toy, early 1950s, Unique Art 200.00   250.00

☐ **Indy Champion Racer,** 1950s, Yonezawa Manufacturing Company, Japan, friction toy 100.00   125.00

☐ **James Bond Car,** friction toy, Japan, 1950s 50.00   75.00

☐ **Jupiter Rocket Launching Pad,** made by T.N. of Japan, lithographed tin, battery powered, beeping countdown, screen flashes, rocket fires, box reads "Two Stage Rocket Launching Pad," early 1960s 250.00   280.00

☐ **Koo Koo Choo Choo,** The Ohio Art Company, #647, c.1960s, metal, plastic, exploding train game, mechanical 10.00   20.00

☐ **Laser 008,** Japan, 7" high 100.00   150.00

☐ **Little Girl in the Whoopee Car,** early 1950s, Marx 50.00   75.00

☐ **Louis Armstrong,** spring-wound toy, Rosho Tested, hat tilts back 75.00   100.00

Price Range

☐ **Major Matt Mason Space Discovery Set,** Mattel, space figures plus vehicles and equipment in a box measuring 20" x 14¾" x 11", carries copyright date of 1968 . . . .   60.00   70.00

☐ **Mars Explorer,** KOP, Japan, battery-operated, light and dark green space toy   200.00   300.00

☐ **Marvelous Mike Electromatic Tractor,** Saunders, lithographed tin, robot seated in tractor which he operates, carries patent date of 1954, 13" x 8½" 130.00   160.00

☐ **Mary Open TV Car,** Asahi Toy Company 25.00   35.00

☐ **Mary Roebling Bank,** limited edition of 200, designated by woman who was a bank president in New Jersey 50.00   100.00

☐ **Mickey the Magician,** late 1950s, Linemar, battery operated 150.00   250.00

☐ **Mickey Mouse Wind-up Car,** 1955, Marx (figure originally was made of tin)   100.00   125.00

☐ **Missile Launching Truck,** Linemar, friction powered, lithographed tin, 5½", c.1965 . . . .   60.00   70.00

☐ **Mister Automic,** tin robot, Cragston . .   1500.00   2500.00

☐ **Money Box,** The Ohio Art Company, #121, c.1950s, multicolored, rectangular, play coins, bills 8.00   12.00

☐ **Mr. Magoo Car,** 1950s, Hubley, tin, battery operated 50.00   75.00

Price Range

☐ **Olive Oyl with Pop-up Squeaker,** 1950s, Linemar 300.00   400.00

☐ **Penny Pineapple Mechanical Bank,** Imswiler, commemorates Hawaii's entering into the union in 1960 . . . .   100.00   150.00

☐ **Milton Berle Car,** 1950s, Marx, car is made of tin and Milton's hat is plastic, 6" long 100.00   125.00

☐ **Popeye Basketball Player,** 1950s, Linemar, battery operated 350.00   500.00

☐ **Popeye on Rollerskates,** 1950s, Japan, Linemar, battery operated 350.00   500.00

☐ **Popeye Sparkler,** 1959, Chein 75.00   100.00

☐ **R17 Volkswagen Space Patrol Car,** TN, Japan, 12" long, battery operated 100.00   200.00

☐ **Robby the Robot Space Patrol,** 12½" long, battery powered, Japan 500.00   750.00

☐ **Roger Robot Giant Playmate,** Whitman, cardboard, box reads "Builds to Four Feet Tall!," has small inset picture of Art Linkletter at lower right and wording, "Giant Toy as Seen on TV," early 1960s 25.00   35.00

☐ **Roto-Robot,** 8½" high, 1950s 35.00   50.00

☐ **Sleeping Beauty,** doll, Disney special edition, 1959, 9" 300.00   400.00

☐ **Snoopy and Woodstock Musical Wind-up Bank,** Japan, 1960s, 6¼" high   25.00   50.00

Price Range

☐ **Space Satellites With Launching Site,**
Marx, lithographed tin, launch pad with
radar screen and rockets, 12", c.1950–55   140.00   160.00

☐ **Space Scout Bubble Gum Bank,** red
cardboard dispenser printed with various scenes of spaceships and astronauts,
3" x 3" x 5", c.1950s 25.00   35.00

☐ **Sparkling Rocket Car,** Bandai, Japan,
early 1950s 50.00   100.00

☐ **The Fishing Bears,** Japan, 1950–1960,
battery powered bank, 5½" high 250.00   350.00

☐ **Tin Man Robot From The Wizard of
Oz,** Remco, battery operated, plastic
with decals, reads "Tin Man Robot" on
chest, has gear panel, reverses direction
when he bumps into something, 21",
1969 . . . .   200.00   250.00

☐ **Unnamed Robot,** made by National of
Japan, lithographed tin, has old-style
TV set built into chest, 1950s variety,
but robot may be more recent, clear face
visor, antenna attached to head, 11" . .   140.00   160.00

☐ **Vatican Guard,** toy soldiers, Britain . . .   10.00   20.00

☐ **Winnie the Pooh Tin Ferris Wheel,**
1964, Japan 50.00   100.00

Entertainment in the '50s and '60s

Introduction

The 1950s saw that entertainment giant, the motion picture, battle it out with the young upstart, television, over a diminishing number of movie patrons, who were finding it more convenient to stay at home and watch Uncle Miltie rather than trek on down to the Rialto.

In an effort to bring back the crowds, filmmakers experimented with new gimmicks—3-D movies, cinerama, Biblical epics and the like. Audiences were amused for a little while, but again drifted back to adjusting the rabbit ears to catch Ed Sullivan's "Toast of the Town." In the end, the movies did what they did best, bring fresh new talent to the big screen. Stars like Marlon Brando, James Dean, and Marilyn Monroe proved to be the drawing card the movies desperately needed.

Not all was glitter up on the screen, however. There is a strong case to be made for the argument that some of the worst motion pictures ever made were released in the '50s. Movies like *Plan 9 From Outer Space, The Blob, I Was a Teenage Werewolf* and *The Three Stooges Go To Mars* were committed to celluloid during this period.

America has long been a nation of people who recognize the best and worst in matters. Consequently, it is no surprise that the most collectible form of cinemabilia from the period not only centers around the great young stars of the day, but also around those items recalling the truly awful "gems" of the day. A poster promoting the low-budget horror flick *The Man Without A Body* (1957) is nearly as popular with collectors as those promoting the films of Brando, et al.

But truly this was the golden age of television. Practically everything was performed live, and TV lacked the "glitz" of today. Programs emitted a spirit of experimentation sorely missing from their modern-day counterparts. This may account for the large number of fan clubs which have emerged in recent years around such long-ago programs as "The Honeymooners," "I Love Lucy" and "Howdy Doody."

Music was also going through a revolution during the '50s, set in motion by the rhythm-and-blues records which were being played by youngsters in reaction to the pat sounds of Rosemary Clooney, Perry Como and Doris Day. It took a singing truckdriver from Tupelo, Mississippi, to turn the music industry around when he set the world on fire with hits like "Heartbreak Hotel" and "Hound Dog." The world would never be the same after Elvis Presley.

By the early '60s, music was again settling into a state of redundancy, only to be re-ignited by four lads from Liverpool. Today Elvis and the Beatles still stand as the greatest acts of the rock era—and the sale of their memorabilia is establishing new world's records daily.

For many of us, entertainment still meant a Saturday afternoon ball game. Television brought sports into our living room in a way radio never could. We saw Willie Mays hit it home, Mickey Mantle slide into third and Floyd Patterson defend his title via the family Dumont.

Prices for '50s and '60s entertainment collectibles are experiencing rapid development. *The Official Price Guide to Collectibles of the '50s and '60s* tells you which items to look for, as well as offers in-depth articles on the hottest categories of entertainment collectibles.

Movies And Television

Movies

DESCRIPTION: Cinemabilia is everything from Dixie ice cream lids featuring photos of yesterday's movie favorites to actual costumes or movie props. Malcolm Willits' Hollywood-based mail-order auctions called Collectors' Showcase (7014 Sunset Boulevard, Hollywood, California 90028), has consistently led the pack by smashing record after glamorous record as he scours the attics of Tinseltown.

The cult popularity of film stars who died early in their careers or through tragic circumstances has continued to mark its sales. The memory of James Dean, who starred in *Giant,* has continued to haunt us despite his few short years in the movie industry. An ordinary paperback from 1953 that was deemed in "so-so condition" was brought up for auction by Malcolm Willits. The paperback carried the autograph of James Dean, who, according to Willits, "just didn't like to sign his name." Thirty years after his death, that autographed but worn paperback sold for $1263.

TYPES COVERED: Posters, inserts, lobby cards, press kits, programs, costumes, magazines.

Price Range

Movie Collectibles

☐ **Alice in Wonderland,** Walt Disney Studio, full-color cel, portrait of the Mad Hatter from Tea Party scene, 1951 ...   300.00   500.00

☐ **The Beatles,** "Yellow Submarine" puzzle, 1968 ....   20.00   25.00

☐ **Ben and Me,** Walt Disney Studio, animation drawing of Ben Franklin with closed eyes, 1953 ....   50.00   75.00

☐ **Cary Grant,** on the cover of *Look,* August '66 ....   3.00   5.00

☐ **Cinderella,** Walt Disney Studio, full-color cel of the cagey cat Lucifer, 1950   300.00   400.00

☐ **Doris Day's** bicycle horn, 1960 ....   50.00   75.00

☐ **Dumbo,** Walt Disney Studio, 8½ x 11 cartoon color & tempera cel of Dumbo and Timothy Mouse, 1950s, ...   1500.00   2000.00

☐ **Egyptian, The,** movie prop game box, 1954 ....   150.00   200.00

☐ **Elizabeth Taylor,** *Cleopatra In Mink* by Cy Rice, 1962, original paperback biography 10.00   20.00

☐ **From All of Us to All of You,** Walt Disney Studio, full-color cel pose of smiling Jiminy Cricket, 1958 ....   150.00   200.00

Price Range

☐ **Gibson Guitar,** "Back To The Future,"
c.1960, model #ES-345, in its original
case with a letter of authencity from the
guitar company who originally rented
the guitar to Universal City Studios   ..   3500.00   4500.00

☐ **James Bond,** "Goldfinger" puzzle, 1965,
Fort Knox finale 10.00   15.00

☐ **James Bond,** game, 1964 ....   15.00   18.00

☐ **James Bond,** thermos, 1964 ....   5.00   8.00

☐ **Lady and the Tramp,** Walt Disney Studio, color-model drawing, full-pose
bulldog, 1955 ....   30.00   55.00

☐ **Ludwig von Drake,** Walt Disney Studio, full-color cel, portrait of Donald
Duck's wacky relative, 1960s 125.00   150.00

☐ **Mickey Mouse's 25th Anniversary,**
Walt Disney Studios, full-color print,
1953 ....   75.00   100.00

☐ **Peter Pan,** Walt Disney Studio, full-
color storyboard litho. crayon, 1953 ..   50.00   75.00

☐ **Peter Pan,** Walt Disney Studio, full-
color print of Tinkerbell w/sticker, 1950   20.00   30.00

☐ **Richard Burton,** on the cover of *The Saturday Evening Post* July 18, '64 ....   3.00   5.00

☐ **Romp In A Swamp,** Walter Lantz Studio, full-color background, interior
scene, 1959 ....   20.00   30.00

☐ **Ronald Reagan,** portrait autographed to
John Ford, 1960s 300.00   400.00

Price Range

☐ **Sleeping Beauty,** Walt Disney Studio, full-color cel of Prince Philip and Aurora, dancing, 1959 . . . . 400.00   600.00

Movie Costumes

(*Note:* These costumes were sold at a Sotheby's collectibles auction in New York City in June 1986.)

☐ **Alice Faye's White Cotton Dress and Feathered Hat,** *Hello Frisco Hello,* 20th Century Fox, 1943, beige chiffon dress with black floral designs trimmed in black velvet with a matching bolero jacket and a large black velvet picture hat covered in black and white ostrich feathers 500.00   600.00

☐ **Anne Baxter's Dress,** *My Wife's Best Friend,* 1954, purple with three-quarter sleeves, self-covered buttons on front, self-covered belt 75.00   95.00

☐ **Bette Davis' Wool Nightgown,** *The Virgin Queen,* 20th Century Fox, 1955, designed by Mary Willis, full sleeves and a double collar trimmed with gold embroidery and sequins and a silk/rayon lining, label with star's name 700.00   730.00

☐ **Charleton Heston's Cotton Toga,** *Ben Hur,* MGM, 1959, designer Elizabeth Haffenden, the woven toga with gold embroidered trim, floral belt and sandals 1000.00   1200.00

☐ **Debbie Reynold's Dancing Costume,** *Singing In The Rain,* MGM, 1952, designed by Walter Plunkett, pink velvet dancing

Price Range

brief with gold lame applied design at the hip representing a basket and pink tulle at the shoulder, label with star's name 1600.00   1700.00

☐ **Elizabeth Taylor's Gowns (2),** *Cleopatra,* 20th Century Fox, 1963, designer Irene Shareff, the first, a gold lame gown with embroidered gold floral motifs ending in gold-embroidered panels over a pleated lame under-skirt; the second, a salmon pink silk Egyptian style gown ending in pleated skirt with embroidered and se- quinned geometric designs, both with labels bearing star's name 5000.00   5500.00

☐ **Jayne Mansfield's Yellow Bathing Suit,** *The Girl Can't Help It,* 20th Century Fox, 1956, the yellow suit with wide straps ending in a skirt, label with star's name   800.00   1000.00

☐ **Jane Russell's Black Leotard,** *The French Line,* RKO, 1953, designed by Jane Rus- sell and Howard Greer, the leotard dec- orated with rhinestones and three large ovals cut out at the torso 3000.00   3300.00

☐ **Judy Garland's Blue Suede Gloves and Boots,** *Annie Get Your Gun,* MGM, 1950, designed by Walter Plunkett and Helen Rose, the boots and gloves trimmed in sequins with a floral design, Judy Gar- land's name inscribed on the bottom of the boots 1700.00   1800.00

☐ **Julie Andrews's Orange Silk Dress,** *Star,* 20th Century Fox, 1968, designer Donald Brooks, the chiffon spaghetti-

Price Range

strap dress with a silk bow at the waist
and beaded layered panels which come
down in a train at the back, with a vel-
vet cape with bead trimming 800.00   900.00

☐ **Julie Andrews's Two-Piece Gray Outfit,** *Sound of Music,* 20th Century Fox,
1965, designed by Dorothy Jeakins, the
fitted quilted jacket with self-covered
buttons down the front and a matching
lined skirt 2500.00   2600.00

Collectors with a Cause

He had appeared in three major movies and over 25 television shows. He had performed in a few Broadway plays,
and had cameo appearances in minor "B" movies. Among
his co-stars were such luminaries as Natalie Wood, Rock
Hudson, Sal Mineo, Elizabeth Taylor and Ronald Reagan.

James Dean

He was hailed by fans and critics alike as the most promising young actor in the somewhat mundane world of early 1950s cinema. *Life* magazine ran a well-received pictorial piece on him, calling it "Hollywood's Moody New Star," and he was interviewed by the prestigious *New York Times*. At 24, James Byron Dean was one of the hottest properties of the movie industry. Dean sprung from the heartland of Indiana into the hearts of American youth. On September 30, 1955, Dean met an untimely end in an automobile accident while en-route to a racing event in which he was to take part.

At this point in his career, only one of his movies, *East of Eden*, had actually been released. Yet public response to his death was strong. With the release of his second film, *Rebel Without A Cause*, four days after his death, a phenomenon never before witnessed in moviedom occurred. Dean's following grew to unbelievable proportions. A *Look* magazine article published in October of 1956 reported that Warner Brothers (the film company under which Dean had signed a nine-year, six-picture contract) had received 7000 letters. There were requests for photos (some sent money); teenagers pleaded for a lock of his hair or just a reply. There were letters from stunned disbelievers who begged to hear that it was all studio hype, hoping to be reassured that the actor was alive. Tribute magazines poured out claims that Dean was still alive, and fans clung to the fallacy that Dean would appear alive again before the public eye. This was not to be. All that was left to come was a third and final motion picture which Dean had finished the day before his death, *Giant*. An NBC television executive at the time remarked that Dean was "hotter than anybody alive."

The public was saddened by the loss of the charismatic Dean, who had left precious few films behind, and suddenly the demand for Dean memorabilia ran high.

Dean was credited with developing the archtypical image of the cool, misplaced youth of the American '50s. His career spawned an eclectic maze of memorabilia, most of which was issued posthumously. What was labeled in 1956 as the "Strange James Dean Death Cult" has grown into a legion of devoted fans—thousands of whom trek to his hometown of Fairmount on the anniversary of his death to attend memorial services, and to walk the streets of Indiana where the legend began. His life, brief as it was, has been the subject of many books and plays, and is the basis of numerous fan clubs dedicated to keeping the actor's memory alive.

"I have to say that I've always admired Mr. Dean, starting in 1954 when I first saw him on TV. I never lost that special feeling," Sylvia Bongiovanni explains. Bongiovanni is president of one of the most respected Dean fan clubs, We Remember Dean International (P. O. Box 5025, Fullerton, CA 92635), founded in 1978. The 45-year-old legal secretary had at the time just finished reading David Dalton's biography, *James Dean, The Mutant King,* and she and another Dean fan decided to form a club to honor the actor. The club, which initially began with five members, now counts actor Martin Sheen and reknowned artist Kenneth Kendall among its nearly 300 members worldwide. Bongiovanni is proud of her club and the closeness she says it has brought her to Dean himself. "Jimmy's brought a lot of people together," she said.

Dean-collecting is a competitive and lucrative field for a great many fans, yet Bongiovanni is one collector who rarely views an item in terms of its monetary value. "I've never even counted the items in my collection—even a rough estimate is difficult. I began collecting Dean items in 1955 before his death."

Some of the unique items the collector holds dear are tape recordings made by those who knew and worked with Dean. There are messages from Julie Harris (his co-star in *East of Eden*), Martin Landau (a friend of Dean's in his early days as a struggling actor in New York), and Bill Bast (former friend and writer). "I asked them to record messages about Jimmy so that I could play it at a We Remember Dean International luncheon in 1985 in Fairmount." She has also

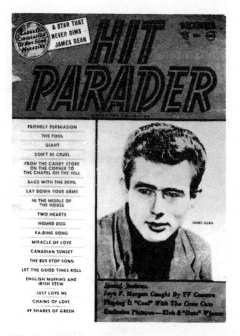

Hit Parader with James Dean on the cover

received letters from friends and associates of Dean. Among these was a letter and two signed photos mailed to her by Elizabeth Taylor. Taylor was appearing in a play in California when Bongiovanni mailed her a letter along with a memento of Taylor and Dean in *Giant.* "I thought I'd never see that again; then, three months later I received it back along with a typed letter and two 8 x 10 photos enclosed of a young Elizabeth Taylor!" Other letters in her collection include correspondence from Bill Bast, noted for his book, *James Dean,* one of the earliest biographies written on the star (published in 1956). "The original paperback sold for 35 cents and has a going value of $25 to $50 now. This is special to me, as it was the first biography I bought," she notes, adding that the hardback version of the book is very difficult to find.

Like many collectors, Bongiovanni has many items that were mass-produced, among them the tribute magazines printed in 1956. The four magazines ran the gamut, from pure sensationalism—*Jimmy Dean Returns, Read His Words From Beyond* (published by Rave)—to the more standard *James Dean Album* (Ideal Publications). "These two publications, along with *The Real James Dean Story* (Fawcett) and *The James Dean Anniversary Book* (Dell) now have a value of $25 to $50 each."

Another mass-produced yet very rare item is a 45-rpm record issued on Romeo Records as a "limited collector's edition." The 45, which sold for the then-exorbitant price of $1.29, was entitled "James Dean on Conga Drums in an ad-lib jam session . . . as he talks and relaxes with friends . . . from an original tape. . . ." The record came with a picture sleeve, a photo of Dean playing the drums, and a blurb on the back describing the sessions. Bongiovanni, like other collectors, admits that the conversation is marginal, yet the record, which she had ordered through movie magazines, now fetches up to $100 in some circles.

Mass-produced medallions advertised in *Modern Screen* magazine and selling for one dollar each have a current value of $50 to $100, and Bongiovanni has one of these as well.

One-of-a-kind items, however, remain her favorites, and she longs to have "a personal item owned by Jimmy." She comes close in this category with a painting she recently acquired. "It was a watercolor painted by Mr. Dean in the late 1940s. I recently purchased it from a former friend of Mr. Dean's." She places an approximate value of $1000 on the painting.

Bongiovanni's deep respect for Dean has led her, like countless others, to make the trek to his hometown. "I've only been there three times," she laments as she begins to describe her visits. "It's just remarkable being there—it takes your breath away—just seeing it all in person. I was with some friends and we went to his grave and I told them to wait a minute, that I'd be right along, and I stood alone; it was my first touching moment. I kept thinking that this was his—that Jimmy was there." But Bongiovanni's impressions should not be construed as maudlin or morbid. In fact, they are quite the opposite. "When WRDI was founded, it gave me something very special and beyond all value: wonderful friends who share their memories and feelings about Jimmy."

Another major collector is Bill Hutchinson, a 29-year-old Griffith, Indiana, resident. Hutchinson's collection includes calendars, fans, shopping bags, magazines and many other mass-produced items; but, as with Bongiovanni and others, it is the hard-to-get items which he cherishes the most. One such artifact is an eighth-grade yearbook with a black and white photo of a very young "Jimmie Dean" inside, looking for all the world like the native Indiana boy that he was. Hutchinson emphasizes the rarity of the yearbook and says the Class of '49 Yearbook (Dean's graduating class) can sell in excess of $400 today.

While personal artifacts such as the yearbook are indeed highly sought, the original movie posters and movie-related memorabilia in general remain at the center of the field. "An original poster for *East of Eden* can go for $350, if it's in fairly good condition." Individual lobby cards have values of $25 and up, depending upon availability and condition, according to the collector.

Among his most unusual artifacts are the Dean masks, described in a *Life* magazine piece in 1956. The masks were life-sized replicas of the actor's head, made with a plastic that looked and felt like actual flesh. The masks, though widely produced at the time, are a rarity today.

Hutchinson has brought his quest for Dean to New York City, even managing to rent the room in the Iroquois Hotel on West 44th Street (between 5th and 6th Avenues) where Dean often stayed. "It looks pretty much the same, and the guy who sometimes used to cut Jimmy's hair still works in the barbershop there; he offered to cut my hair, and he told me these little stories about him, reminiscing about him. I always try to get that room when I go there."

New York City collector David Loehr is renowned as the foremost expert on Deanophilia, and was a photo consultant for David Dalton's second book on Dean, *James Dean: American Icon*. Loehr collects like a curator for his museum-like collection of Dean, devoting much time to tracking-down items. He is also responsible for bringing the true Dean fan just a little bit closer to the actor. Each year David Loehr conducts a seven-hour walking tour through the streets of James Dean's New York. At no cost (except for bus fare and optional dinner money), Loehr leads the faithful, equipped with maps, through the bars, cafes, apartments and theaters that the actor frequented in the city.

How did it all come about for Loehr? "I began in 1974, when I first read the Dalton biography, *The Mutant King*. I hadn't even seen any of his movies until then. Then I saw *East of Eden*." So impressed was Loehr that he began to pick up whatever he could find on the actor at flea markets, book shops and the like. From that beginning, Loehr has amassed an astounding collection of some 2500 items. "I've got lots of things—the photos, books, magazines, busts, plates, cups, even half a dozen of the Kenneth Kendall sculpted busts."

Loehr's collection of Dean memorabilia is far from complete, however, and he is constantly seeking out new items. He notes that, even today, items are being produced. "Now there's more stuff—plates, figurines, even replicas of clothing he wore. Several companies have marketed copies of the red jacket (worn by Dean in the climactic moments of *Rebel Without a Cause*), and there's a duplicate of the black leather jacket he wore that goes for around $300 now." Even Stetson, the respected western hat manufacturer, has jumped into the act by remaking the style worn by Dean when he portrayed ranchhand Jett Rink in the movie *Giant*. The new models start at $125.

Loehr's apartment is completely covered with his Dean items: magazines, statues, souvenir trinkets, even gumcards. "There were four cards that were part of a movie-star series made in 1956," he explained. "Original cards go for a starting value of $20–$25 each." Countless movie posters adorn the walls. "The amount of Dean movie memorabilia is amazing, and the prices are simply astronomical. *Rebel Without A Cause* is the hardest film to find original material on. "Rebel" posters (originals) can and do sell for $1000 in some markets.

Price values aside, Loehr's collection and his yearly Dean walks are a true labor of love, a dedication to Dean that transcends the myths and legends Dean left behind. Those myths and legends are still the subject of dispute to those who recall the childhood of James Byron Dean. "He was a normal Indiana Hoosier farm child," begins Ann Warr. "I didn't know him personally, but I watched him play basketball and my husband and I used to see him ride up and down Main Street on his motorcycle. My sister went to school with him though," she adds matter-of-factly.

Warr, a Fairmount native, is a leading historian in the town, and president of The Fairmount Historical Museum, Inc. (203 East Washington Street), in which there is a room reserved for the memorabilia of Fairmount's favorite son. "We were dedicated on September 21, 1975." (The museum is open from May until October.) "The Dean memorabilia really came about when they closed the old high school in 1970 and turned it into a junior high. School administrators had all the old high school memorabilia put away, storing it under the auditorium stage (the stage being the very first one Dean ever set foot on), and we had to find a way to preserve the artifacts of our old school." Warr pauses. "Then, when we got the artifacts and decided to display them, we had all these things from Jimmy's days in the school— athletic trophies, newspaper clippings, class pictures, yearbooks."

The old Fairmount High School closed its doors forever in 1986, and, like many of Dean's fans, Warr is concerned about what will happen to the building and its stage. "There's been all this talk of the museum moving there, but we just can't move all over again," she says sadly. "I feel very comfortable with what we have done here. This is not a James Dean museum, but we promote him in the best possible ways that we can."

Some of her favorite curios came to her through Dean's father, Winton. "He just came by one day in 1979 with all his son's artifacts that he said he wanted to see stay here in Fairmount, in the museum. He left us a lot of Jimmy's personal items. We never heard from him since," she says sadly. Some of the items he left were Dean's racing trophies, bongos, and a black and gold basketball sweater.

To those who knew Jimmy well, the words moody and arrogant often applied to Dean don't apply. "He played just like all the boys," remembers Adeline Nall. "He wasn't this lonely little child all the time—not at all." Nall is a warm and gracious woman, adored by Dean's fans almost as much as Dean himself. She was his school drama teacher, a woman for whom Dean had much respect. Since his death, Nall has conducted her own walking tours through Jimmy's school, has acted on many committees, and has kept in active touch with numerous fan clubs throughout the world. Nall accompanied Dean on several occasions as he went up for auditions and contests. The bond she shared with the actor is intensified in her own collection and memorabilia. Dean's watercolor painting of an orchid Nall had received as a gift from her drama class is among her most cherished items.

"He was a very sensitive young boy. I know he would have gone into directing had he lived." There is a sadness in Nall's voice as she thinks back on the dreams and goals she and Dean worked on and shared during their association. "Jim Dean would be flattered to know the type of fans he still has."

Among those select few who took part in and witnessed Dean's sudden rise to fame are the Winslows, the relatives who raised him. At the age of nine, the unexpected death of his mother had resulted in the young boy's departure from his father and their California home. He was sent to his Aunt and Uncle Winslow's Indiana farm; Dean's separation from his father was to be almost permanent. Dean's younger cousin, Mark Winslow, recalls life with Dean fondly. "He was like an older brother," he said.

Mark was still a child at the time of Dean's death, yet he recalls the actor's visits home clearly, particularly Dean's last visit, in February 1955. It was a visit with photographer Dennis Stock, whose photos depicting Dean in his hometown were publicized in March 1955. Several of the photographs were of Dean and the young Mark Winslow.

Winslow has lent his own precious-few artifacts to the museum. "His first motorcycle was Czechoslovakian. Dad (Dean's Uncle Marcus) bought it for him—it was a '46 model—and I put it on display at the museum along with the chaps he wore in *Giant* and a pair of his jeans." There are also some of Dean's personal books, and a brown suede jacket the actor particularly favored.

Winslow is a remarkably kind man who takes an active interest in Dean fandom. "They are a respectful group of people of all ages. You wouldn't believe the fans we get worldwide, from Japan and England (Dean is real big in England), and Spain."

Says Winslow, "He certainly inspired a lot of people. It's gratifying to see the way he changed a lot of lives in a positive way. It's good that the public can get involved. Jimmy was a good person."

Some three decades later, the rebel has found a cause.

The Tragedy of a Heroine

When Marilyn Monroe died of an overdose of sleeping pills at the age of 36 back in 1962, the movie industry and millions of devoted fans were thrown into shock. The "blonde, little-girl-like woman" who had flirted and flaunted on the screen was alive no more.

She starred in films with Tony Curtis *(Some Like It Hot)* and Jane Russell *(Gentlemen Prefer Blondes),* and appeared on the now-famous nude calendar, examples of which have sold

Marilyn Monroe

at auction for $250. Clearly, Marilyn, along with her memorabilia, was not for the stingy or the tight-fisted. One of the more sought-after items in the Marilyn collection is a poster of Marilyn with Rock Hudson, which sells for around $150. Original posters and lobby cards go for $50 to $80.

Her first movie was *Love Happy,* which she made in 1950 with Groucho Marx. "Hardly a day went by when she wasn't in the papers," says collector Donald Smith of Missouri. "There were clippings, photos, scripts, posters, books. Marilyn Monroe was the centerfold of the movie industry."

"I don't really know why I collect Marilyn Monroe memorabilia," says Donald, but "I think she was fascinating."

Donald started collecting Marilyn items when he was 10 years old, shortly after Marilyn's death. "I collected Marilyn when she wasn't popular, starting in 1962," he said. "I have all of her movies, calendars, and many posters."

Donald attributes much of the new interest in Marilyn Monroe and her life and collectibles to the recent connection between her and the Kennedys. "And those George Barris photographs, too. He kept them for such a long time and never released them until recently."

New information about Marilyn keeps cropping up, even some 25 years after her death. For instance, her controversial letter to acting coach Lee Strasburg begging to be released from a mental institution (valued by one gallery at $18,000) brought back the ghost of Marilyn Monroe for a little while. The fact that the letter was withdrawn from sale did nothing to lessen the interest in Marilyn.

It seems that, as the years go by, Marilyn keeps attracting crowds, even if now it is at auction galleries.

Magazine Covers

	Price Range	

Esquire

☐ **September, 1951** (color print of Marilyn Monroe)	45.00	55.00

Modern Screen

☐ **October, 1953** (cover)	45.00	55.00
☐ **October, 1955** (cover)	35.00	45.00
☐ **November, 1962** (cover)	30.00	40.00

Movieland

☐ **October, 1952** (cover)	40.00	50.00
☐ **October, 1953** (cover)	45.00	55.00
☐ **February, 1954** (cover)	45.00	55.00

Marilyn Monroe calendar

	Price Range	
Movie Life		
☐ **November, 1952** (cover)	40.00	50.00
☐ **April, 1955** (cover)	25.00	35.00
Movie Pix		
☐ **October, 1952** (cover)	40.00	50.00
☐ **April, 1953** (cover)	35.00	45.00

	Price Range	

Movie Spotlight

☐ **October, 1952** (cover) 40.00 50.00

Movie Stars Parade

☐ **October, 1953** (cover) 40.00 50.00

Saturday Evening Post

☐ **May 19, 1956** (article about Marilyn
Monroe by Pete Martin) 20.00 30.00

Screen Life

☐ **November, 1953** (cover) 45.00 55.00

Screen Stories

☐ **August, 1956** (cover) 45.00 55.00

Silver Screen

☐ **October, 1953** (cover) 45.00 55.00

☐ **April, 1954** (cover) 50.00 70.00

Movie Costumes

(*Note:* These costumes were sold at a Sotheby's collectibles auction in New York City in June 1986.)

☐ **Marilyn Monroe's Bathing Suit,** *There's
No Business Like Show Business,* 20th Century Fox, 1954, designed by William
Travilla and Charles Lamaire, black
bathing suit, a white sequinned bathing
cap, a white-with-black-polka-dots
wrap, a black belt, two bows and a tie,
label with star's name 1600.00 1700.00

Price Range

☐ **Marilyn Monroe's Green Silk Robe,**
There's No Business Like Show Business, 20th
Century Fox, 1954, designed by William
Travilla, the robe with oriental motifs
and a matching belt, label with star's
name 2100.00   2300.00

☐ **Marilyn Monroe's Leotard,** *Gentlemen
Prefer Blondes,* 20th Century Fox, 1953,
black and gold sequinned leotard with
tassles-and-rhinestones   trim   at   the
neckline, label with star's name 2100.00   2300.00

☐ **Marilyn Monroe's Pink Cotton Dress,**
Niagara, 20th Century Fox, 1952, linen
tight-fitting dress with a halter top,
label with star's name 2800.00   2900.00

☐ **Marilyn Monroe's Silk Pajamas,** *Seven
Year Itch,* 20th Century Fox, 1955, designer William Travilla, the raw silk
pink pajamas with collared V-neck and
a "Jax" label 2500.00   2800.00

Movie Posters

BACKGROUND: In 1909, the Motion Picture Patents
Company standardized both the size and purpose of posters.
A three-sheet is 41" x 81"; a two-sheet is 30" x 40"; a one-
sheet is 27" x 41"; an insert is 14" x 36"; a display card is
22" x 28"; a window card is 14" x 22"; and a lobby card is
11" x 14".

Between 1937 and 1961 almost 200,000,000 movie posters were produced in this country. The value of such posters
existed only so long as the film stayed popular. After all,
movie posters were meant to sell the movie, not themselves.

The production of window cards declined in the 1960s when TV became the preferred medium to use when advertising a new movie. The three-sheets and six-sheets phased out during the 1970s.

Lobby cards usually came in numbered sets of eight, and depict a series of scenes from the movie the set promotes. The first card in the set is usually the title card, while the other cards are scene cards and feature minor figures. The title cards are sometimes worth more than the scene card.

(*Note:* The letter "R" after a date signifies that the price listed is for only that year of release, not earlier or subsequent releases.)

Movie Ad Press Kits

BACKGROUND: These are packages of black and white ads used by the theaters to advertise films as well as suggestions to help boost customers, like staging a James Dean or Marilyn Monroe look-alike contest.

	Price Range	

1950s

☐ **"A Bullet For Joey,"** A. Trotter, Edward G. Robinson, George Raft	8.00	12.00
☐ **"Across The Wide Missouri,"** Clark Gable	10.00	15.00
☐ **"The Bad And The Beautiful,"** Lana Turner, Kirk Douglas, Walter Pidgeon, Dick Powell	10.00	15.00
☐ **"Bitter Creek,"** Wild Bill Elliott	8.00	12.00
☐ **"Blowing Wind,"** Gary Cooper, Barbara Stanwyck	10.00	15.00
☐ **"Dangerous When Wet,"** Esther Williams, Fernando Lamas	8.00	12.00

	Price Range	
☐ **"Dragnet,"** Jack Webb, Ben Alexander	10.00	15.00
☐ **"Escape From Fort Bravo,"** William Holden	8.00	12.00
☐ **"Executive Suite,"** William Holden, Barbara Stanwyck, Shelley Winters, Nina Foch, Paul Douglas	10.00	15.00
☐ **"The Far Country,"** James Stewart	10.00	15.00
☐ **"The Flame And The Flesh,"** Lana Turner	10.00	15.00
☐ **"Gun Fury,"** Rock Hudson, Donna Reed	10.00	15.00
☐ **"The Homesteaders,"** Wild Bill Elliott	8.00	12.00
☐ **"I'll Cry Tomorrow,"** Susan Hayward	10.00	15.00
☐ **"The Indian Fighter,"** Kirk Douglas . .	10.00	15.00
☐ **"Island In The Sky,"** John Wayne	10.00	15.00
☐ **"It Could Happen To You,"** Judy Holliday, Peter Lawford	10.00	15.00
☐ **"Johnny Guitar,"** Joan Crawford	10.00	15.00
☐ **"Jupiter's Darling,"** Esther Williams, Howard Keel	8.00	12.00
☐ **"Kansas Pacific,"** Sterling Hayden	8.00	12.00
☐ **"The Left Hand Of God,"** Gene Tierney, Humphrey Bogart	10.00	15.00
☐ **"Man With The Gun,"** Robert Mitchum	8.00	12.00
☐ **"Man Without A Star,"** Kirk Douglas	10.00	15.00
☐ **"The Moonlighter,"** Fred MacMurray, Barbara Stanwyck	10.00	15.00

	Price Range	
☐ **"The Naked Spur,"** James Stewart, Janet Leigh	10.00	15.00
☐ **"Never Let Me Go,"** Clark Gable, Gene Tierney	10.00	15.00
☐ **"The Man Form Laramie,"** James Stewart	10.00	15.00
☐ **"Personal Affair,"** Gene Tierney	8.00	12.00
☐ **"Roman Holiday,"** Audrey Hepburn, Gregory Peck	10.00	15.00
☐ **"Sabrina,"** Audrey Hepburn	10.00	15.00
☐ **"Sadie Thompson,"** Rita Hayworth ..	10.00	15.00
☐ **"Shane,"** Van Helflin, A. Ladd, J. Arthur	10.00	15.00
☐ **"Shoot First,"** Joel McCrea	8.00	12.00
☐ **"Six Bridges To Cross,"** Tony Curtis ..	8.00	12.00
☐ **"Solid Gold Cadillac,"** Judy Holliday, Paul Douglas	10.00	15.00
☐ **"Strange Lady In Town,"** Greer Garson, Dana Andrews	10.00	15.00
☐ **"Summertime,"** Katherine Hepburn ..	10.00	15.00
☐ **"Ten Wanted Men,"** Randolph Scott, Richard Boone	8.00	12.00
☐ **"Texas Lady,"** Claudette Colbert	8.00	12.00
☐ **"Topeka,"** Wild Bill Elliott	8.00	12.00
☐ **"Vera Cruz,"** Gary Cooper, Burt Lancaster	10.00	15.00
☐ **"Violent Men,"** Glenn Ford, Barbara Stanwyck	10.00	15.00

Price Range

1960s

	Price Range	
☐ **"A Man Called Dagger,"** Terry Moore, 1967	4.00	6.00
☐ **"Bonnie and Clyde,"** Warren Beatty, 1967	15.00	25.00
☐ **"Counterpoint,"** Charlton Heston, 1967	4.00	6.00
☐ **"Custer of the West,"** Robert Shaw, 1968	4.00	6.00

Inserts

(14" x 36")

☐ **"Abbott and Costello Go To Mars,"** 1953, Universal Pictures	50.00	60.00
☐ **"Abbott and Costello Meet Dr. Jekyll and Mr. Hyde,"** 1953, Universal Pictures, Bud Abbott, Lou Costello, Boris Karloff	95.00	115.00
☐ **"Anniversary, The,"** Bette Davis, 1967	15.00	25.00
☐ **"Anything Goes,"** Bing Crosby, 1956	45.00	55.00
☐ **"Birds, The,"** Tippi Hedren, 1963	180.00	220.00
☐ **"Bullitt,"** Steve McQueen, 1968	45.00	55.00
☐ **"Carbine Williams,"** James Stewart, 1952	40.00	50.00
☐ **"Cash McCall,"** Natalie Wood, 1960 ..	20.00	25.00
☐ **"Coogan's Bluff,"** Clint Eastwood, 1968	45.00	55.00
☐ **"Daniel Boone Frontier Trail Rider,"** Fess Parker, 1968	15.00	25.00
☐ **"Fighting 69th,"** James Cagney, 1956R	50.00	100.00

	Price Range	
☐ **"Firecreek,"** Fonda/Stewart, 1968	15.00	25.00
☐ **"Four Horseman of the Apocalypse,"** Glenn Ford, 1961	15.00	25.00
☐ **"Friendly Persuasion,"** Gary Cooper, 1956	45.00	55.00
☐ **"Gallery of Horror,"** Lon Chaney, 1967	20.00	30.00
☐ **"Go Man Go,"** Harlem Globetrotters, 1954	10.00	20.00
☐ **"Heart Is A Lonely Hunter,"** Alan Arkin, 1968	10.00	20.00
☐ **"Hell's Angels,"** Tom Stern, 1969	30.00	40.00
☐ **"Honeymoon Machine,"** Steve Mc-Queen, 1961	12.00	18.00
☐ **"Hootenanny Hoot,"** Johnny Cash, 1963	20.00	30.00
☐ **"Ice Station Zebra,"** Rock Hudson, 1969	40.00	50.00
☐ **"Lady L,"** Sophia Loren, 1966	15.00	25.00
☐ **"Morituri,"** Marlon Brando, 1965	10.00	20.00
☐ **"Muscle Beach Party,"** Funicello/Avalon, 1964	30.00	40.00
☐ **"Paint Your Wagon,"** Clint Eastwood, 1969	40.00	50.00
☐ **"The Rainmaker"** Katharine Hepburn, 1956	50.00	100.00
☐ **"Rare Breed,"** James Stewart, 1966	30.00	50.00
☐ **"Return of Dracula,"** Francis Lederer, 1958	30.00	50.00

	Price Range	
☐ "Saginaw Trail," Gene Autry, 1953 . . .	20.00	30.00
☐ "Satan's Satalites," Judd Holden, 1962	30.00	40.00
☐ "Seven Thieves," Joan Collins, 1959 . .	12.00	18.00
☐ "The Swan," Grace Kelly, 1956	60.00	80.00
☐ "The Swimmer," Burt Lancaster, 1968	15.00	25.00
☐ "Sword and The Rose," Richard Todd, 1953	14.00	16.00
☐ "Three Stooges Go Around The World In A Daze," 1963	50.00	60.00

Lobby Cards

(Individual 11" x 14")

	Price Range	
☐ "African Queen," Humphrey Bogart, 1952, #2	40.00	50.00
☐ "Bus Stop," 1956, 20th Century Fox, Marilyn Monroe, Don Murray, scene card, #5	25.00	65.00
☐ "Donovan's Brain," Nancy Davis (Reagan), 1953	45.00	55.00
☐ "How To Marry A Millionaire," Marilyn Monroe, 1953	40.00	50.00
☐ "The Misfits," 1961, United Artists, Clark Gable, Marilyn Monroe	40.00	60.00
☐ "Mogambo," 1953, MGM, Clark Gable, Grace Kelly, Ava Gardner, scene card	25.00	75.00
☐ "On The Waterfront," 1954, Columbia Pictures, Marlon Brando, Karl Malden, Eva Marie Saint	40.00	60.00

Price Range

☐ **"Rachel, Rachel,"** Paul Newman, 1968   10.00   15.00

☐ **"The Seven Year Itch,"** 1955, 20th Century Fox, Marilyn Monroe, Tom Ewell   30.00   60.00

☐ **"Three Stooges Go Around The World In A Daze,"** 1963 . . . .   25.00   35.00

☐ **"Wabash Avenue,"** 1950, 20th Century Fox, Betty Grable, Victor Mature 40.00   60.00

Lobby Cards

(Sets of Eight)

☐ **"Asphalt Jungle,"** 1950, MGM 100.00   150.00

☐ **"Bridge On The River Kwai,"** 1958, Columbia Pictures 50.00   100.00

☐ **"Breakfast At Tiffany's,"** 1961, Paramount Pictures 30.00   50.00

☐ **"Bullitt,"** Steve McQueen, 1968 . . . . . .   50.00   100.00

☐ **"Casino Royale,"** Peter Sellers, 1967 . .   35.00   45.00

☐ **"Country Girl,"** 1954, Paramount Pictures 50.00   100.00

☐ **"Circus World,"** John Wayne, 1965 . . .   35.00   45.00

☐ **"Executive Suite,"** 1954, MGM 15.00   25.00

☐ **"Grapes of Wrath,"** 1956, 20th Century Fox 100.00   200.00

☐ **"Great Escape,"** 1963, United Artists . .   75.00   125.00

☐ **"Green Fire,"** 1954, MGM 40.00   60.00

☐ **"Jailhouse Rock,"** 1957, MGM 100.00   150.00

	Price Range	
□ "Legend Of The Lost," 1957, United Artists	50.00	100.00
□ "Critic's Choice," Lucille Ball/Bob Hope, 1963	30.00	40.00
□ "Daniel Boone Frontier Trail Rider," Fess Parker, 1968	25.00	35.00
□ "Donovan's Reef," John Wayne, 1953	45.00	55.00
□ "North To Alaska," John Wayne, 1960	50.00	70.00

One-Sheet Posters

(27" x 41")

□ "Advise and Consent," Henry Fonda, 1962	15.00	17.00
□ "African Queen," Humphrey Bogart, 1968R	100.00	150.00
□ "After The Fox," Peter Sellers, 1966 ...	30.00	40.00
□ "Barbarella," Jane Fonda, 1968	100.00	150.00
□ "Bedazzled," Raquel Welch, 1968	20.00	30.00
□ "Blow Up," Vanessa Redgrave, 1967 ..	35.00	45.00
□ "Bonnie and Clyde," Warren Beatty, 1967	60.00	80.00
□ "Casino Royale," Peter Sellers, 1967 ..	45.00	55.00
□ "Circus Girl," K. Soederbaum, 1956 ..	20.00	30.00
□ "Circus World," John Wayne, 1965 ...	30.00	50.00
□ "Fearless Vampire Killers," 1967, Sharon Tate	100.00	200.00

Price Range

☐ **"How The West Was Won,"** Henry Fonda/John Wayne, 1963 .... 40.00 45.00

☐ **"Country Girl,"** Grace Kelly, 1954 .... 80.00 120.00

☐ **"Critic's Choice,"** Lucille Ball/Bob Hope, 1963 .... 30.00 40.00

☐ **"Dallas,"** Gary Cooper, 1956R 25.00 35.00

☐ **"Diamond Head,"** Charlton Heston, 1962 .... 15.00 25.00

☐ **"Dinosaurus,"** Ward Ramsey, 1960 ... 45.00 55.00

☐ **"The Dirty Dozen,"** Lee Marvin, 1967 45.00 55.00

☐ **"Doctor Blood's Coffin,"** Kieron Moore, 1961 .... 20.00 30.00

☐ **"Dr. No/From Russia With Love"/** combo, 1965R 45.00 55.00

☐ **"Dr. Who and the Daleks,"** Peter Cushing, 1966 .... 80.00 120.00

☐ **"Dr. Zhivago,"** Julie Christie, 1965 ... 80.00 90.00

☐ **"Dracula Has Risen From the Grave,"** Christopher Lee, 1969 .... 20.00 30.00

☐ **"Easy Rider,"** Peter Fonda, 1969 ...... 40.00 50.00

☐ **"Fanny,"** Leslie Caron, 1961 .... 20.00 30.00

☐ **"First Men in the Moon,"** Harry Hausen, 1964 .... 40.00 50.00

☐ **"Flying Leathernecks,"** John Wayne, 1951R 45.00 55.00

☐ **"Frankenstein's Daughter,"** John Ashley, 1959 .... 40.00 50.00

	Price Range	
☐ **"Funny Girl,"** Barbra Streisand, 1968	25.00	35.00
☐ **"Goodbye Columbus,"** Ali MacGraw, 1969	20.00	30.00
☐ **"Good, Bad And The Ugly,"** Clint Eastwood, 1968	140.00	160.00
☐ **"Gorgo,"** Bill Travers, 1961	50.00	70.00
☐ **"The Graduate,"** Dustin Hoffman, 1967	20.00	30.00
☐ **"Greatest Show On Earth,"** C.B. DeMille, Dir., 1952	50.00	70.00
☐ **"Guess Who's Coming To Dinner,"** Hepburn/Tracy, 1967	30.00	40.00
☐ **"Guest, The,"** Alan Bates, 1965	15.00	25.00
☐ **"Hellfighters,"** John Wayne, 1969	50.00	70.00
☐ **"Hello Dolly,"** Barbra Streisand, 1969	45.00	55.00
☐ **"Jeanne Eagles,"** Kim Novak, 1957 . . .	55.00	65.00
☐ **"The King And I,"** Yul Brynner, 1956	100.00	150.00
☐ **"La Dolce Vita,"** Fellini, 1961	125.00	175.00
☐ **"The Leech Woman,"** Coleen Grant, 1960	60.00	70.00
☐ **"Lilith,"** Warren Beatty, 1964	25.00	35.00
☐ **"The Lion In Winter,"** Katherine Hepburn, 1968	50.00	60.00
☐ **"Lust For Life,"** Kirk Douglas, 1962R	20.00	30.00
☐ **"Man In The Grey Flannel Suit,"** Gregory Peck, 1956	50.00	70.00

	Price Range	
☐ **"Man Without A Body,"** Robert Hutton, 1957	45.00	55.00
☐ **"Music Man,"** Robert Preston, 1962	35.00	45.00
☐ **"Night Creatures,"** Peter Cushing, 1962	20.00	30.00
☐ **"Northwest Mounted Police,"** Gary Cooper, 1958R	120.00	130.00
☐ **"Oedipus The King,"** Orson Wells, 1968	25.00	35.00
☐ **"Only Game In Town,"** Elizabeth Taylor, 1969	25.00	35.00
☐ **"Ski Party,"** Frankie Avalon, 1965	20.00	30.00
☐ **"Revenge Of Frankenstein,"** Peter Cushing, 1958	80.00	120.00
☐ **"Safe At Home,"** Mantle/Maris, 1962	100.00	150.00
☐ **"Summertime,"** Katherine Hepburn, 1955	90.00	110.00
☐ **"Who's Afraid Of Virginia Wolf,"** Taylor/Burton, 1966	40.00	50.00

Posters

	Price Range	
☐ **"Beauty and the Beast,"** Joyce Taylor, 22 x 28, 1962	15.00	25.00
☐ **"Becket,"** Richard Burton, 14 x 22, 1964, (1967R)	15.00	20.00
☐ **"The Birds,"** 46½ x 63, striking color French poster for Hitchcock's classic	75.00	100.00
☐ **"Charge of the Light Brigade,"** Vanessa Redgrave, 14 x 22, 1968	10.00	15.00

Price Range

☐ **"Cinderfella,"** Jerry Lewis, Rockwell art, 22 x 28, 1969 . . . .   45.00   55.00

☐ **"Cleopatra,"** Claudette Colbert, 22 x 28, 1952R 100.00   150.00

☐ **"Deadline U.S.A.,"** Humphrey Bogart, 22 x 28, 1952 . . . .   100.00   150.00

☐ **"Flower Drum Song,"** Nancy Kwan, 22 x 28, 1962 . . . .   10.00   20.00

☐ **"Flying Fontaines,"** Michael Callan, 22 x 28, 1959 . . . .   20.00   30.00

☐ **"Follow The Fleet,"** Astaire/Rogers, 30 x 40, 1953R 180.00   220.00

☐ **"For The First Time,"** Mario Lanza, 22 x 28, 1959 . . . .   25.00   35.00

☐ **"Funny Face,"** Astaire/Hepburn, 22 x 28, 1957 . . . .   100.00   150.00

☐ **"Gay-Purr-Ee,"** Judy Garland, 22 x 28, 1962 . . . .   20.00   30.00

☐ **"Gigi,"** Leslie Caron, 22 x 28, 1959 . . . .   35.00   45.00

☐ **"Golden Age of Comedy,"** Laurel and Hardy, 22 x 28, 1958 . . . .   15.00   25.00

☐ **"High Time,"** Bing Crosby, 22 x 28, 1960 . . . .   20.00   30.00

☐ **"Inside Daisy Clover,"** Natalie Wood, 22 x 28, 1966 . . . .   35.00   45.00

☐ **"The Jungle Book,"** 65½ x 44½, full-color standee lobby display in 2 sections, on heavy board, for Disney 45.00   65.00

Price Range

☐ **"Left Handed Gun,"** Paul Newman, 22 x 28, 1958 . . . . 20.00 30.00

☐ **"Legend Of The Lost,"** John Wayne, 22 x 28, 1957 . . . . 45.00 55.00

☐ **"Lilith,"** Warren Beatty, 22 x 28, 1964 25.00 35.00

☐ **"Love Is My Profession,"** Brigitte Bardot, 22 x 28, 1959 . . . . 20.00 30.00

☐ **"Man With The Golden Arm,"** Frank Sinatra, 22 x 28, 1956 . . . . 55.00 65.00

☐ **"The Misfits,"** Gable/Monroe, 22 x 28, 1961 . . . . 150.00 200.00

☐ **"Oklahoma,"** Gordon MacRea, 22 x 28, 1956 . . . . 90.00 110.00

☐ **"Oklahoma,"** Gordon MacRea, 30 x 40, 1956 . . . . 120.00 130.00

☐ **"One, Two, Three,"** James Cagney, 22 x 28, 1961 . . . . 40.00 60.00

☐ **"Paint Your Wagon,"** Clint Eastwood, 1969 . . . . 40.00 50.00

☐ **"Psycho,"** Anthony Perkins, 14 x 22, 1960 . . . . 120.00 130.00

☐ **"Raiders, The,"** Robert Culp, 30 x 40, 1964 . . . . 10.00 20.00

☐ **"Ride The Wild Surf,"** Fabian, 22 x 28, 1964 . . . . 20.00 30.00

☐ **"Ring Of Fear,"** Mickey Spillane, 22 x 28, 1954 . . . . 25.00 35.00

Price Range

☐ **"South Pacific,"** Mitzi Gaynor, 22 x 28, 1964R 25.00   35.00

☐ **"Storm Center,"** Bette Davis, 22 x 28, 1956 . . . .   50.00   70.00

☐ **"Story Of 3 Loves,"** Kirk Douglas, 22 x 28, 1953 . . . .   30.00   40.00

☐ **"Straight Jacket,"** Joan Crawford, 22 x 28, 1964 . . . .   30.00   40.00

☐ **"Sun Also Rises,"** Errol Flynn, 14 x 22, 1957 . . . .   20.00   30.00

☐ **"Tarzan's Savage Fury,"** Lex Barker, 22 x 28, 1952 . . . .   40.00   50.00

☐ **"Tennessee's Partner,"** Ronald Reagan, 22 x 28, 1968R 125.00   175.00

☐ **"Tom Jones,"** Albert Finney, 22 x 28, 1963 . . . .   15.00   25.00

☐ **"Top Hat,"** Astaire/Rogers, 22 x 28, 1953R 180.00   220.00

☐ **"Town Without Pity,"** Kirk Douglas, 22 x 28 . . . .   35.00   45.00

Programs

☐ **"Cardinal, The,"** Romi Schneider, 1964   8.00   12.00

☐ **"Cleopatra,"** Elizabeth Taylor, 1964 . . .   20.00   30.00

☐ **"Is Paris Burning?"** Alain Delon, 1966   8.00   12.00

☐ **"It's A Mad Mad Mad World,"** all-star cast, 1964 . . . .   10.00   15.00

Television

DESCRIPTION: Collectors are hot on the trail of items spun-off from 1950s and '60s TV shows like "Mr. Ed," "Star Trek" and "Dark Shadows," shows that have always enjoyed near-cult followings. In 1965, the Ideal Toy Company produced the "Man From U.N.C.L.E." game; today it is selling for around $20 at flea markets. The secret agent and espionage genre of the time continues to develop a footing with collectors ("Sorry about that, chief!"). Thanks to reruns in syndication, "Star Trek," "Mr. Ed" and the Mouseketeers are still around.

TYPES COVERED: "Dark Shadows," "Howdy Doody," "Man From U.N.C.L.E.," "Mr. Ed," Mouseketeers, Roy Rogers and Dale Evans, "Star Trek."

BACKGROUND: Technological efforts of the early TV days of old TV sets and premiums from the pre-World War II shows like "Space Control" and "Captain Video" attract high prices simply because they began during the days of radio serials and are considered the oldest and rarest TV collectibles.

While in 1946 there were just six TV stations in the eastern region of the United States, by 1951 TV broadcasts reached all over the country. The Milton Berle program was a hit from 1948 to 1956, and programs like Ed Sullivan's "Toast of the Town" as well as professional wrestling matches were almost as popular.

TV's Golden Age is considered to be 1953 to 1956. Newscasts were only 15 minutes long (who needed more than that?), and "Philco Theater," "Playhouse 90" and "Kraft Theater" were all introduced. From 1951 to 1957, "I Love Lucy" was at the top of the ratings, and it is a well-known fact that more viewers tuned in to watch Lucy have a baby than to watch Eisenhower's inauguration the next day.

By late 1958, the famous quiz show scandals were appearing on TV: a report of show producers allegedly supplying quiz show contestants with the answers was aired. Shortly thereafter, in 1960, the networks had discovered the profits gained by spectacular newscasting, and the newcasts were expanded.

It would be only a few short years later that the nation would watch—many times over—as a handsome young president was shot and killed in Dallas, Texas, right in their own living rooms. The horrors of Vietnam and the violence incurred by the movement of civil rights, the excitement of men on the moon and the political intrigue of Watergate soon appeared live whenever we pulled out the "on" button. Watching television had become that automatic.

Price Range

Television Collectibles

☐ **Alphabet Game,** c.1950s, "Pinkey Lee's" 7.00   14.00

☐ **Atomic Man,** Script, 1955, Gene Nelson, Faith Domerque, 89 pp. 15.00   25.00

☐ **"Atomic Submarine,"** script, 1959, Dick Foran, Bob Steele, Joi Lansing, 116 pp. 40.00   50.00

☐ **Avenger,** cap pistol, Kilgore, c.1959 ... 4.00   6.00

☐ **Beany and Cecil,** "Match It" game, 1961, 14" x 8" 10.00   14.00

☐ **Beany and Cecil,** "Match It" puzzle, 1961 .... 20.00   30.00

☐ **Beany and Cecil,** music box 5.00   10.00

Annie Oakley comic book

	Price Range	
☐ **"Ben Casey, M.D.,"** game, Bing Crosby Production, based on TV program, pictures Vincent Edwards on cover, box measures 9" x 17½", 1961	20.00	30.00
☐ **Ben Gazarra and Chuck Connors,** arrest and trial game, 1963	8.00	12.00
☐ **"Beverly Hillbillies,"** card game, 1963	15.00	25.00
☐ **"Bewitched,"** large wonder book, 1965	2.00	4.00
☐ **BooBoo The Doodle Cat,** yarn doll, 1961	4.00	6.00
☐ **"Branded,"** game, 1966	5.00	10.00
☐ **Bride of Frankenstein,** 15" paper doll with clothes, 1964	5.00	7.00

	Price Range	
☐ **Buffy** ("Family Affair"), paper doll, 1968	5.00	8.00
☐ **"Captain Video" Pursuit Ship,** plastic, three pieces, 4"	25.00	35.00
☐ **"Captain Video" Space Ships,** Lido/ Dumont TV, set of eight in box, plastic, box measures 8" x 10", c.1950	125.00	135.00
☐ **Casper,** game, 1959	6.00	10.00
☐ **Clark Kent,** "Superman", button, 1966, ⅞"	20.00	25.00
☐ **Crime Busting With The Green Hornet,** coloring book, Watkins-Strathmore, 1966, 8½" x 11"	10.00	15.00
☐ **Cecil,** talking sea serpent, puppet, 1961	40.00	50.00

Dark Shadows—Tales From Syndication and Beyond

"When the moon is full, and the night air is clear, creatures of the darkness emerge from the shadows of their sleep to walk the earth, witness to that which lies hidden to those who walk by day and sleep by night. . . ."

Although not exactly your standard fare in the world of comic books, "Dark Shadows," a Gold Key comic book series, often used this introduction in its story lines, lines borrowed from one of the most innovative television serials of the mid-'60s.

The show on which these books were based was of course "Dark Shadows," which first aired on the ABC television network June 27, 1966, and ran nearly five years as a daily serial. "Dark Shadows" used the traditional genre of the soap opera to deal with a most untraditional theme, the supernatural. Daily episodes revolved around a host of curses that plagued the once-affluent Collins family. Frequent characters included gypsies, unhappy spirits, men tor-

Barnabas Collins of "Dark Shadows"

mented by the full moon, and America's most marketable vampire since Dracula, Barnabus Collins (played by Shakespearean actor Jonathan Frid).

The show garnered a phenomenal following almost from the start. It is said that by the summer of 1969 (the height of popularity), at least 20 million viewers were hooked on the supernatural occurrences that befell the residents of Collinwood. It wasn't until 1971, after some 1245 episodes, that "Dark Shadows" returned to the crypt from whence it came. It left behind not only success stories (it helped launch acting careers for household names David Selby and Kate Jackson), but two major motion pictures, as well as a vast amount of memorabilia. Even today "Dark Shadows" fans continue to buy, sell and trade as a part of what amounts to a great resurgence of interest in the show.

Part of this resurgence is due to the 20th anniversary of the show's premiere and part is due to its current syndication on the PBS network and various television stations across the country. For a good many viewers, this is the first opportunity to see the show since its original run. "A lot of the people also watching are kids," "Dark Shadows" buff Kathy Resch explains.

Kathy is no stranger to "Dark Shadows." Resch founded one of the first of several fan clubs for the show (The World of Dark Shadows, Box 2262, Mission Station, Santa Clara, CA 95055). Resch's publication offers fans a chance to showcase original work and keep up-to-date on current activities of the club and, of course, the actors who participated in the show. She estimates her membership to be at least 500.

Resch's interest evolved from her dealings with other fans at various science fiction and horror conventions. Her collection grew from the few items she had since the show's original run to the large collection it is today. Among her items is one of the rarest prizes to the "Dark Shadows" fan, a plastic music box. Manufactured in 1971, the Josette Music Box (so named after Barnabas Collins' long lost love, Josette), is a replica of one used on the show and was available only through mail order. "I sent off for it when it first went on sale; now I wish I had bought 10 more," she said. For those few lucky enough to own one, the box currently goes for $200 to $500.

While items such as the music box fetch high prices on the market, a lot of memorabilia can still be had at reasonable prices. A series of paperbacks (32 in all) written by Canadian author Dan Ross (who used his wife's name, Marilyn, as a pen name) sold well over 40 million copies. These books often turn up periodically in used book stores and are generally available for $2–$8. Like most books in a series, first printings are worth the most. The first five printings in the "Dark Shadows" series, which appeared before the introduction of Barnabas and featured drawings on the cover are particularly valuable. After the successful introduction of Barnabas, those first five were reissued with photos on the cover (as were all later editions).

Resch also speaks highly of the Gold Key comics—which, oddly enough were printed for another five years after the series was cancelled. First issues included a fold-out photo, which has raised the prices from $15 to $20. Later issues are still found at prices of $2–$5.

Resch's appreciation of the show led her to the founding of ShadowCon in 1977. As the convention drifted away from "Dark Shadows" specifically and began to concentrate on the horror genre itself, she began a convention that would cater to "Dark Shadows" fans alone. The result was The Dark Shadows Festival (Box 92, Maplewood, NJ 07040), now in its fourth year. The festivals became so popular that other collectors became involved in putting them on.

One of these collectors, John Pierson, became chairman. Pierson refers to himself as "a second generation fan." "I was in high school in 1976 and worked for a local TV station," he says. "I had remembered the show as a kid, but I never took time out to watch it, so at the station I worked for I got to watch the show during my breaks. They took it off after a year, and I was pretty annoyed because I never got to follow it." Four years later, the show resurfaced and Pierson got involved all over again. He soon learned about the festivals, and plunged head-first into them. He affectionately refers to the festivals as "one big party," and his name has become synonomous with them. The weekend convention features major guests (Jonathan Frid and Joan Bennet, to name two), lectures, auctions, contests, and dealer tables where the collector/fan many sell or trade memorabilia. The 1985 convention attracted 800 people.

Among Pierson's favorite items from the show is the vast amount of photographs he has acquired. Since the show was filmed live, fans would more often than not be on hand at the taping, sometimes with cameras in hand. Some of Pierson's own favorite shots are of the actors "hanging around backstage." Pierson also prizes his audio material. "I collect records," he explains, and "Dark Shadows" produced a slew of recorded materials. "The 'Dark Shadows' soundtrack album was one of the biggest-selling television soundtracks ever; it reached the Billboard Top Twenty in 1969," Pierson says. The album, produced by Phillips Records, can sell for up to $15, depending on condition. Under the musical guidance of Robert Cobert, "Dark Shadows" music was produced on a variety of 45s. Among these was a duet done by David Selby (Quentin) and Nancy Barret (Charity) entitled "I'll Want to Dance With You"—not exactly the hit "Quentin's Theme" (done by Charles Randolph Grean Sounds) had been when released in 1969.

Pierson's wealth of knowledge extends far beyond the audio and photographs to include the realm of mass-produced items. The show's popularity had much to do with the marketability of its key character, Barnabas. Today, a host of "Dark Shadows" fans are drawn to Barnabas memorabilia, such as the Barnabas cane, an inexpensive reproduction of the one he used on the show. One piece of Barnabas memorabilia that stands out for its rareness is the Barnabas ring. "There was an offer on the back of a bubblegum wrapper that you could order by mail the Barnabas ring. (The ring was silver with a black onyx and adorned the vampire's hand). It's quite rare, never really turns up, and being that it is so small, it tended to get lost easier than the music box."

Even though Pierson's collection is constantly changing, there are still certain items that elude him. "The number one item that I want is the 'Dark Shadows' Fan Club kit." "Dan Curtis (the show's producer) sanctioned it in 1968. You would write to the network and they'd mail a form which you in turn filled out and mailed back to get this kit. The kit had color post cards, a big fold-out with the family mansion, Collinwood, and there were little postage-size stamps with the stars' pictures on them." These kits were never for sale commercially, and were, as Pierson is quick to point out, a bit misleading. "There was never really a major fan club for the show at that time."

Collecting from the show can indeed become a time-consuming project, and collector Steven Hall is more than aware of that fact. Hall has always been involved in "Dark Shadows" fandom. "As a young boy I would hurry home from school to watch the show," he says. "I got into buying and reading the books." Hall began to collect in 1970, and has amassed a collection of what he calls "all the good stuff," including duplicates which he sells or trades.

Hall attributes scarcity of some items to geographics. "Distribution has a lot to do with current availability. The gum cards (there were two series, one red from 1968 and one green from 1969) were hard to get in the south and southwest." Generally, the gum cards are still fairly easy to obtain with prices that Hall says vary from 50 cents to a dollar each.

Hall's eclectic collection contains curios such as the color Quentin postcards. There were 12 in a set, and they can fetch up to $16. Another unique item is the GAF View Master set. It included 21 color photos and came with a 16-page folio. "It currently sells from $30 to $50," Hall adds.

Steven Hall, like many collectors, has a favorite item, and his is a large poster from the 1970 movie *House of Dark Shadows.* Movie memorabilia can fetch high prices today, with posters from either *House* or *Night of Dark Shadows* selling for $25 to $50 each, not to mention the rising prices in lobby cards, stills, pressbooks and other film promotional items.

Dale Clark's collection contains a much-coveted prop. Collector and fan club organizer, Dale Clark publishes *Inside the Old House* (11518 Desdemona Drive, Dallas, TX 75228), a newsletter for "Dark Shadows" buffs. His prized item is a shawl that Diana Vincent Millay used in her role as Laura Collins. "I bought it at an auction at a 'Dark Shadows' convention," he says, adding that his timing "couldn't have been better." The shawl went up for bid just as the convention's special guests (actors who appeared on the program) were arriving. Naturally, everyone was more interested in the actors, "so practically everyone left the room, which game me the perfect opportunity to win the bidding," said Dale. "I got the shawl for practically nothing" ($10).

Original scripts, often signed by the actors who handed them to fans after a day's filming, have fetched high prices, although Clark says collector interest in acquiring scripts is because of the information they reveal. "I enjoy reading them to see the difference between what was originally written and what was actually aired," he said. "I have a collection of about 60 or so."

Two games produced for children are among Clark's collection. The "Dark Shadows" game (a traditional board game Clark describes as a cross between Life and Monopoly) was manufactured in 1968 by Whitman. The second game, and one that holds more attraction to collectors, is "The Barnabas Collins—Dark Shadows" game, made by Milton Bradley in 1969. This game called for players to take turns attempting to assemble plastic skeletons. While the artwork on the box appeals more to collectors, a set of plastic fangs included with each game has a lot to do with the value placed on this collectible. Both games, if in good shape, can sell for $20 to $35 each.

While prices vary and items come and go on the want lists of many collectors, one thing is certain. "Dark Shadows" continues to grow. Of the series, collector Pierson says, "Sure it was outrageous, bizzare and absurd. But it was believable." The actors, writers and producers took it seriously, and "that's why it worked." The new and old "Dark Shadows" fans continue to take it seriously. Maybe that's why it still works today.

Price Range

"Dark Shadows" Collectibles

(*Note:* The following items are from Steven Hall's Dark Shadows Collector #1, 11634 Sagepark Lane, Houston, TX 77089.)

☐ **Barnabas Collins,** paperback book, by Marilyn Ross 1.00   3.00

☐ **Barnabas Collins,** game, comes with skeleton pieces for players to try to assemble 10.00   35.00

☐ **Dark Shadows,** 1969, record album features eerie music with an occasional voice-over by David Selby ("Quentin") and Jonathan Frid ("Barnabas") 25.00   35.00

☐ **The Mystery of Collinwood,** paperback by Marilyn Ross .... .50   2.00

More Television Collectibles

☐ **Drop In For Dinner,** ("Addams Family"), lithographed pinback, Filmways TV Productions, ⅞", c.1968 .... 6.00   8.00

☐ **Donna Reed,** 15" paper doll with clothes, 1964 .... 5.00   7.00

☐ **"Family Affair,"** coloring book 5.00   7.00

☐ **Fast Draw McGraw,** 18" figure, 1959   15.00   18.00

☐ **"Flintstones,"** Silly Sun Pik Camera, 1964 .... 10.00   12.00

"Felix the Cat" record

	Price Range	
☐ **Flintstones, A Great Punchout Book,** Whitman/Hanna-Barbera, 11" x 22", 1961	40.00	50.00
☐ **"Flying Nun,"** lunch box, 1968	7.00	9.00
☐ **Flying Nun,** game, 1968	10.00	12.00
☐ **Gene Autry,** board game, boxed, "Bandit Trails"	70.00	100.00
☐ **"Gentle Ben,"** lunch box and thermos, 1968	5.00	7.00
☐ **Gentle Ben,** thermos, 1968	3.00	5.00
☐ **Gunsmoke,** frame tray puzzle, 1960 . . .	5.00	7.00
☐ **Hopalong Cassidy,** alarm clock	200.00	300.00
☐ **Hopalong Cassidy,** wristwatch	100.00	150.00
☐ **Hopalong Cassidy Gum Box,** this is the box the 1950 gum cards were sold in	80.00	100.00

WHEN YOU CALL ME AN IDIOT, SMILE.

Don Adams "Get Smart" card

Price Range

☐ **Hopalong Cassidy,** wind-up band-
piano toy, mint condition 350.00   450.00

"Say Kids, What Time Is It?"

"It's Howdy Doody time! It's Howdy Doody time!"

Howdy Doody, beloved puppet star of the popular TV
show of the '50s, is now the focal point of some very serious
toy collectors. Jim Dixon, a Howdy Doody collector, used
to be a baseball card collector, "Until I realized you had to
be a millionaire to have a good collection of old baseball
cards." He turned to collecting standard gauge trains, and
soon found himself giving up for the same reason. "Then
I remembered how much I'd loved Howdy Doody when I
was a kid, and decided to concentrate on Howdy Doody collectibles," he said. The Howdy Doody Club may be small,
with only 40 members, but it consists of serious collectors.
(For information on the association, write to Jeff Judson,
RD2, Box 87, Flemington, NJ 08822. Membership dues is

$12 a year, and the newsletter, *Howdy Doody Times,* containing trivia and information on Howdy Doody and collectibles, is mailed to members every month.)

"Howdy Doody is very collectible today," Jim said. "Prices are going sky-high. The Howdy Doody fever has caught on like wildfire." Jim said he has one of the largest collections of toys around, plus all of the comic books. Some collectible items he looks for are games, posters, Golden Books, puppets, wristwatches, and promotional items put out by Wonder Bread, Welch's Jelly, and Royal pudding.

Howdy Doody was on TV from 1947 until 1960. It was again on TV in 1976, but was quickly cancelled due to lack of interest among the children of the '70s. For 13 years, however, Howdy Doody and Buffalo Bob Smith, Clarabelle, Phineas T. Bluster, and all the other Howdy Doody characters held sway over audiences of children across America. The Howdy Doody puppet used from 1948 on was designed by two former Walt Disney studios artists. Howdy had red hair, a freckled face, a wide grin, a red kerchief and plaid shirt. The show was made up of puppets and their human counterparts, chief among them Buffalo Bob Smith, who, along with Howdy, made the show the most popular with kids on television. Some of the other puppets include Don Jose Bluster, Flub-a-Dub, Dilly Dally, Captain Scuttlebutt, John J. Fadoozle and Double Doody (Howdy's twin brother). Welch's Jelly sponsored the show from 1951 to 1955, and put out such items as jelly glasses, posters, cookbooks, and giveaway spoons and dolls. Poll Parrot was also an advertiser on the show. Jim notes that the age of particular items may be determined by the copyrights on them. Items marked Bob Smith or Martin Stone Associates date from 1948–1951, while items marked Kagran Corp. are from the 1951–1956 era. California National Products is from 1956–1960, and anything marked NBC dates from 1960 to the present.

Rare items include the Howdy Doody Tin Litho Clock-A-Doodle, a Pinhead and Foodini Tin Litho (Jack-in-the-Box), which is extremely rare, and a Howdy Doody wood jointed puppet, worth about $100. Many of these collectibles are worth hundreds of dollars. More common items include comic books, which sell for up to $35, records, books, and advertising.

For newcomers to the field of Howdy Doody collecting, Jim advises, "Place an ad in different magazines, such as the *Antique Trader.* You'll find Howdy Doody collectibles that way, and usually for a reasonable price. At auctions you'll pay through the nose." "Know copyrights," he adds "and avoid copies of Howdy Doody items."

Jeff Judson, Jim Dixon and other Howdy Doody collectors are trying to ensure Howdy's immortality by saving long-lost items from the early years of black-and-white TV. Those old shows, including "Howdy Doody," represent our history in entertainment. As Howdy would say, "What time is it, kids? It's Howdy Doody time!"

Howdy Doody Collectibles

	Price Range	
□ **Howdy Doody,** tin litho clock and doodle game, mint condition, c.1950–60s	500.00	550.00
□ **Howdy Doody,** Effanbee doll, fully dressed and in mint condition, ...	1000.00	1200.00
□ **Howdy Doody,** 10" wood jointed doll, mint condition . . . . (*Note:* For more Howdy Doody items, see listings of *Little Golden Books* and Premiums sections.)	80.00	120.00

More Television Collectibles

□ **Huckleberry Hound,** schoolbag, vinyl, 1960	12.00	15.00

Howdy Doody
Welch's ad

Howdy Doody
comic book

Howdy Doody record

Howdy Doody handkerchief

Howdy Doody playing cards

	Price Range	
☐ **Huckleberry Hound,** Silly Sun Pix Camera, 1964	10.00	12.00
☐ **"I Love Lucy,"** 3-D comic book, with original glasses	40.00	60.00
☐ **Kato's Revenge Featuring The Green Hornet,** coloring book, Watkins-Strathmore Publishing Co., 1966	50.00	60.00

	Price Range	
☐ **Kitty Kat** ("Addams Family"), lithographed pinback, Filmways TV Productions, ⅞", c.1968	6.00	8.00
☐ **"Laugh-In,"** lunch box, 1968	8.00	10.00
☐ **Lurch** ("Addams Family"), lithographed pinback, Filmways TV Productions, ⅞", c.1968	6.00	8.00
☐ **Magilla Gorilla,** Silly Sun Pix Camera, 1964	10.00	12.00

"Leave It to Beaver" book

Lone Ranger comic book

To Trap a Spy—Collecting "The Man From U.N.C.L.E."

During the early 1960s, the American public became obsessed with the secret agent/spy genre. One of the major reasons was the popularity on these shores of author Ian Fleming's Agent 007, better known as James Bond. The Bond movies—a mix of high adventure and comic relief—developed a strong and loyal following with American movie-goers.

Television followed suit, and soon dozens of spy shows jammed the network airwaves. One of the series determined to rise above the banal production of most crime shows at the time was "The Man From U.N.C.L.E." Premiering on September 22, 1964, and running for four years. the hour-long NBC drama not only set the style for the spies to come, but dominated the medium as well.

"U.N.C.L.E." borrowed heavily from the Bond success. The show was filled with gadgets and the ever-present beautiful girl in trouble. Fleming himself contributed the

The Men from U.N.C.L.E.

name of lead character Napoleon Solo to the show. When illness forced Fleming to leave the project, producers Norman Felton and Sam Rolfe continued to incorporate the Bond influence. Fleming's initial involvement in the show is a source of pride to "U.N.C.L.E." fans, and script notes or letters from him are highly coveted items.

Centering around two agents who worked for a CIA-like bureau called "U.N.C.L.E." (United Network of Criminal Law Enforcement), the series starred Robert Vaughn as the sophisticated, suave Napoleon Solo and David McCallum as the intellectual Illya Kuryakin, a man of few words, much action and inherent good looks. The casting was a stroke of pure genius. Solo appealed to the slightly older group while the British McCallum soon found himself a teen idol of sorts. Somewhere in the midst of this success, an "U.N.C.L.E." market was born.

A look at the current "U.N.C.L.E." merchandise want-lists reveals a multitude of available memorabilia. There were "U.N.C.L.E." badges, books, coloring books, games, toy guns, hats, trench coats, vests and lunch boxes. There was even a company (Cormier Hosiery Mills of Laconia, NH) that produced "U.N.C.L.E." hosiery. "U.N.C.L.E." memorabilia went so far as the long-since-forgotten "Transmitter Toffee Bar" candy, which was made by the Cavenham Confectionary Ltd. The same company also marketed chocolate "U.N.C.L.E." badges.

While a good deal of this memorabilia met its demise in dumpsters or tummies across the country, an astounding amount was saved. The show's current revival, due to such factors as syndication, a televised movie, *The Return Of The Man From U.N.C.L.E.*, aired in 1983, and the general revival of the '60s itself, has seen the market of "U.N.C.L.E." memorabilia on a continual rise.

Time was when "U.N.C.L.E." items were yours for the asking. Collector Lynda Mendoza offers this explanation of how she amassed her collection. "At one time people would just say—'You want that? Here take it.'—and they'd give it away."

Mendoza began collecting "U.N.C.L.E." seriously in 1979, although she does have several items saved from the show's original run. It wasn't until she saw McCallum on stage that her respect for his talent drew her into collecting his memorabilia, a lot of which is, understandably, "U.N.C.L.E."-related.

While serving as a secretary for an "U.N.C.L.E." fan club, she began to toy with the idea of forming her own club. On October 1, 1985, *The McCallum Observer* (known as the "official" publication on McCallum's career) first appeared. The club now boasts a subscription number close to 250, and the newsletter appears bimonthly. Not only does the newsletter cover McCallum's career then and now, but it also features photos and classified for the "U.N.C.L.E." collector. Those wishing to subscribe may write to *The McCallum Observer* at P. O. Box 165, Downers Grove, IL 60515.

Among Mendoza's prize possessions are the personal letters written to her by McCallum and the "U.N.C.L.E." producers, Felton and Rolfe. "Norman Felton wrote me something like six pages," she said. (Felton is a key link in "U.N.C.L.E." clubs, volunteering much time to preserving the "U.N.C.L.E." legacy.) "You can't put a price on something like that," Mendoza said.

Besides her personal artifacts, Mendoza's collection turns up some interesting and hard-to-come-by, mass-produced items, among them the Illya Puppet. Made of rubber, the hand-held puppet was manufactured by A. C. Gilbert Company and is considered a rare find. Perhaps the oddest curio she has saved is the box in which a Halloween "U.N.C.L.E." costume originally came, made by J. Halpern Company in the mid-'60s. Mendoza holds onto the box with the hope that someday the costume itself may turn up.

Not all items are as hard to come by, however. According to Mendoza, there are the fortunate dealers who have obtained mass lots. "I know of dealers who actually have gone through factories and warehouses, and dredge up this stuff in sealed boxes."

While dealers and collectors may still run across the Whitman "U.N.C.L.E." books (a hardbound series of which there were three issued), or Ace paperbacks at the local garage sale, the "U.N.C.L.E." suitcase finds its way into the hard-to-get set. The cardboard spy suitcase was chock-full of "U.N.C.L.E." items: matches, a gun with a silencer, badges, a camera and a walkie-talkie set, and more. Mendoza is still trying to complete the set.

In the world of collecting, the fan club offers a perfect opportunity for collectors and dealers to share current information and obtain items for their own collections. Some clubs hold conventions, and these are the best places for a polished collector to find that one item she or he has longed for, or for the amateur collector to get a crash course on the subject itself. A club which holds conventions yearly for the "U.N.C.L.E." fan is The "U.N.C.L.E." HQ Club (Darlene Kepner, 5 Chenault Court, Buffalo Grove, IL 60089). Aside from publishing a bimonthly newsletter, "U.N.C.L.E." HQ holds a convention known as Spy Con, a convention brimming with "U.N.C.L.E." memorabilia, contests, guests and film-fests, not to mention an array of dealers who carry other spy-related articles as well. "It's an exciting way to learn the market of "U.N.C.L.E." memorabilia," says Kepner, the club secretary. "We started out four years ago with just three dealers, and last year we had 27 tables!"

Competition among collectors can sometimes prove fierce. "At our Spy Con there was an "U.N.C.L.E." thermos for sale. It went out so fast we didn't even get a chance to see it, really. This collector bought it and just ran out the door, he was so pleased to get it." It reportedly went for $15, not bad for an item that 15 years ago was probably dropped on the playground.

Kepner's prize book, *Illya—That Man From U.N.C.L.E.*, originally published in 1966, is proof of the rise in value "U.N.C.L.E." memorabilia has seen. Kepner saw a copy recently and marveled at the price it fetched. "It went for $20 at Spy Con," she said, adding, "it has a nice collection of photos of David McCallum."

In her collecting treks, Kepner has seen the Barbie-sized "U.N.C.L.E." dolls sell for $45. The dolls, in character costume and complete with tiny guns, were not the big hits their manufacturer, A. C. Gilbert, expected them to be, and as such they are currently hot items on the market.

Though Kepner collects all sorts of "U.N.C.L.E."-related items (including an original script autographed by McCallum from a theater production and for which she paid $75), there are the collectors who focus on one specific type of item. Susan Cole is in this category. Cole is the president of "U.N.C.L.E." HQ and specifically collects paper. In fact, her basement, the "U.N.C.L.E." HQ office, is literally brimming with "U.N.C.L.E." paper; books, comics and posters. Another of Cole's "specialties" is the "U.N.C.L.E." charity auction, at which cherished "U.N.C.L.E." items are auctioned off at the Spy Con for the March Of Dimes. Her relentless pursuit of interesting items to donate have turned up those items many collectors dream of owning, including "U.N.C.L.E." movie posters. (There were three American movies based on the TV show, and the paper items from these are quite rare.) Selling for high prices, the movie memorabilia includes a Japanese poster promoting one of the films, commanding $165 at auction. A "Man From U.N.C.L.E." bowling jacket donated by producer Felton brought $135 at one of the auctions.

As we leave the land of the "Man From U.N.C.L.E.," one can rest assured that the agents of "U.N.C.L.E." continue to do battle with the evil THRUSH (The Technological Hierachy For the Removal of Undesirables and the Subjugation of Humanity) in syndication land, just as surely as the collectors of "U.N.C.L.E." continue their never-ending search for the men from "U.N.C.L.E."

"Man From U.N.C.L.E." game, 1965, $15.00–$18.00

Price Range

"Man From U.N.C.L.E." Collectibles

☐ **Man From U.N.C.L.E.,** book, 48 pps,
MGM photo cover, 1965 . . . .   2.00   3.00

☐ **Napoleon Solo** ("The Man From
U.N.C.L.E."), black-and-white pinback,
3½", 1965 . . . .   60.00   80.00

More Television Collectibles

☐ **Morticia Addams** ("Addams Family"),
lithographed pinback, Filmways TV
Productions, ⅞", c.1968 . . . .   6.00   8.00

☐ **"That Girl,"** sunglasses display, 1960s   20.00   24.00

America's Number One Mouseketeer

"M-I-C-K-E-Y! M-O-U-S-E! Mickey Mouse!"

Back in the mid-'50s, the Mouseketeers made their song famous, and the most famous Mouseketeer of all was Annette Funicello, the vivacious, dark-haired girl who went on to star in Disney feature films, many beach movies, and who continues in the public eye today as the spokesman for Skippy Peanut Butter and other products.

Annette Funicello is now 44 years old, the mother of three children, Gina, Jackie and Jason Gilardi, and the object of a fan club dedicated to her life and career.

Rita Rose, long-time fan of Annette and President of the Annette Funicello Fan Club, doubles as a newspaper reporter in real life. She has been a friend of Annette's for many years and wanted to keep her accomplishments in the world of show biz alive and well. She writes and publishes the club's newsletter, *The Annette Featurette,* a journal chock-full of stories, pictures and information issued three times a year.

Annette Funicello ad

Dues for new members are $10, with a $7 renewal fee after members have received six publications from the club. Members also receive a 5 x 7" photo, three snapshots, a photo membership card, a biography, and "extras." Members also have the opportunity to participate in all club contests and projects, and contribute stories, poems, sketches and photos for the journal. Fans are kept up-to-date on how to order Annette's records, and books and other items are also available. For her part, Annette answers questions in her exclusive column, "Personally Yours." Memorabilia is the keystone of the club's interest. Items for sale or trade are listed in the *Bulletin Board Classified* newsletter. Rita is unwavering in her devotion to the former Mouseketeer. "Annette is a warm, friendly person," she said. "She takes an interest in the club, which now has 300 members, and is a main contributor to it." Rita says that, as a result of increased interest in the '50s and '60s, people are becoming interested in Annette, her Disney movies and beach movies, and "especially because the Mouseketeers and other movies are being run on the Disney channel now."

Rita founded the club in 1961, which puts it in its 25th year. "I think it's great that another generation is learning to like Annette and her work all over again," Rita says. Annette was 9 years old when she joined the Mickey Mouse Club. She went on to appear in numerous Disney films, including *Johnny Tremain* (1957), *The Shaggy Dog* (1961) and *Babes in Toyland* (1961). From there she went beachside, starring in such films as *Bikini Beach* (1964) with Frankie Avalon.

In 1965, Annette Funicello married and settled down to raise her children. "She didn't do much of anything else," Rita said of those years. It wasn't until the '70s when she re-emerged on television, promoting products such as Clairol, Mennen Baby Products and Skippy Peanut Butter. Her exposure in commercials led to the recording of a country music album a few years ago.

"The Annette Funicello Fan Club hopes to hold its first convention in the summer of '88, at Disneyland." At the gathering, all forms of Funicello collectibles will come to the fore. A sampling of what Rita has collected includes records ("Tall Paul" and "Jo-Jo The Dog-Faced Boy" being favorite 45 rpms), paper dolls, coloring books, sheet music and comic books. There are coloring books and comic books from both the Mouseketeer period and the beach movies, Rita says. Annette was also frequently the subject of stories published in the early '60s teen magazines, such as *Teen Screen* and "*16*." These magazines according to Rita, are routinely worth from $5 to $15.

Even though Annette has long since hung up her mouse ears, she remains no stranger to show business. A new beach movie, starring Annette Funicello and Frankie Avalon as middle-aged parents with children who give their parents as many headaches as Annette and Frankie did 25 years ago, is planned for next year.

Rita invites members to "come along and sing our song and join our family" by writing to the Annette Funicello Fan Club, 10075 Dedham Drive, Indianapolis, IN 46229.

Mouseketeers Collectibles

	Price Range	
☐ **Annette Funicello,** paper doll, mint condition	45.00	55.00
☐ **"How to be a Mouseketeer,"** record album, 1962	55.00	75.00
☐ **Mickey Mouse,** bubble bath, 4½ oz. (3.50), "Avon," 1969	9.00	12.00
☐ **Mickey Mouse,** coloring book, "Avon," 1969	4.00	5.00
☐ **Mickey Mouse,** "Politoy," die-cast plastic automobile, Italian, marked #W600, c.1960	10.00	14.00
☐ **Mickey Mouse Club,** dotto dot book, 1957	2.00	3.00
☐ **Mouseketeers,** paper dolls, c.1957–58	50.00	60.00
☐ **Mouseketeer,** coloring book, 1957–58	5.00	15.00

More Television Collectibles

☐ **"Munsters,"** coloring book, 1965	6.00	10.00
☐ **Popeye,** 12" plastic firefighter, early 1960s	12.00	15.00
☐ **Popeye,** 10" plastic airplane, early 1960s	12.00	15.00
☐ **Popeye,** punch-me bag, 1960s	12.00	15.00

Walt Disney Magazine, 1957

Official Mickey Mouse Club book, 1950

"Happy Trails to You!"

Roy and Dale, born in 1912 as Leonard Slye and Frances Octavia Evans, who starred in such great Western classics as *Pals of the Golden West* and starred in their own TV series, the "Roy Rogers Show," from 1952 to 1954, have ensured their immortality with their showmanship. Now their personal mementos are safeguarded as well.

There is a place southeast of L.A. which is something of a mecca for fans of these two sagebrush stars who rode the silver screen. It is in Victorville, tiny home of the Roy Rogers and Dale Evans Museum. You'll know it when you get there because a 50-foot replica of Trigger, permanently reared upon his hind legs, is visible from the highway.

Roy Rogers and Dale Evans

Roy Rogers comic book

Roy Rogers pinback

Since 1976 the museum has admitted several hundred admirers each day to look at the famous couple's boots, costumes, scripts, movie posters, cars, saddles, awards, and more.

The museum houses the 1963 Pontiac convertible which Roy used in parades; silver dollars are mounted on the dashboard and throughout the interior of the car. Door handles are pistol handles, and on the front bumper rests a huge pair of sterling silver-tipped steer horns. Rifles are mounted on the back and sides, and a sterling silver saddle is mounted between the two front seats.

A $50,000 item in the museum is Roy's parade saddle, which is displayed behind thick glass. It is embellished with silver, gold and rubies.

Family photos and personal items also abound, as well as collectibles and artifacts belonging to other Western film stars. There is an Iron Eyes Cody room, William S. Hart's easy chair, Tom Mix's hat, gun and chaps, Buck Jones' saddle, and a piano belonging to Hoot Gibson. Sure attention-getters are Trigger, Buttermilk, Trigger, Jr., and Bullet, all stuffed and mounted.

The museum is open year-round, seven days a week, from 9 to 5, and there is a nominal admission fee.

	Price Range	
Roy Rogers Memorabilia		
☐ **Roy Rogers,** toy guitar with "RR" on it	40.00	50.00
☐ **Roy Rogers and Dale Evans,** thermos, 1955	30.00	35.00
☐ **Roy Rogers,** lunch box	6.00	8.00

"Star Trek" Collectibles

Memorabilia from one of the most popular television programs to come out of the '60s, "Star Trek," didn't begin appreciating in value until the program met with major success after it went into syndication. The market continues to be very strong in the '80s, buoyed by the release of full-length feature films starring the original cast.

Price Range

☐ **Star Trek,** leaf photo cards, 72-card set, withdrawn from the market because of contractual disputes, black-and-white photos from the television series, captions in black panels below picture, story on back, 1967, 2⅜" x 3⁷/₁₆" 600.00   800.00

☐ **Star Trek,** magazine, "Castle of Frankenstein," #11, Spock on cover 12.00   16.00

Cast of "Star Trek"

	Price Range	

Scripts

☐ **"All Our Yesterdays,"** 1968, by Jean Lisette Aroeste, third season, 68 pp. 40.00 60.00

☐ **"The Alternative Factor,"** 1966, by Don Ingalls, first season, 56 pp 40.00 60.00

☐ **"Amok Time,"** 1967, by Theodor Sturgeon, second season, 67 pp. 40.00 50.00

☐ **"And The Children Shall Lead,"** 1968, by Edward J. Lakso, third season, 71 pp. 40.00 60.00

☐ **"Apple, The,"** 1967, by Max Ehrlich, second season, 71 pp. 45.00 55.00

☐ **"Arena,"** 1966, by Gene Coon, first season, 63 pp. 50.00 60.00

☐ **"Balance of Terror,"** 1966, by Paul Schneider, first season, 68 pp. 65.00 75.00

☐ **"Bread and Circuses,"** 1967, by Gene Roddenberry and Gene L. Cook, second season, 65 pp. 45.00 55.00

☐ **"Catspaw,"** 1967, by Robert Bloch, copy #2, 67 pp. 45.00 55.00

☐ **"The Cloud Miners,"** 1968, by Margaret Armen, 68 pp. 25.00 35.00

☐ **"The Corbomite Maneuver,"** 1966, by Jerry Sohl, first season, 67 pp. 60.00 80.00

☐ **"Court Martial on Star Base 811,"** 1966, 74 pp. 40.00 60.00

☐ **"Dagger Of The Mind,"** by S. Wincelberg 30.00 40.00

	Price Range	
☐ **"Day Of The Dove,"** 1968, by Jerome Bixby, third season, 67 pp.	15.00	25.00
☐ **"The Enemy Within,"** by R. Matheson	35.00	55.00
☐ **"Enterprise Incident,"** by D.C. Fontana	25.00	35.00
☐ **"Friday's Child,"** 1967, by D.C. Fontana, second season, 68 pp.	45.00	55.00
☐ **"I, Mudd,"** 1967, by Stephen Kandel and David Gerrold, second season, 69 pp.	45.00	55.00
☐ **"Man Trap,"** by George C. Johnson . . .	50.00	60.00
☐ **"Miri,"** 1966, by Adrian Spies, copy #4, first season, 70 pp.	75.00	100.00
☐ **"Mirror, Mirror,"** 1967, by Jerome Bixby, 67 pp.	45.00	55.00
☐ **"Obsession,"** 1967, by Art Wallace, 143 pp.	55.00	65.00
☐ **"Shore Leave,"** 1966, by Theodore Sturgeon, copy #7, first season, 64 pp. . . .	65.00	75.00
☐ **"The Tholian Web,"** 1968, by Judy Burns and Chet Richards, third season, 61 pp.	45.00	55.00
☐ *Trek,* the Magazine for Star Trek Fans		
March 4, 1967, ...	25.00	30.00
July 15, 1967	5.00	10.00
November 18, 1967	25.00	30.00
June 22, 1968	5.00	10.00
August 24, 1968	20.00	25.00

More Television Collectibles

Soupy Sales pinback

TV's Top Stars magazine

	Price Range	
☐ **Tom Corbett Space Cadet,** coloring book, Saalfield, 1952, 16 pp., 10¾" × 14"	20.00	30.00

	Price Range	
☐ **"Tom Corbett Space Cadet,"** lunch box, 1952	20.00	25.00
☐ **"Tom Corbet Space Cadet,"** school bag, plastic sides supplemented with fabric, the sides imprinted with illustrations of space vehicles and a Tom Corbett Space Cadet, c.1950s, 10" x 14"	40.00	50.00
☐ **"Tom Corbett Space Cadet,"** thermos, 1952	20.00	25.00
☐ **"Wild Bill Hickok,"** thermos, 1955 . . .	6.00	8.00
☐ **Wyatt Earp,** frame tray puzzle, 1957 . .	5.00	6.00
☐ **Yogi Bear,** 21" plastic garden tool, 1960s	5.00	6.00
☐ **Yogi Bear,** game, 1961	8.00	10.00

Uncle Fester ("Addams Family") pinback, $6.00–$8.00

Zorro hat

Music

DESCRIPTION: Rock 'n' Roll has been considered an outgrowth from rhythm and blues music. But when did rock 'n' roll really begin?

It is actually a combination of many forms of music: hillbilly, folk and most certainly R&B. In 1953, the term "rock and roll" first came into use. When Ed Sullivan put Bill Haley and the Comets on his television show, the nation was introduced to rock 'n' roll. It was the beginning of a musical rollercoaster which has yet to cease.

Featured in this section are articles on the two biggest forces in the rock collecting era, Elvis Presley and the Beatles. Articles on the revival of interest in the Monkees, as well as an interview with Phil Schwartz of the Keystone Record Collectors Club, also highlight this section.

TYPES COVERED: Records (45 rpms, albums, extended play records), spinoff collectibles (gum cards, toys, dolls, etc.), teen magazines, memorabilia originally owned by well-known performers.

Records

	Price Range	
☐ **Avalon, Frankie,** "Just Ask Your Heart"/"Two Fools," Chancellor, 45 rpm, 1959	4.00	6.00
☐ **Avalon, Frankie,** "Why"/"Swingin' On A Rainbow," Chancellor, 45 rpm, 1959	15.00	35.00
☐ **Avalon, Frankie,** "Venus"/"I'm Broke," Chancellor, 45 rpm, 1959	3.00	6.00
☐ **Avalon, Frankie,** "Gingerbread"/"Blue Betty," Chancellor, 45 rpm, 1958	4.00	6.00
☐ **Avalon, Frankie,** "Bobby Sox To Stockings"/"A Boy Without A Girl," Chancellor, 45 rpm, 1959	3.00	6.00
☐ **Beach Boys,** "Good Vibrations"/"Let's Go Away For Awhile," Capitol, 45 rpm, 1966	4.00	6.00

Daytrippin'—Collecting the Beatles

Periodically in the history of show business, an "act" reaches heights that can only be called phenomenal. Although a fair share of individual artists (recent examples being Michael Jackson and Bruce Springsteen) have reached this level, only one band has ever achieved this status—the Beatles.

The Beatles provided the soundtrack for the turbulent '60s. Few adults now in their 30s and 40s can think of a personal incident that occurred without acquainting it to a Beatle song. Like the Kennedy assassination barely two months earlier, nearly everyone who lived through Beatlemania can remember where they were and what they were doing when the Beatles first hit American shores with their infamous appearance on the "Ed Sullivan Show." In the months and years that followed, the Beatles' private lives rarely escaped the limelight, and their every word or song was scrutinized by everyone, from professors to critics to teenagers and the PTA. Until they disbanded in 1970, the Beatles broke virtually every record in entertainment history.

When the murder of John Lennon in December of 1980 tragically ended forever any possibilities of a reunion, the true Beatle fan sought consolation amid a wealth of recorded material and an incredible amount of memorabilia. Beatle memorabilia is not only hot property, but a thriving industry which shows no signs of waning. Sotheby's, the renowned auction gallery, discovered this in a series of what has become known as "Rock 'n' Roll Memorabilia Auctions." The gallery has seen a dramatic rise in interest in rock memorabilia—the majority of which is Beatle-related.

Dana Hawkes, who heads Sotheby's New York Collectibles Department, speaks about the current interest. "The first one that Sotheby's, New York, had was held in 1983,

Beatles Gold album for "Hey Jude" sold at Sotheby's

John Lennon's Rolls sold for $2.3 million at Sotheby's

but we really put our name on the map for rock 'n' roll memorabilia when we sold items from the collection of John and Yoko." Items closely related to the Beatles tend to draw the highest bids. "Original drawings, lyrics—they all go for more than regular items offered," Hawkes says. She remarks, however, that "it's still hard to judge what an item will go for as it's such a volatile type of market." Original items sold at a Sotheby's 1986 auction drew stellar prices. John Lennon's school book *(Latin For Today)* signed twice by Lennon while a student at Quarry Bank High School in 1954, and containing humorous pen and ink doodles by the future Beatle, sold for $3740. A gold display album for "The Beatles Magical Mystery Tour" presented to Lennon sold for $4675. A Beatle Fan Club letter, typewritten and signed by George Harrison in 1964, thanking two young fans for "the lovely tie and pin" sold for $1100 (this lot also included a sheet of paper autographed by all four Beatles).

While letters and gold records seemed to command high prices, one type of item which does exceedingly well on the marketplace is original song lyrics. Two Sotheby's lots comprised of Beatle lyrics, both penned by Lennon, sold at amazing prices. The lyrics for "It's Only Love" (circa 1965), which contained nine lines of unpublished verse, sold for $7150. One of the highest prices realized for a Beatle song lyric was for the two verses of "Help!", written on scrap cardboard. Matted with an autographed magazine photo of Lennon, the lyric sold for $9350.

Beatle novelties did not sit idle at Sotheby's sale either. A lot comprised of a pair of sterling silver Apple cufflinks and an Apple wristwatch with a suede band sold for $935. (Apple Corps. was the name of the Beatle business company.) A sleeveless pink cotton promotional dress, which depicted portraits and facsimile signatures of the group, sold for $1540. Of the remarkable prices being set for Fab Four memorabilia, Hawkes of Sotheby's remarked, "The desirability of the rock 'n' roll memorabilia has created stronger and stronger prices over the years."

While auctions containing Beatle items focus attention on the field, the prices are often out of the reach of the average collector. To help bridge the gap between the $9000 autograph and the increasingly difficult chore of finding Beatle memorabilia at garage sales, there is the Beatle dealer/collector. One person bridging this gap is Rick Rann. Rann's *Beatlelist* catalog, which he sends out upon request (Beatlelist, P. O. Box 877, Oak Park, IL 60303) offers a vast array of all-original Beatle merchandise for sale.

Rann has attended over 30 Beatle conventions, even in Japan, where he notes that Beatle interest is "very strong." Rick Rann is a walking encyclopedia on Beatle merchandise and prices. Rann says many inaccuracies occur in the realm of Beatle collecting, and he is quick to dispell the myths which surround Beatle memorabilia. "Most people think that anything with the Beatles on it is worth a lot of money," he begins, citing records as an example.

According to Rann, due to the overwhelming amount of Beatle records sold in the mid-'60s, most Capitol Beatle albums are commonplace—garnering only $10–$20 at most on the market today. There are exceptions, however, and Rann knows them all.

"The 45 picture sleeve can be a rarity," he explains. "The sleeve for 'Can't Buy Me Love' is worth $150–$200. Beatle picture sleeves have been reproduced, and Rann is quick to forewarn collectors. "Chances are if the little dome which appears above the word 'Capitol' is blurred, it's probably a reproduction, although certain originals may have been blurred also. Check the condition of the paper and the weight," he advises, as these are all strong indicators of its age.

"Promotional records are always of value" he goes on to say. A six-song mini-ep made for jukebox distribution can command $200 if complete. "The promotional singles almost all had different promotional labels; they are worth $50–$150. Between 1964–1970, Capitol only issued four promotional singles and these are quite rare."

Rann's wealth of Beatle recording knowledge predates their signing with Capitol Records. "The Decca records single by Tony Sheridan and The Beat Brothers (which utilized the group as back-ups) is worth up to $2000, depending on condition." It was released in 1962 and contained "My Bonnie" b/w "When The Saints Go Marching In." However, the promotional version is only worth $600. "They must have flooded the market with promos," Rann deduces. After the band became an international success story, Decca re-released the 45, this time crediting the performance to the Beatles. It is a far more common issue.

Another pre-Capitol Beatle collectible is the VeeJay album. The album, issued in 1963 and called "Introducing the Beatles," is worth a couple of hundred dollars. Once again, after the band became popular, the company reissued the album in 1964 and its market value is relatively inexpensive. "The easiest way to tell which version you have is to turn the record over. If it has the songs listed on the back, it's a 1964 issue. If, however, the back cover features photos of other VeeJay artists and albums like Jimmy Reed, then you are holding a rare record." Condition is always an important contributing factor to value, as is whether the record was pressed in stereo or mono. "Stereo's worth more for the early '60s records as they weren't common."

Another VeeJay rarity is the 45 issue on VeeJay of "Please, Please Me." The reason for this is the misspelling of the group's name. It appears with two T's in Beatles. "It's worth about $250. No one in the U.S. knew who they were in 1963," Rick laughed.

The pride and joy of Rann's personal collection are his paper artifacts. "I have ticket stubs, some of which are used and some aren't. They're hard to find and I'd never sell them." Original paper items are hard to authenticate, and Rann is more than cautious when he finds something. "They are easy to duplicate. If I can't tell for sure, then I compare it to something I know is real, such as tickets and items that I have taken out of original scrapbooks people kept at the time. I look at the ink, the weight—everything." Rann knows of several cases in which over-exuberant fans have been taken by an unscrupulous Beatle counterfeiter who charges exorbitant prices for repro items. "There is no end to what these people have done," he says. "Sometimes they even get the dates wrong," he adds, recalling one such ticket stub which circulated with the wrong date printed on it.

Rann favors mass-produced items for the beginning collector, as it is easier to reproduce picture sleeves and ticket stubs than it is to reproduce a lunch thermos. "Also, those items that still have their original tags are extremely rare. Sweatshirts with tags can start at $50, and the wigs can go for that price also. Several years ago, someone unearthed caseloads of the wig, driving prices of it down to $35. But now, they're becoming hard to find again."

"There's so much stuff to collect, you could be collecting this for 15 years and somebody will come along with more!" The actual amount of Beatle items produced in 1964 alone can boggle the mind. There were Beatle boots, sneakers, jewelry, tablecloths, games, ties, even ice cream crunch bars (yes, Rann has a few wrappers in his collection), and candy cigarettes. "There were little boxes of candy cigarettes with cartoon figures of each Beatle on the boxes," Rann continued. When it comes to unusual items, Rann has turned up some pretty off-the-wall items in even odder places. "A friend of mine several years ago came across boxes for Beatle shampoo! He found all these empty boxes in an alley, of all places. Someone was probably storing stuff in them. When he went back, they were all gone. I've never seen shampoo—it could quite possibly be an item that was never distributed. But I still have the box he gave me." One hair product that was certain to have been marketed was the Beatle hairspray. Several cans have found their way into Rann's collection, and he places a value of $300 apiece on them.

"Memorabilia," he explained, are the kinds of things that got tossed—that's why these things are so rare. People usually kept their records—but lunchboxes or board games or dolls, they just got tossed." Beatle dolls are among these. Essentially, there were two types of dolls that did well on the market. The Remco doll (which featured each Beatle with his respective instrument) sells for $200–$250 a set. The Car Mascot dolls (a 16-inch doll with a "Bobbing Head") sells for the astronomical price of $1200 to $1500 a set.

Keeping in line with hard-to-find memorabilia, Rann brings up the Beatle Color Form kits. "A teenager in 1965 wouldn't buy them, and that item can get $100–$150 now. I had put one in my catalog and it sold right away. I wish I could find 100 of them." Wallpaper is another Beatle curio. "I bought a tube in 1982, and I sectioned it off so as to include a complete pattern (measuring 20 inches by 21 inches), and I've sold them all. You could probably ask $200—at least—for a roll now."

The field of Beatle collecting is filled with people of all ages. Take, for example, Beatle collector Tony Saks. Saks, who calls himself "The World's Oldest Beatle Maniac," may just be. The 78-year-old semi-retired guitar teacher from Norfolk, Virginia, owns the only guitar in the world personally autographed "in gold," by all four Beatles.

Traveling around the world to various Beatle festivals, often as an invited guest, Saks shares his mementos with thousands of fans yearly, who pose for photos with the famed Rickenbacker guitar. "I feel like I am a one-man ambassador, spreading the gospel of the Beatles!" he exclaims.

Saks' fortunate encounter with music history began in 1964 when, at the invitation of a Rickenbacker guitar official, he and his wife, Grace, drove to New York City to help demonstrate guitars and see, as he says, "a bunch of rock 'n' rollers." The "bunch of rock 'n' rollers" turned out to be the Beatles on their first American visit. Saks spoke to John, Paul and Ringo (George, who was laid up with a cold, was unavailable at the time), as they tried out the Rickenbacker guitar. Saks immediately purchased the guitar the Beatles had tried out for $467, with the thought of selling it to a student when he returned home. His students, on the other hand, begged him to hang on to the instrument. Some six months later, when the group played in Maryland, Saks had the opportunity to meet with all four. It was here that the guitar was signed. From that meeting, Saks became hooked on the band, saving photos and clippings, while proudly displaying his guitar. "I never even had to buy one record," he said. "People are always giving them to me. Last year in Miami I was presented with a 24-karat gold display album of 'The White Album.'"

Saks' guitar is such a valued item that the Beatlemaniac can't even lay claim on its value, saying, "I got several offers—for thousands and thousands of dollars—but oh God, I could never sell that guitar. I'm not interested in money; I don't need money—as long as I've got pocket money I'm happy. I have all these beautiful memories." One of his most beautiful is of his recent encounter with Lennon's eldest son, Julian, who also signed the guitar for Saks. "He (Julian) was in town on his first tour. When I found out, I got in touch with the guys who were doing the show. We met him backstage, and I had brought my guitar." Saks speaks in an excited tone as he relates the moment. "Do you know, he was stunned. He couldn't say anything. I got my pen ready, and when he saw that guitar, all he could do was say, 'I don't believe it, I don't believe it.' He even followed me back through the crowd to look at it again after he signed it, kind of touching the spot where his father had signed it."

Saks is like the proverbial kid in the candy shop when it comes to his cherished signed guitar. "I get such a kick from it," he says. "I enjoy seeing people happy. They love to pose with the guitar (even celebrities have posed, including "Star Trek" creator Gene Roddenberry, Roy Rogers, and talk-show host Gary Collins). I've always admired the boys," Saks said of the Beatles. Reflecting, he adds, "I often wonder what the heck I'm doing. I've been called a hoax, a liar, I've been mentioned in Derek Taylor's book on the Beatles. I've been on 'To Tell the Truth.' You have no idea. But I'm invited to Beatle shows to honor their name," he pauses, and adds, "Sometimes they (fans) even want my autograph."

Not every Beatle collector can come up with an item such as the Saks guitar, but there is a viable market for the collector of any size and budget. To help sift through the ever-changing world of Beatle fandom, there exist numerous fan clubs, which publish current news on the Beatles, photos, prices, and an in-depth look at the world of Beatlemania as it exists today. *Good Day Sunshine* is a fine example of one such newsletter. Published bimonthly, *Good Day Sunshine* (397 Edgewood Avenue, New Haven, CT 06511) is a labor of love, with 2800 members, headed by collector Charles F. Rosenay!!!, an enthusiastic Beatlemaniac, who bears a more-than-eerie resemblance to Paul McCartney.

Besides publishing *Good Day Sunshine,* he is also the producer of one of the largest Beatle conventions on the East Coast. Under the business name of "Liverpool Productions," Rosenay's conventions include special guests (like ex-Beatle

Beatle collector Charles F. Rosenay

drummer Pete Best, for whom Rosenay arranges many personal appearances in America), film footage, contests, continuous music, and a showcase for Beatle dealers. What started as a childhood obsession has become Rosenay's life. "Somewhere down the road the regular releases of Beatle albums weren't enough, and just having mono and stereo copies or imports weren't enough either, so my collecting ventured into the 'underground' world of unreleased Beatles material (culled from concerts, studio sessions, alternate versions, outtakes, etc.). My passion became and continues to be finding rare recorded material not commonly nor commercially available."

Rosenay's love of the Beatles has made for an amazing collection. "It would just be impossible to compile a list of my favorite items, but a few come to mind." One such item is a model which he describes quite humorously as "an atrociously painted plastic model kit, which I assembled as a child (of Paul)." Other choice items include "a John Lennon-autographed promotional poster given to me by a friend of John's, and a Christmas card that (Beatles manager) Brian Epstein sent out on behalf of his Liverpool lads, as well as the first two singles of the Beatles' I remember getting ('She Loves You' on the Swan label and 'I Want To Hold Your Hand' on Capitol.)" He is quick to point out that "these items are mostly of sentimental value and don't really reflect a typical collection, nor do they all have a set market value—but they are special to me."

Rosenay's collection runs the gamut, from an autographed picture of the four Beatles which he "lucked upon when buying an entire collection of '60s paraphernalia," to the quite popular Beatles board game produced by Milton Bradley and known as the "Flip Your Wig Game." "It's still playable with all its game pieces, but it doesn't really hold one's interest beyond the first few seconds anymore. I've tried to play recently . . . and anyway, the box states it's for ages 7–15." The game can be worth approximately $75 now.

"I have some items in storage, like the famed 'Butcher Block'-cover album as it came to be known." The cover was an original for "The Beatles Yesterday and Today" album, and was released in 1965. The Capitol album shot originally issued depicted the band in butcher smocks cheerfully holding chunks of red meat and half-assembled dolls. Some 60,000 copies were released with this photograph before public rage forced a recall. New photos were hastily pasted on originals not yet sold, and the new photo appearing was of the band situated around an open travel trunk. Many copies of this photo have been peeled to reveal the original photo underneath. It sells for at least $400 today. Says Rosenay of the covers, "They're status symbols among collectors."

Rosenay prefers the sentimental value of the "I Love the Beatles" buttons. Like the song says, "All You Need is Love," and to the true Beatle fan, like Rosenay, that's all it was really about in the first place.

Beatles Memorabilia

(*Note:* The following items appeared as lots at a recent Rock 'n' Roll memorabilia auction held by Sotheby's in New York City.)

	Price Range	
☐ **Album Cover,** "Help!", signed in blue ballpoint by all four members of the Beatles, c.1965, 20" x 19"	700.00	900.00
☐ **Album Cover,** "White Album," the inner cover autographed by all four Beatles in blue ballpoint, triple matted and framed with a plaque inscribed Beatles "White Album" c.1968, 19½" x 30"	800.00	1200.00
☐ **Album Jacket,** "Double Fantasy," autographed by John Lennon and Yoko Ono, the album slick signed on the cover	850.00	950.00
☐ **Album Slick,** "Butcher Cover," c.1966, the unreleased slick for "Yesterday and Today" album, double matted and framed with an engraved plaque, 21" x 17"	600.00	800.00
☐ **Cards,** gum cards, set of 65, question and answer series, color, Topps, 1964	50.00	70.00

Price Range

☐ **Card,** original Beatles autographed Cavern Club membership card, 1962, Liverpool, 4" x 2½" 800.00 1000.00

☐ **Celluloid,** "Lucy in the Sky," 1968, depicting Lucy riding a horse, matted and framed, 9¾" x 13½" 1000.00 1200.00

☐ **Jacket,** Beatles black Chinese-style jacket with mandarin collar and wide sleeves photo-printed with a design of Beatles photograph and press clippings on the lining, can be worn on the reverse, c.1960 .... 2600.00 3000.00

☐ **Letter,** January 24, 1964, the letter written to a fan in blue ink on blue air mail stationary, inscribed "with best wishes to our Austrian fan, Anne! Wishing you all the very best of luck for the future, Love from the Beatles. John Lennon, Paul McCartney, George Harrison, Ringo Starr," 9½" x 8" 1000.00 1500.00

☐ **Letter,** Beatles fan club typewritten letter, 1964, written to Jane and Nigel, thanking them for the "lovely green tie and pin ... I wish that I could come to each house and thank each fan that sent me a present, but I know that this is not possible, so I hope that this letter will make up for it. All my love, George Harrison" with his signature 800.00 1500.00

☐ **Lyrics,** John Lennon's handwritten lyrics for "It's Only Love," c.1965, the lyrics written in blue ballpoint pen and in black ink on a sheet of plain white

Price Range

paper, with many alterations and differences from the recorded version of the song, written on the reverse in John Lennon's hand in black ink with nine lines of unpublished lyrics, 8" x 6" ...   6500.00   7500.00

☐ **Magazine Photograph,** autographed by John Lennon, 1969, the Richard Avedon psychedelic John Lennon photograph signed "Love from John Lennon," 1969, 20½" x 16½" 1000.00   1800.00

☐ **Newsletter,** complete set of *Melody Makers* newsletter, dating from 1963 to 1969, with such headlines as "Beatles Make History," "Beatles Ape Monkees" and "Hendrix Double Hit Bid" 800.00   950.00

☐ **Painting,** "All You Need is Love," Alan Aldridge, 1968, gouache and inks on board, the word LOVE painted in shades of tangerine orange and brilliant red, placed over a purple heart speckled with stars and a moon and interwined with flowers and ribbons, signed lower right, 16" x 20" 4000.00   5000.00

☐ **Painting,** "Cry Baby Cry," Alan Aldridge, 1968, gouache and inks on board, the colorful depiction of a giant baby who cries tears that turn into fish and flow into a sea on which Paul McCartney floats in a rowboat, signed lower right, 27" x 20" 5000.00   6000.00

☐ **Painting** (Watercolor) of the Beatles, autographed, 1965, inscribed "To Patricia love from The Beatles XX," signed by

Price Range

all four members of the band, signed
lower right Patricia Kane '65, 20½" x
13½" 500.00   1000.00

☐ **Painting** (Mixed Media) of John Lennon
and Yoko Ono, Anne Meisel, 1969, depicting portraits of John Lennon and
Yoko Ono and the two of them walking
to a distant castle, signed lower left by
the artist, 23½" x 16½" 1500.00   2000.00

☐ **Painting** (Mixed Media), "The Beatles,"
Anne Meisel, 1968–69, depicting all
four members of the Beatles within
symbolic images such as Paul with the
Yellow Submarine, John with Straw-
berry Fields, and Ringo with Lucy in the
Sky With Diamonds, 19" x 24" 1000.00   1200.00

☐ **Painting** (Oil) of the Beatles, George
Underwood, depicting the four members of the Beatles, on canvas, signed on
the left by the artist, 18" x 24" 1500.00   2000.00

☐ **Postcard,** John and Cynthia Lennon,
March 1968, the short note on a postcard written and addressed to Victor
Spinetti from John and Cynthia when
they were in India, with Indian stamps,
cancel date 5 Mar 68, signed John & Cyn
XX 1000.00   1800.00

☐ **Posters,** set of four Richard Avedon psychedelic posters, 1968, 27" x 19", together with a Richard Avendon "The
Beatles" black-and-white poster, 1967,
15" x 39½" 650.00   750.00

Price Range

☐ **Program,** "The Beatles Show," August 12th, 1963, at the Odean, Llandudno, autographed by all four members of the band, Dakotas: Tommy Quickly, The Lanas, and Billy Baxter 800.00   950.00

☐ **Record Jacket,** 45 rpm, "Starting Over," autographed by John Lennon, signed on the cover John Lennon, '80, and the caricature signature of John, Yoko, and Sean 800.00   900.00

☐ **Ticket,** "Ready, Steady Go," 1963, signed twice by George Harrison, Ringo Starr, and Brian Epstein with two promotional photographs of Ringo Starr and George Harrison 600.00 1000.00

☐ **Watercolor Design,** for the exterior of Apple Boutique, late 1960s, Simon and Marijke, depicting a women playing a horn within psychedelic surroundings of setting suns and a distant temple, signed lower left by the artist, 17" x 14" 1000.00 1500.00

☐ **Watercolor and Marker Design for a John Lennon Piano,** late 1960s, probably Simon and Marijke of the Fool, the brightly colored piano painted with a landscape of flying saucers, fire and winged goddesses in shades of orange, yellow, blue and green, signed lower right S & M '68, matted and framed, 15¼" x 18¼" 1000.00 1500.00

Price Range

Beatles Collectibles

(*Note:* The following items are from Rick Rann's Beatle-list, P. O. Box 877, Oak Park, IL 60303.)

☐ **Beatles Wallpaper,** a complete 21″ x 21″ panel 25.00

☐ **Beatle Coin Purse** 20.00

☐ **Beatle Writing Tablet,** ⅝″ thick 25.00

☐ **Ringo Revell Model Kit,** unassembled in original box with instructions 90.00

☐ **Beatle Lunchbox,** blue, 1965 . . . .   65.00

☐ **Beatle Thermos,** 1965 . . . .   40.00

☐ **Flip Your Wig Game,** complete 60.00

☐ **John Remco doll,** with instrument 65.00

☐ **Beatle Hairbrush,** 1964, in original package 10.00

Additional Beatles Collectibles

Beatles Records

☐ **"She Loves You"/"I'll Get You,"** Swan, 45 rpm, 1964, white label 35.00   45.00

☐ **"She Loves You"/"I'll Get You,"** Swan, 45 rpm, 1964, black label 3.00   6.00

☐ **"Can't Buy Me Love"/"You Can't Do That,"** Apple, 45 rpm, 1964 . . . .   3.00   5.00

☐ **"Love Me Do"/"P.S. I Love You,"** Tollie, 45 rpm, 1964, promo 45.00   55.00

☐ **"Love Me Do"/"P.S. I Love You,"** Tollie, 45 rpm, 1964, commercial 4.00   7.00

The Beatle Book,
published by Lancer Books in 1964

Beatles cards

Complete Beatles story

A No. 1 issue of
Beatles 'Round the World,
from 1964

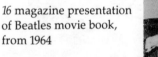

16 magazine presentation
of Beatles movie book,
from 1964

Autographed photo of Beatles,
with George's and John's
signatures reversed

"Introducing the Beatles" record album

	Price Range	
☐ **"Love Me Do"/"P.S. I Love You,"** Tollie, 45 rpm, 1964, picture sleeve	20.00	30.00
☐ **"A Hard Day's Night"/"Should Have Known Better,"** Capitol, 45 rpm, 1964	3.00	5.00
☐ **"I Feel Fine"/"She's A Woman,"** Capitol, 45 rpm, 1964	3.00	5.00
☐ **"Eight Days A Week"/"I Don't Want To Spoil The Party,"** Capitol, 45 rpm, 1965	4.00	6.00
☐ **"Ticket To Ride"/"Yes It Is,"** Capitol, 45 rpm, 1965	4.00	6.00
☐ **"Help"/"I'm Down,"** Capitol, 45 rpm, 1965	3.00	5.00
☐ **"Yesterday"/"Act Naturally,"** Capitol, 45 rpm, 1965	3.00	5.00
☐ **"We Can Work It Out"/"Day Tripper,"** Capitol, 45 rpm, 1965	3.00	5.00
☐ **"Paperback Writer"/"Rain,"** Capitol, 45 rpm, 1966	3.00	5.00

	Price Range	
☐ "Penny Lane"/"Strawberry Fields Forever," Capitol, 45 rpm, 1967	4.00	6.00
☐ "All You Need Is Love"/"Baby You're A Rich Man," Capitol, 45 rpm, 1967, promo	50.00	70.00
☐ "All You Need Is Love"/"Baby You're A Rich Man," Capitol, 45 rpm, 1967	4.00	6.00
☐ "Hello Goodbye"/"I Am The Walrus," Capitol, 45 rpm, 1967, promo	50.00	70.00
☐ "Hello Goodbye"/"I Am The Walrus," Capitol, 45 rpm, 1967	3.00	5.00
☐ "Hey Jude"/"Revolution," Apple, 45 rpm, 1968	5.00	7.00
☐ "Get Back"/"Don't Let Me Down," Apple, 45 rpm, 1969	5.00	7.00
☐ "ComeTogether"/"Something,"Apple, 45 rpm, 1969	4.00	6.00

More Records

☐ Brummels, Beau, "Laugh Laugh"/"Still In Love With You Baby," Autumn, 45 rpm, 1965	3.00	5.00
☐ Brummels, Beau, "Just A Little"/ "They'll Make You Cry," Autumn, 45 rpm, 1965	3.00	5.00
☐ Brummels, Beau, "You Tell Me Why"/ "I Want You," Autumn, 45 rpm, 1965	3.00	5.00

Price Range

☐ **Bee Gees,** "New York Mining Disaster 1941"/"I Can't See Nobody," ATCO, 45 rpm, 1967 ....   2.00   4.00

☐ **Bee Gees,** "To Love Somebody"/"Close Another Door," ATCO, 45 rpm, 1967   2.00   4.00

☐ **Bee Gees,** "Holiday"/"Every Christian Lion Hearted Man Will Show You," ATCO, 45 rpm, 1967 ....   3.00   5.00

☐ **Bee Gees,** "(The Lights Went Out In) Massachusetts"/"Sir Geoffrey Saved The World," ATCO, 45 rpm, 1967 ...   2.00   4.00

☐ **Bee Gees,** "Words"/"Sinking Ships," ATCO, 45 rpm, 1968 ....   2.00   4.00

☐ **Bee Gees,** "I've Got A Message To You"/"Kitty Can," ATCO, 45 rpm, 1968 ....   2.00   4.00

☐ **Bee Gees,** "I Started A Joke"/"Kilburn Towers," ATCO, 45 rpm, 1969 ......   2.00   4.00

☐ **Bee Gees,** "First of May"/"Lamplight," ATCO, 45 rpm, 1969 ....   2.00   3.00

☐ **Berry, Chuck,** "Maybellene"/"Wee Wee Hours," Chess, 45 rpm, 1955 ....   5.00   10.00

☐ **Berry, Chuck,** "Johnny B. Goode"/ "Around And Around," Silver-and-Blue Chess-Top label, 45 rpm 5.00   7.00

☐ **Big Bopper** (Jape Richardson), "Chantilly Lace"/"Purple People Eater Meets The Witch Doctor," Mercury, 45 rpm, 1958 ....   4.00   6.00

Purple People Eater pinback

Pat Boone 45

Price Range

☐ **Big Bopper,** "Big Bopper's Wedding"/"Little Red Riding Hood," Mercury, 45 rpm, 1958 .... 3.00 5.00

☐ **Boone, Pat,** "Ain't That A Shame"/ "Tennessee Saturday Night," DOT, 45 rpm, 1955 .... 3.50 4.50

☐ **Boone, Pat,** "At My Front Door"/"No Other Arms," DOT, 45 rpm, 1955 .... 3.50 4.50

☐ **Boone, Pat,** "Gee Whittakers"/"Take The Time," DOT, 45 rpm, 1955 ...... 3.50 4.50

☐ **Boone, Pat,** "Tutti Fruitti"/"I'll Be Home," DOT, 45 rpm, 1956 .... 2.00 4.00

☐ **Boone, Pat,** "Long Tall Sally"/"Just As Long As I'm With You," DOT, 45 rpm, 1956 .... 2.00 4.00

☐ **Boone, Pat,** "I Almost Lost My Mind"/"I'm In Love With You," DOT, 45 rpm, 1956 .... 2.00 4.00

☐ **Boone, Pat,** "Don't Forbid Me"/ "Anastasia," DOT, 45 rpm, 1956–57 .. 3.00 4.00

☐ **Boone, Pat,** "Love Letters In The Sand"/"Bernadine," DOT, 45 rpm, 1957 .... 3.00 4.00

☐ **Boone, Pat,** "April Love"/"When The Swallows Come," DOT, 45 rpm, 1957 3.00 4.00

☐ **Boone, Pat,** "Moody River"/"A Thousand Years," DOT, 45 rpm, 1961 ..... 3.00 4.00

Price Range

☐ **Brown, James,** "I Got You (I Feel Good)"/"I Can't Help It," King, 45 rpm, 1965 . . . .   3.00   6.00

☐ **Brown, James,** "It's A Man's Man's Man's Man's World"/"Is It Yes Or Is It You?", King, 45 rpm, 1968 . . . .   4.00   6.00

☐ **Brown, James,** "Cold Sweat," King, 45 rpm, 1967 . . . .   4.00   6.00

☐ **Brown, James,** "Papa's Got Brand New Bag/Pt.2," King, 45 rpm, 1967 . . . .   4.00   6.00

☐ **Brown, James,** "Say It Loud," King, 45 rpm, 1968 . . . .   4.00   6.00

☐ **Campbell, Glen,** "Galveston," Capitol, 45 rpm, 1968 . . . .   2.00   5.00

☐ **Campbell, Glen,** "Witchita Lineman," Capitol, 45 rpm, 1968 . . . .   2.00   5.00

☐ **Campbell, Glen,** "By The Time I Get To Phoenix," Capitol, 45 rpm, 1967 . . . . .   3.00   5.00

☐ **Cash, Johnny,** "I Walk The Line"/"Get Rhythm," Sun, 45 rpm, 1956 . . . .   3.00   6.00

☐ **Charles, Ray,** "What'd I Say," ABC-Paramount, 45 rpm, 1959 . . . .   4.00   6.00

☐ **Charles, Ray,** "Busted," ABC-Paramount, 45 rpm, 1963 . . . .   4.00   6.00

☐ **Charles, Ray,** "Hit The Road Jack," ABC-Paramount, 45 rpm, 1961 . . . . . .   4.00   6.00

☐ **Checker, Chubby,** "The Twist"/"Toot," Parkway, 45 rpm, 1960 . . . . . .   4.00   6.00

	Price Range	
☐ **Checker, Chubby,** "The Twist"/ "Toot," Parkway, 45 rpm, 1961	4.00	5.00
☐ **Coasters,** "One Kiss Led To Another"/"Brazil," ATCO, maroon label, 45 rpm	10.00	15.00
☐ **Coasters,** "Down In Mexico"/"Turtle Dovin'," ATCO, maroon label, 45 rpm	10.00	20.00
☐ **Darin, Bobby,** "Mack The Knife"/"Was There A Call For Me," ATCO, 45 rpm	4.00	8.00
☐ **Darin, Bobby,** "Dream Lover"/"Bull Moose," ATCO, 45 rpm	4.00	8.00
☐ **Domino, Fats,** "Ain't It A Shame"/"La La," Imperial, 45 rpm, 1955	5.00	15.00
☐ **Domino, Fats,** "I'm Walkin"/"I'm In The Mood For Love," Imperial, 45 rpm, 1957	4.00	10.00

Dick Clark Volume 2

Price Range

☐ **Domino, Fats,** "I'm In Love Again"/"My Blue Heaven," Imperial, 45 rpm, 1956 ....   4.00   6.00

☐ **Domino, Fats,** "Blueberry Hill"/ "Honey Chile," Imperial, 45 rpm, 1956   4.00   6.00

☐ **Domino, Fats,** "Blue Monday"/ "What's The Reason I'm Not Pleasing You," Imperial, 45 rpm, 1957 ....   4.00   6.00

☐ **Domino, Fats,** "Valley of Tears"/"It's You I Love," Imperial, 45 rpm, 1957 ..   4.00   6.00

☐ **Domino, Fats,** "Whole Lotta Loving"/"Coquette," Imperial, 45 rpm, 1958 ....   3.00   5.00

☐ **Fabian,** "Hound Dog Man"/"This Friendly World," Chancellor, 45 rpm, 1959 ....   2.00   5.00

☐ **Fabian,** "Turn Me Loose"/"Stop There," Chancellor, 45 rpm, 1959 ....   3.00   5.00

☐ **Fabian,** "Tiger," Chancellor, 45 rpm, 1959 ....   3.00   5.00

☐ **Fleetwoods,** "Mr. Blue"/"You Mean Everything To Me," Dolton, 45 rpm ..   4.00   6.00

☐ **Fleetwoods,** "Come Softly To Me"/"I Care So Much," Liberty, 45 rpm, 1959   4.00   8.00

☐ **Four Seasons,** "Sherry"/"I've Cried Before," VeeJay, 45 rpm, 1962 ....   4.00   6.00

☐ **Four Seasons,** "Big Girls Don't Cry"/"Connie-O," VeeJay, 45 rpm, 1962 ....   3.00   5.00

Price Range

☐ **Four Seasons,** "Walk Like A Man"/"Lucky Ladybug," VeeJay, 45 rpm, 1963 ....   3.00   5.00

☐ **Francis, Connie,** "Who's Sorry Now"/"You Were Only Fooling," MGM, 45 rpm, 1958 ....   4.00   6.00

☐ **Francis, Connie,** "Who's Sorry Now," MGM, EP 8.00   12.00

☐ **Francis, Connie,** "Who's Sorry Now," MGM, album 25.00   35.00

☐ **Francis, Connie,** "My Happiness"/"Never Before," MGM, 45 rpm, 1958 ....   4.00   5.00

☐ **Francis, Connie,** "Lipstick On Your Collar"/"Frankie," MGM, 45 rpm, 1959   4.00   5.00

☐ **Francis, Connie,** "Among My Souvenirs"/"God Bless America," MGM, 45 rpm, 1959 ....   3.00   5.00

☐ **Francis, Connie,** "Everybody's Somebody's Fool"/"Jealous Of You," MGM, 45 rpm, 1960 ....   3.00   5.00

☐ **Francis, Connie,** "Where The Boys Are"/"No One," MGM, 45 rpm, 1961   3.00   4.00

☐ **Francis, Connie,** "Don't Break The Heart That Loves You"/"Drop It, Joe," MGM, 45 rpm, 1962 ....   3.00   4.00

☐ **Halley, Bill And The Comets,** "Rock Around The Clock"/"Thirteen Women," Decca, 45 rpm, 1955 ....   8.00   16.00

Price Range

☐ **Halley, Bill And The Comets,** "Shake, Rattle And Roll"/"A.B.C. Boogie," Decca, 45 rpm, 1954 . . . .   4.00   8.00

☐ **Hendrix, Jimi,** "All Along The Watchtower"/"Burning Of The Midnight," Reprise, 45 rpm, 1968 . . . .   3.00   5.00

☐ **Holly, Buddy,** "Peggy Sue"/"Everyday," Coral, 45 rpm, 1957 . . . .   6.00   12.00

☐ **Holly, Buddy,** "Rave On"/"Take Your Time," Coral, 45 rpm, 1958 . . . .   8.00   12.00

☐ **Holly, Buddy,** "Early In The Morning"/"Now We're One," Coral, 45 rpm, 1958 . . . .   8.00   12.00

☐ **Holly, Buddy,** "It Doesn't Matter Anymore"/"Raining In My Heart," Coral, 45 rpm, 1959 . . . .   8.00   12.00

☐ **Knight, Gladys And The Pips,** "Every Beat Of My Heart"/"Room In Your Heart," VeeJay, 45 rpm, 1961 . . . .   4.00   6.00

☐ **Knight, Gladys And The Pips,** "I Heard It Through The Grape Vine," Soul, 45 rpm, 1967 . . . .   4.00   6.00

☐ **Lee, Brenda,** "Rockin' Around The Christmas Tree"/"Papa Noel," Decca, 45 rpm, 1960 . . . .   3.00   5.00

☐ **Lee, Brenda,** "I Want To Be Wanted"/"Just A Little," Decca, 45 rpm, 1960   3.00   4.00

☐ **Lee, Brenda,** "I'm Sorry"/"That's All," Decca, 45 rpm, 1960 . . . .   3.00   5.00

Price Range

☐ **Lee, Brenda,** "Fool No. 1"/"Anybody But Me," Decca, 45 rpm, 1961 . . . .   3.00   4.00

☐ **Lee, Brenda,** "Break It To Me Gently"/"So Deep," Decca, 45 rpm, 1962   3.00   4.00

☐ **Lewis, Jerry Lee,** "Whole Lot Of Shakin' Going On"/"It'll Be Me," Sun, 45 rpm, 1957 . . . .   5.00   8.00

☐ **Lewis, Jerry Lee,** "Great Balls of Fire"/"You Win Again," Sun, 45 rpm, 1957 . . . .   5.00   8.00

☐ **Lewis, Jerry Lee,** "Breathless"/"Down The Line," Sun, 45 rpm, 1958 . . . .   4.00   6.00

☐ **Little Richard,** "Maybe I'm Right"/"I Love My Baby," Peacock, 45 rpm, 1956   20.00   30.00

☐ **Little Richard,** "Tutti Fruitti"/"I'm Just A Lonely Guy," Specialty, 45 rpm, 1956   5.00   9.00

☐ **Little Richard,** "Keep A Knockin'"/"Can't Believe You Wanna Leave," Specialty, 45 rpm, 1957 . . . .   4.00   6.00

☐ **Little Richard,** "Good Golly Miss Molly"/"Hey Hey Hey Hey," Specialty, 45 rpm, 1958 . . . .   4.00   6.00

☐ **Mathis, Johnny,** "Wonderful Wonderful"/"When Sunny Gets Blue," Columbia, 45 rpm, 1957 . . . .   4.00   5.00

☐ **Mathis, Johnny,** "It's Not For Me To Say"/"Warm and Tender," Columbia, 45 rpm, 1957 . . . .   4.00   5.00

Price Range

☐ **Mathis, Johnny,** "Chances Are"/"The
Twelfth of Never," Columbia, 45 rpm,
1957 .... 4.00 5.00

All Aboard for the "Last Train to Clarksville"

In the beginning, the recipe was simple. Take four relatively unknown boys—two actors and two musicians—and cast them as plastic replicas of Britain's biggest selling import of the '60s, the Beatles. There was to be a cute one like Paul (only his name was Davy). There was to be a loveable comic like Ringo (but his name was Micky). There was to be a mystical one like George (his name was Peter). And finally, there was even one tall, gangly guy named Michael who was every bit the deadpan wit that John was. Mix in an NBC television series which revolved around the life of a rock'n' roll group circa 1966, blend in the studio techniques

The Monkees

of director James Frawley, and you had it—a pasteurized, Americanized TV show that derived a great deal from such Beatles movies as *A Hard Day's Night* and *"Help!"*

The recipe's ingredients combined to form the Monkees, who have been humorously called the "Pre-Fab Four."

After the TV series debuted on September 12, 1966, the group took off. By late 1966, Monkees albums were outselling the Beatles on some markets. The Monkees' debut album remained at the top of the charts for 13 weeks, and the first single, "Last Train to Clarksville," sold over 50,000 copies within weeks of its release. Then, the news hit: the Monkees didn't even play their own instruments. They in fact had the finest studio musicians and songwriters behind them. "Just who did these guys think they were?" the music industry asked. The Monkees were a sham, and the declamations went on and on. While the Monkees faced a verbal lambasting from an angry press, an oblivious nation of pre-teens showed they cared not and fell head-over-heels for Davy, Micky, Mike and Peter.

The band put out an admirable effort at taking control of their music late in 1967, but by then their appeal was wearing. The Monkees were tired and disillusioned. One by one they quit; Peter Tork went first, followed by Nesmith, leaving only Micky Dolenz and Davy Jones to carry on, playing together occasionally in a series of musical lineups, including a quartet which featured Tommy Boyce and Bobby Hart, the group's chief songwriters during their peak of popularity.

After 20 years of legal problems, character assaults and a general bad news stigma which seemed to plague the Monkees, the group is back—three of them, that is—in the world of pop music. Giving in to fans' demands on the 20th anniversary of their TV debut (1986), the Monkees scheduled a small reunion tour on which they were slated to play a few state fairs and small venues. Not expecting much, Tork, Jones and Dolenz set out in the late spring of '86. And then something happened. MTV, the music video network, obtained clearance to air the 58 episodes of "The Monkees" television series. Suddenly it was 1966 all over again. The tour was extended, and again, just like in the '60s, there were young girls screaming everywhere. Reissues of Monkees albums climbed their way up the charts and there, for all the world to see, were the Monkees, on stage and playing their own instruments! The group's outlandish antics and quaint, outdated charm earned them a new generation of followers. Even the press was on their side this time. The great big Monkees machine chugged into action once more.

If liking the Monkees wasn't enough, collecting Monkee memorabilia became the rage of the year. With the tour being one of the year's hottest news items in the industry, and the Monkees themselves achieving stellar status, the demand for the '60s stuff soared. Collectors and dealers alike were virtually harassed as they found it increasingly difficult to keep up with the sudden demand. A story circulated about a collector who decided the time was right to sell off his large collection. Within one week of his ad's appearance in a Monkee fanzine he was beseiged by 125 inquiries. Monkeemania has struck paydirt, 20 years after the fact, and there is little in the current world of pop to compete with it.

The die-hard fans couldn't be happier. "The Monkees were a bit cooler than most people thought," says collector Fred Velez. "I had the stuff by the Beatles, but the Monkees were a little bit more special to me." An original fan, Velez began collecting in 1967. "My first piece was the second Monkees album. I got it by winning a contest at a fair. For some reason, I chose the album over the other prizes." From that humble beginning, Velez's collection has grown. "I don't have the luxury of displaying my stuff," he noted, regarding his somewhat crowded living quarters. "I have two old Monkees posters on the walls." Most of his over-500 items are stored away. In reference to the revival, he says, "I've tapered off on original memorabilia right now for the obvious reasons—it's in such demand again. But the new stuff (items related to the '86 tour) is inexpensive and easy to get."

Although Velez has seen the group on their current tour, he, like many, laments that he never had the chance to see them during their heyday in the '60s. With this in mind, it is little wonder he cherishes his '60s tour books. Another favorite and rather unique item for Velez is a 1969 tour booklet. "A while ago I saw Peter Tork perform live as a solo and I brought along the book. It had a questionnaire on the then-current Monkees Fan Club and how to join it. They asked you questions like 'Who's your favorite Monkee?' and I had Peter sign that line." During the past few years, he has gotten to know Peter. "He's a great human being and a talented artist," And what of the tour booklet? "I'd never sell it," he says.

What makes Monkees collecting so appealing to many fans are these personal tie-ins, and the chance to still be able to meet them. Unlike the Beatles, the Monkees were and are far more accessible to the general public. Velez's collection also includes an autographed picture sleeve for "Oh My My" b/w "I Love You Better" released in April 1970 by Dolenz and Jones as the Monkees. "I saw Micky at a club in New York where he and Davy were doing solo gigs and I had him autograph it," Velez says proudly.

Velez's love for the group has gotten him involved with outside projects, like emceeing at Monkees conventions, as well as the task of taking bids at a Monkees auction. "Davy had graciously contributed items from his own collection to an auction, where the proceeds go to a charity of Davy's choice." The bids on the items were remarkably high. "There was a program for 'Godspell' (which Jones, who is no stranger to theater, had performed in). Another high bid went for three shirts. These were shirts which the Monkees wore for publicity shots," Velez said. "He (Davy) had three of them—Peter Tork's went for $500."

Is there one item that Fred Velez would like to own himself from the Monkees' own personal collection? "Mike's (Nesmith) wool hat," he is quick to answer. "It's a real personal item." The wool hat was Nesmith's trademark, and since he wore it incessantly, the producers of the show had originally given him the name "wool hat" for the series before a disgruntled Nesmith began objecting to the moniker. "I'd love to own that hat," sighs Velez, adding almost as an afterthought, "I used to try to dress just like him when I was a kid."

Dress just like the Monkees? Yes, indeed. In the mid-'60s, there was a line of Monkees clothing marketed by JC Penney's: raincoats, shirts, the "stovepipe" pants, sweaters, and vests. "I found recently a vest with the Monkees' logo printed on the inside tag," says Maggie McManus. "I bought it a little while ago at a record convention for $40." Maggie McManus calls herself a "second generation fan," and has been the editor of one of the largest fan clubs newsletters for the group since June 1977. *Monkee Business* (2770 South Broad Street, Trenton, NJ 08610) is available for $8.00 a year. "I was 16 when I started it," she said. "Initially it was intended to be a little magazine where fans could write who had Monkees experiences to share. At the time, there was little being done on the Monkees. There wasn't the large resurgence, so no one in the media had paid any attention to us, and it just evolved. We had grown to several hundred members, but as soon as the series hit MTV, it began to really take off. We're up to nearly 10,000 members, with a hundred or so new members joining each week!"

McManus is proud of her Monkees connections. "I've known Peter now a long time," she says. Her contact has paid off. At a recent Philadelphia convention, all three of the touring Monkees appeared. "Our conventions used to have 300–400 people total in attendance; our last convention had 1000–1400 people a day." Convention co-partner Ed Reilly said that Monkees goods were selling like never before. "One guy at the last convention turned up with two plastic models of the Monkeemobile in their box, still sealed," Reilly recalled. "He wanted $500 each, and someone whipped out their charge card and bought them."

McManus, who owns one of the most extensive collections of Monkee collectibles, favors collecting magazines. "I really enjoyed the old teen magazines," she muses. "Those magazines nowadays at conventions are worth $8–$15 at least."

John Sheridan's ties in the world of Monkees memorabilia run to the slightly offbeat. A musician in his own right, the collector has been involved in Monkeemania, a Monkee look-alike, sound-alike band, and has had the chance to perform with Monkees members Tork and Jones on two separate occasions. "I played guitar for Davy Jones in 1984," he explained. "He was in New York City and appearing on the 'Uncle Floyd TV Show.'"

Sheridan's first appearance on stage with a Monkee happened at a Monkees convention. "Peter Tork was supposed to be there. But no one had any idea when, even though it was advertised. We were all thinking, 'where is he?', and eventually someone had to drive into the city and pick him up. Meanwhile, there was this talent contest happening onstage and Monkeemania was also on stage at the time. Then it was announced that there was one last contestant who really didn't want to get up there. And all of a sudden, Peter Tork came through the wings. He acted like he was really a contestant in a talent contest, he acted nervous-like." He did his poem entitled, "Peter Percival Patterson's Pet Pig Porky" (a nonsensical bit of prose which led into the song "Pleasant Valley Sunday" on their album). What followed was Tork backing up Sheridan's group through a memorable rendition of "Pleasant Valley Sunday."

Sheridan's knowledge of Monkees recorded material is vast. "There were five variations of the 45 picture sleeve to 'Last Train to Clarksville.' The first issue was a black-and-white photo tinted brown. It had a red border and was on semi-glossy paper. The third one was the same photo (the band was standing on what appeared to be a Western set, on a porch, looking up), only it was color. It says on the bottom of the sleeve, 'write to the Monkees Fan Club' and has an address. (It's printed on the back of the sleeve as well.) The fourth one was yet another sleeve with the same photo, only it says 'Ask for the Monkees Album' on one side with the fan club on the other." As for the fifth variation, "it was a reissue from '69 or '70. It was standard paper with no information on the back and looked cheap." This final pressing had the Colgems logo on the label.

Another Monkees rarity in the recorded category is the original pressing of the first Monkees album. The initial pressing has the misspelling of Michael Nesmith's song "Papa Jean's Blues" (the correct spelling was "Gene's."). Later issues were corrected.

Among the most unusual of the Monkees records were the Post cereal box specials. "I have one or two of them and what's interesting about them was by the time they came out Peter Tork had already left the group, so there were these neat little drawings of the other three on them." These 33⅓ rpm records "were a little piece of cardboard that you cut off the cereal box and played on your parents stereo."

Sheridan has also found a real gem—a bona fide Monkees model guitar manufactured by Gretsh instruments at the height of Monkeemania. "It retailed then for somewhere around $350 to $500 when new," he says. "It's actually a good guitar.

"I also have a few rare music books. I have the book for the 'The Birds, The Bees and The Monkees' album, which is very desirable because it has full-color photos taken from the Monkees movie *Head.* Memorabilia for the movie is worth a considerable amount. Released in 1968, the movie enlisted the aid of then-unknown screenwriter Jack Nicholson, and had among the cast Frank Zappa and Annette Funicello. Poor advertising at the start, as well as a fad-ing fire in Monkeemania, made the film a dismal flop. Like many underrated films of its day, however, *Head* has been a cult favorite for years.

Printed memorabilia is another strong area in the Sheridan collection. *Tiger Beat,* which was the leading fanzine at the time, put out authorized Monkee magazines. "They were called 'Monkee Spectaculars' and there were 16 issues in all. The first issue was early '67 and the last was in 1968. The final issues were nice because they had photos from *Head* in it, stuff that was scrapped from the movie's final version." At the time, fanzines sold for 50 cents each. At Monkees conventions they can now get $15.

And as could be guessed, there were the inevitable Monkees gum cards. "There were three series," Sheridan says. "The first series was stills from the TV show's pilot episode. They also included black-and-white publicity stills. The second and third series were done in color, and date from the '67 series episodes primarily."

Sheridan is hesitant to say what effect the current Monkees reunion will have on the wildly-fluctuating prices of Monkees memorabilia within the next year or so. In a market which sees complete gum card series go from $13 to $25, and plastic model kits net $500, there is little question that, regardless of the final outcome, Monkees collectibles have at long last arrived on the market.

Hey! Hey! They're the Monkees—and they're back!

Monkees Collectibles

	Price Range	
☐ **Cereal Box Cards,** 2" x 3½", color photo and autograph, featuring Davy or Peter	1.00	3.00
☐ **Gum Cards,** "C" series, complete set ..	13.50	25.00
☐ **Gum Cards,** second series, Canadian set	6.00	15.00
☐ **Gum Card Wrappers** red (1966)	5.00	10.00

	Price Range	
blue (1967)	5.00	10.00
yellow (1967)	5.00	10.00
☐ **More of the Monkees Gum Card Box**	20.00	30.00
☐ **More of the Monkees Jukebox Mini LP,** with title cards	40.00	50.00
☐ **Screen Life,** July, 1968 (Monkees cover)	10.00	15.00

16 teen magazine

Monkees "I'm A Believer" record

Price Range

More Records

☐ **Nelson, Ricky,** "A Teenager's Romance"/"I'm Walking," Verve, 45 rpm, 1957 . . . .   5.00   7.00

☐ **Nelson, Ricky,** "Be Bop Baby"/"Have I Told You Lately That I Love You?," Imperial, 45 rpm, 1957 . . . .   4.00   5.00

☐ **Nelson, Ricky,** "Stood Up"/"Waitin' In School," Imperial, 45 rpm, 1957 . . . . . .   4.00   5.00

☐ **Nelson, Ricky,** "Poor Little Fool"/"Don't Leave Me This Way," Imperial, 45 rpm, 1958 . . . .   4.00   5.00

☐ **Nelson, Ricky,** "Never Be Anyone Else"/"Sweeter Than You," Imperial, 1959 . . . .   4.00   5.00

☐ **Nelson, Ricky,** "Travelin' Man"/"Hello Mary Lou," Imperial, 45 rpm, 1961 . . .   3.00   5.00

☐ **Nelson, Ricky,** "Young World"/"Summertime," Imperial, 45 rpm, 1961   3.00   5.00

☐ **Pitney, Gene,** "Only Love Can Break A Heart"/"If I Didn't Have A Dime," Musicor, 45 rpm, 1962 . . . .   3.00   4.00

☐ **Pitney, Gene,** "It Hurts To Be In Love"/"Hawaii," Musicor, 45 rpm, 1964 . . . .   3.00   4.00

☐ **Pitney, Gene,** "I'm Gonna Be Strong"/"Alladin's Lamp," Musicor, 45 rpm, 1964 . . . .   3.00   4.00

	Price Range	
☐ **Platters,** "Twilight Time," Mercury, 45 rpm, 1958	4.00	5.00
☐ **Platters,** "The Great Pretender"/"I'm Just A Dancing Partner," Mercury, 45 rpm, 1955	5.00	7.00
☐ **Platters,** "You'll Never Know"/"It Isn't Right," Mercury, 45 rpm, 1956	4.00	5.00
☐ **Platters,** "Smoke Gets In Your Eyes"/"No Matter What You Are," Mercury, 45 rpm, 1958	3.00	5.00

Elvis Presley: The King of Rock 'n' Roll Collectibles

It's 1956 and you're cruising the main drag with the usual crowd when suddenly a new song comes over the car's radio. You are mesmerized by this soulful voice singing about some place called "Heartbreak Hotel" where "the desk clerk's dressed in black." This is the first Elvis Presley song you've ever heard, but somehow you know that your life will never be the same.

Elvis Aaron Presley (born January 8, 1935 in Tupelo, Mississippi) rocked his way right into the American music scene like no one before him. And at the time of his death in 1977 he would be called over and over again "the most successful performer of all time." With a career that spanned over 21 years, and which carried him through 107 records which made the Top 40 charts and 33 motion pictures, there is no doubt that Presley's legend will continue to live on for decades to come.

Today this legend lives on via the never-ending tribute albums being released, as well as hundreds of thousands of Elvis collectibles dating all the way back to the beginning.

Elvis Presley

"He was the epitome of the American dream. He had the talent, the right looks and the right attitude. A lot of people with looks couldn't sing and a lot of the ones who could sing didn't have his looks. For 21 years he was the All American Boy. He was a hero to the boys and a hearthrob to the girls." The speaker is collector Sean Shaver, who readily admits to being an original Presley fan.

Shaver's association to Presley is a rather unique one indeed. "Back in '67 I hurt myself, and I had to lie around on a couch all day. You can grow crazy doing that, so I started my own Presley fan club." It was at this point that Shaver began showing up at places to take Presley's photo. From that time until Presley's death, Shaver amassed a photograph collection of some 80,000 photographs of Presley. "Even though I was never hired by Presley, he began referring to me as his unofficial photographer . . . I was as close to Presley's inner circle as you could get. I guess it was just a hobby that got way out of control."

Shaver's collection also includes memorabilia from the Elvis Presley movies. "The first four movies (generally thought to be Presley's best cinematic endeavors) are worth the most. "There's a 27 x 41 one sheet for 'Jailhouse Rock' that's worth several hundred dollars today. They had two different one sheets for 'Jailhouse Rock.' That one was the oil painting, and the drawing which is beautiful and in real good color can sell for almost as much. The early films can sell for $125 at least." According to Shaver, Presley movie memorabilia can range from $80 to $100 depending on the film. "From '65–'68, those were the lean years (for Presley's reputation among music buffs). I mean, I bought Sun records (Sun was Presley's original record label which sells today for $300 to $400 apiece) for 50¢ each because Elvis was making movies like *Girls, Girls, Girls*."

Regardless of the quality of Elvis films, Shaver remains a loyal collector. "I have almost everything—nobody has it all," he quickly adds, while discussing the remarkable amount of memorabilia produced. A quick scan of the early items includes charms, pillows, hats, shoes, wallets, scrapbooks, lipstick (sold in "Hound Dog Orange" and "Cruel Red"), even Presley guitars. Marketed by Elvis Presley Enterprises, the official marketing firm behind most '50s memorabilia, the guitar was sold in a plain box. Today the guitar with booklet is valued as high as $800.

"It seems like everybody's collecting Elvis," exclaims Wendy Sauers. Sauers, a 28-year-old Bewisburg, Pennsylvania, resident, has quickly earned status among Presley fans. The author of *Elvis Presley* (published by McFarland Press), Sauer's wealth of knowledge stems from her great admiration for Presley. She is often found doing radio shows on "The King," touting her own large album collection, which includes many rare releases. "It's getting harder all the time to get the early stuff; you can't get anything unless you pay $125–$200 or so for it," she says, regarding the exorbitant prices that early Presley memorabilia can get on the market.

Sauers is particularly fond of a cardboard standee of Presley that she recently acquired. "It's a cut-out figure (cardboard) of Elvis used to display and promote Priscilla's book, and I've been offered $175 for it already!" The book, *Elvis and Me,* written by Presley's ex-wife Priscilla Beaulieu, is a fairly recent publication, making the value of the promotional box a particularly high one.

Other items in Sauer's eclectic grouping include fan club pictures. "Back in '56 the original clubs (which cost right around a dollar to join) sent out these three or four 8 x 10 glossies, and those are really rare today. You just can't seem to find that stuff today."

"I was a great one as a kid to send off for a picture of Elvis. A lot of those mail order offers have become quite valuable." Elvis expert and collector Rosalind Cranor had amassed quite an impressive collection of Elvis memorabilia before she went away to college. Upon her return years later, there were the boxes all tucked away in an attic full of her Presley mementoes. "I have always been a collector," she adds.

Cranor, the author of *Elvis Collectibles* (published by Collector Books in 1983) is currently rewriting her book as prices continue to rise in the ever-changing world of Presley collectibles. (The current book is by Overmountain Press and will be available soon.) Among Cranor's best bets for highly sought items is the Presley doll. "That doll, made in 1957, would be worth around $1,000 to $1,500 now, depending on if it is still in the box or not. The box in which the Presley doll came was a plain pink box with a place cut out in it so you could see the doll.

"There were two record players put out in '56; one was more expensive, though. One had a three-record EP set that came with it and the other had a two-record set that came with it. I've seen original ads for them and one was about $29 or so. The only thing they had was a gold facsimile of his signature on the bottom of it, just said 'Elvis Presley,' that's it." Apparently this is of little dissatisfaction to Presley fans; the record players fall into a price range of $500 to $800.

"Just about anyplace in the country there's an Elvis collector," laughs Ted Young. Young (162 Hendrix Drive, Oakridge, Tennessee 37830) has been an Elvis collector for many years. "I didn't come along as a big Presley fan until '67. I knew all about him, but I could never really afford to collect then. At that point in time ('67) I got started on the records and I couldn't stop." By Young's own estimate his collection holds some 3,000 items. "I cherish all my items deeply," he said. Among the hundreds of items in his collection are the unopened bottle of "Teddy Bear Perfume," worth somewhere around $125, and the Presley novelty hat. "I have one with the original price tag on it. It is black with red trim. There's a bunch of figures on it, and it has sayings all over it like 'Love Me Tender,' and there's music notes, hound dogs. It is a very colorful item; it sold for around $1.98 and now it's worth around $50."

Some of Young's oddities include an Elvis Presley drinking glass which Young is particularly keen on. "It came out in '56; it's really beautiful. There was also a dinner plate with the same emblem. It had a gold painted figure outlined in black and white."

In a collection as large as Young's, paper artifacts are an integral part. "I have hundreds of items, boxes of them, there were so many items. There were magazines I didn't even know existed. There was this one magazine called *Hep Cats;* there were only three issues put out and Elvis domi-

nated the cover of all three issues. They were made in
'56–'57 and they go for anywhere from $20 to $75 dollars.
If Elvis dominated the cover it can be worth up to $75 easy."

For collectors like Ted Young, Elvis Presley will always
reign as the king of '50s and '60s collectibles.

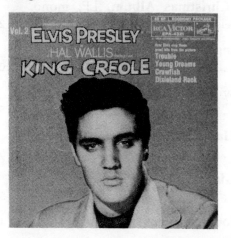

Volumes 1 and 2 of the hit songs from *King Creole*

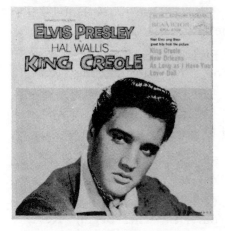

Elvis Presley Music Memorabilia

	Price Range	
☐ **"Change of Habit,"** Elvis Presley, 22 x 28, 1969	20.00	30.00
☐ **Elvis' Christmas Album,** LP, mono, 1951, reissue, photo on back	20.00	30.00
☐ **"Flaming Star,"** Elvis Presley, 22 x 28, 1960	100.00	120.00
☐ **"Follow That Dream,"** Elvis Presley, 1962	50.00	70.00
☐ **"Girl Happy,"** Elvis Presley, 22 x 28, 1962	50.00	70.00
☐ **Girls, Girls, Girls,** Elvis Presley, 22 x 28, 1962	50.00	70.00
☐ **Roustabout,** Elvis Presley, 22 x 28, 1964	40.00	60.00

Elvis Presley Records

☐ **Presley, Elvis,** "Heartbreak Hotel"/"I Was The One," RCA, 45 rpm, 1956 ..	5.00	10.00
☐ **Presley, Elvis,** "I Want You, I Need You, I Love You"/"My Baby Left Me," RCA, 45 rpm, 1956	5.00	10.00
☐ **Presley, Elvis,** "Don't Be Cruel"/ "Hound Dog," RCA, 1956	6.00	10.00
☐ **Presley, Elvis,** "Love Me Tender"/ "Anyway You Want Me," RCA, 1956	5.00	10.00
☐ **Presley, Elvis,** "All Shook Up"/"That's When Your Heartaches Begin," RCA, 45 rpm, 1957	5.00	8.00

Price Range

☐ **Presley, Elvis,** "Hard Headed Woman"/ "Don't Ask Me Why," RCA, 45 rpm, 1958 . . . . 6.00   8.00

☐ **Presley, Elvis,** "Jailhouse Rock"/"Treat Me Nice," RCA, 45 rpm, 1957 . . . . 5.00   8.00

☐ **Presley, Elvis,** "It's Now Or Never"/"A Mess Of Blues," RCA, 45 rpm, 1960   4.00   6.00

☐ **Presley, Elvis,** "It's Now Or Never"/"A Mess Of Blues," RCA, 45 rpm, 1960, stereo single 80.00   150.00

☐ **Presley, Elvis,** "Are You Lonesome To-night?"/"I Gotta Know," RCA, 45 rpm, 1960 . . . . 4.00   6.00

☐ **Presley, Elvis,** "Are You Lonesome To-night?"/"I Gotta Know," RCA, 45 rpm, 1960, stereo single 80.00   150.00

Elvis Presley Movie Memorabilia

☐ **Stay Away Joe,** 1965 . . . . 30.00   50.00

☐ **Wild in the Country,** 1961 . . . . 50.00   70.00

☐ **Jailhouse Rock,** 1957, MGM 100.00   150.00

☐ **Viva Las Vegas,** Elvis Presley/Ann Margaret, 1964 . . . . 50.00   60.00

Rockin' Around the Clock

If Phil Schwartz could find one record in a pile of old platters in a junk store today, it would be a pristine copy of "Can't Help Loving That Girl" by the Hide-A-Ways. "It is a really rare one," Phil says, "issued on a small label called Ronni in the Philadelphia area in 1955." Saying that it was basically distributed "out of the back of a stationwagon,"

Phil, a Lancaster, Pennsylvania record collector, would love to get his hands on the hard-to-find disc. "It has a beautiful harmony sound."

Phil, who is the secretary of the Keystone Record Collectors Club (P. O. Box 1516, Lancaster, PA 17604), has a weekend "oldies" show on a local radio station, and it's not uncommon for listeners to be treated to the all-but-forgotten sounds of some of the lesser-remembered groups and performers of the '50s and '60s. Phil is a collector who constantly haunts the proverbial rock 'n' roll attic in quest of songs to add to his collection.

"People often ask me how many records I have in my collection and I tell them that a good collection stresses quality rather than quantity," Phil explains, admitting that he owns in excess of 50,000 records. He says that he's been a record collector since he was four years old, "which means I've been doing this for some 30 years."

He collects all forms of music committed to wax in the '50s and '60s, and says that he continues to buy records which appeal to him musically as well as for their potential future worth. His personal favorites, however, are the early rhythm-and-blues records of the late '40s and early '50s, the sort of records which led to the development of what we now recognize as rock 'n' roll. "The rhythm and blues pre-rock 'n' roll records of 1945–55 are still the big money records as far as investing goes," the collector explains. The vast majority of the early R & Bs were issued on 78 rpm records as this was still the most common form of record in use (although 45 rpms emerged just after World War II).

Schwartz says that just the opposite is true about rock 'n' roll records of the late '50s. By this point, 45s were becoming widely accepted, and companies produced 78s in lesser quantities. "The major trade dropped the 78 trade around 1958. The smaller companies were pressing them until about 1960." Rock classics like "Why Do Fools Fall In Love?" by Frankie Lymon and the Teenagers and "Love Me Tender" by Elvis Presley featured on 78s are very hot items.

Also popular are picture sleeves. "Sometimes a record's picture sleeve is worth more than the record it originally covered because the sleeves were often cut up or hung on a fan's wall. The first five Elvis records issued with his Sun label singles are very sought-after."

Awareness in record collecting is making it more difficult for collectors like Phil to find those great gems of yesterday these days. "I used to go out at four in the afternoon to yard sales and pick up great stuff," he laments. "Now you have to be out there by seven in the morning to find anything."

Unlike some collectors, Schwartz prefers to listen to his own records than to tapings. "I bring them along when I do my radio show and play them. I'm not abusive with them, but I also don't think you should put them on a shelf and put cellophane around them and never touch them."

His choices for the best songs of the '50s and '60s period? " 'Try the Impossible' by Lee Andrews and the Hearts, 'Golden Teardrops' by the Flamingos, and 'Island of Love' by the Shepherds."

Sports

Note. With appreciation to Dr. James Beckett, the following is an abridged chapter of information taken from his books, the *Official 1987 Price Guide to Baseball Cards,* and the *Official 1987 Price Guide to Football Cards,* published by The House of Collectibles.

Baseball card picturing Ted Williams

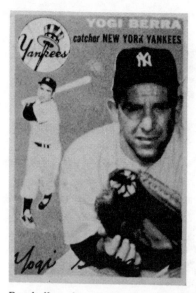

Baseball card picturing Yogi Berra

Baseball card picturing Phil Rizzuto

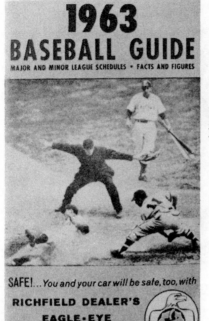

1963 Baseball Guide,
published by Premo *Sports*
Publications, Inc.

1968 Official Yankee Schedule,
endorsed by American Airlines
and Krueger Beer

Baseball Cards

"Can a Batter Swing at the Same Pitch Twice?"

To the kids of the 1950s, they were the best buy in town. For the five cents you put down at the corner store, you received a pack of bubble gum containing the pictures of as many as ten Major League baseball players. With each new pack, your expectations soared—maybe it contained a Mickey Mantle, a Willie Mays, or a Roy Campanella. Yes, maybe even a Ted Williams! This time you were lucky: "Theodore Samuel Williams, outfield, Boston Red Sox. Ted is one of the greatest hitters of all time," a Topps card told us. "In '41, he hit .406. Named the Most Valuable Player in '46 and '49. He has the highest Lifetime Batting Average of any active player. Bats left. Throws right." Thumbing through your pack, you quickly discover other "secrets." Yogi Berra's real first name is Lawrence. Pitcher Ed Roebuck of the Brooklyn Dodgers learned to throw by knocking tin cans off a fence. Yankees' Phil Rizzuto was turned down by the Dodgers because he was too short (5 feet, 6 inches). Packs of baseball cards constituted gold mines of information for the young sports fan. They told us everything we wanted to know. "Can a batter swing at the same pitch twice?" a 1955 Topps card number 130 asked (picturing Phillies' Mayo Smith). Answer: "Yes, if he doesn't hit it the first time."

According to Dr. James Beckett, the 1980s have seen a rebirth and explosion of interest in all cards, but especially cards of the 1950s. Up until 1955, it was Bowman and Topps competing, and the competition brought out the best in the competitors. "We've got the same thing going on now. There's a competition now between Topps, Donruss, and Fleer, which has increased interest in the '80s just like it did in the '50s," says Dr. Beckett.

Companies producing a set for a given year do not print a card for every single player on the team. They are, typically, choices that are made, even though the choice is not always the best player. However, the companies in those days were required to have the players under contract in order to print them on a card. "In the 1950s," says Beckett, "there was a lot of competition between Topps and Bowman over the player rights."

The number of cards produced in a set has gradually increased from the 1950s to the 1980s, and so has the number of teams. It is obvious there is presently a strong superstar orientation in baseball cards—with the biggest names commanding the biggest buck. "That was not as much true in the '50s as it is in the '80s," says Beckett. "The difference between the highest price and the lowest price is great. The hobby just wasn't that well developed then." "There wouldn't be price guides or an organized hobby if all cards were worth the same amount," adds Beckett.

For the 1980s, it is a much more developed hobby. Every card is a different price. "Generally," says Beckett, "the higher prices go for the superstars—the most popular players." Specifically, when you bought a pack of cards for a dime or nickel, you got whatever cards were in the package. They were all produced pretty much in the same amounts. But when you wanted to trade or sell your Mickey Mantle, it was not for just any other player. It would be someone of equal stature. Kids aren't going out and buying too many $50 cards today, but they're buying all the nickel cards, thinking that maybe in 10 years they'll become $50 cards just like the nickel cards of 10, 20 or 30 years ago.

"There is a high number phenomenon in baseball card collecting," Dr. Beckett explains. "Essentially, later in the year the numbers at the end of the series were produced in lesser quantities." Dr. Beckett says this usually was because it was late in the summer and companies did not want to have unsold products. The print quantities of those higher numbers would be lowered, and those numbers not only are harder to get but they are higher in value as well. Says Beckett, "This was a very sticky thing with kids in the '50s and '60s. You'd get all these cards, and then maybe your candy store wouldn't get the last numbers because they thought 'nobody's going to buy baseball cards anymore. The kids are back in school, so we're not even going to order them.' "

There are exceptions to that rule, however, like the Bowman baseball set from 1950. The lower numbers are more valuable because the lower numbers were not in the stores for a very long time, and they were immediately followed by the next group of cards.

Some of the same phenomena holds true for football cards, but to a lesser extent. "Football, as a sport, is very popular, but it has never caught up with baseball cards," says Beckett. "Football cards are a distant second place."

The scope of baseball card collecting today is overwhelming. To talk with a full-fledged enthusiast is to hear mentioned hundreds of players long forgotten. Most of all, it is to realize how truly dedicated card collectors are to the game of baseball. They don't merely collect baseball—they think, live, and breathe baseball. The cards epitomize the glamour of the game—the teams, the scores, and the players. Dizzy Dean, Dixie Walker, Jackie Robinson, Stan Musial, Whitey Ford, Duke Snider, Roy Sievers, and Hank Greenberg—as long as there are baseball card collectors, these names will remain immortal. Come to think of it, there's even a stick of gum in those packages too!

Topps—1955

The cards in this 206-card set measure 2⅝" by 3¾". Both the large "head" shot and the smaller full-length photos used on each card of the 1955 Topps set are in color. The card fronts were designed horizontally for the first time in Topps' history. The first card features Dusty Rhodes, hitting star for the Giants 1954 World Series sweep over the Indians. A "high" series, 161 to 210, is more difficult to find than cards 1 to 160. Numbers 175, 186, 203, and 209 were never issued. To fill in for the four cards not issued in the high number series, Topps double-printed four players, those appearing on cards 170, 172, 184, and 188.

Complete Set: M-850.00; VG-E-375.00; F-G-75.00

		MINT	VG-E	F-G
	Common Player (1–150)	1.25	.60	.12
	Common Player (151–160)	2.50	1.15	.25
	Common Player (161–210)	3.75	1.75	.37
☐	1 Dusty Rhodes	4.50	1.00	.30
☐	2 Ted Williams	45.00	20.00	4.50
☐	3 Art Fowler	1.25	.60	.12
☐	4 Al Kaline	18.00	8.50	1.80
☐	5 Jim Gilliam	2.75	1.25	.27
☐	6 Stan Hack	1.25	.60	.12
☐	7 Jim Hegan	1.25	.60	.12
☐	8 Harold Smith	1.25	.60	.12
☐	9 Robert Miller	1.25	.60	.12
☐	10 Bob Keegan	1.25	.60	.12
☐	11 Ferris Fain	1.25	.60	.12
☐	12 Vernon Thies	1.25	.60	.12
☐	13 Fred Marsh	1.25	.60	.12
☐	14 Jim Finigan	1.25	.60	.12
☐	15 Jim Pendleton	1.25	.60	.12
☐	16 Roy Sievers	1.50	.70	.15

	MINT	VG-E	F-G
☐ 17 Bobby Hofman	1.25	.60	.12
☐ 18 Russ Kemmerer	1.25	.60	.12
☐ 19 Billy Herman	2.50	1.15	.25
☐ 20 Andy Carey	1.50	.70	.15
☐ 21 Alex Grammas	1.25	.60	.12
☐ 22 Bill Skowron	2.75	1.25	.27
☐ 23 Jack Parks	1.25	.60	.12
☐ 24 Hal Newhouser	2.25	1.00	.22
☐ 25 John Podres	2.25	1.00	.22
☐ 26 Dick Groat	2.00	.90	.20
☐ 27 Bill Gardner	1.50	.70	.15
☐ 28 Ernie Banks	16.00	7.50	1.60
☐ 29 Herman Wehmeier	1.25	.60	.12
☐ 30 Vic Power	1.25	.60	.12
☐ 31 Warren Spahn	12.00	5.50	1.20
☐ 32 Warren McGhee	1.25	.60	.12
☐ 33 Tom Qualters	1.25	.60	.12
☐ 34 Wayne Terwilliger	1.25	.60	.12
☐ 35 Dave Jolly	1.25	.60	.12
☐ 36 Leo Kiely	1.25	.60	.12
☐ 37 Joe Cunningham	1.50	.70	.15
☐ 38 Bob Turley	2.25	1.00	.22
☐ 39 Bill Glynn	1.25	.60	.12

	MINT	VG-E	F-G
☐ 40 Don Hoak	1.25	.60	.12
☐ 41 Chuck Stobbs	1.25	.60	.12
☐ 42 John (Windy) McCall	1.25	.60	.12
☐ 43 Harvey Haddix	1.50	.70	.15
☐ 44 Harold Valentine	1.25	.60	.12
☐ 45 Hank Sauer	1.50	.70	.15
☐ 46 Ted Kazanski	1.25	.60	.12
☐ 47 Hank Aaron	50.00	22.00	5.00
☐ 48 Bob Kennedy	1.25	.60	.12
☐ 49 J.W. Porter	1.25	.60	.12
☐ 50 Jackie Robinson	35.00	16.50	3.50
☐ 51 Jim Hughes	1.25	.60	.12
☐ 52 Bill Tremel	1.25	.60	.12
☐ 53 Bill Taylor	1.25	.60	.12
☐ 54 Lou Limmer	1.25	.60	.12
☐ 55 Rip Repulski	1.25	.60	.12
☐ 56 Ray Jablonski	1.25	.60	.12
☐ 57 Bill O'Dell	1.25	.60	.12
☐ 58 Jim Rivera	1.25	.60	.12
☐ 59 Gair Allie	1.25	.60	.12
☐ 60 Dean Stone	1.25	.60	.12
☐ 61 Forrest Jacobs	1.25	.60	.12
☐ 62 Thornton Kipper	1.25	.60	.12

	MINT	VG-E	F-G
☐ 63 Joe Collins	1.50	.70	.15
☐ 64 Gus Triandos	1.50	.70	.15
☐ 65 Ray Boone	1.25	.60	.12
☐ 66 Ron Jackson	1.25	.60	.12
☐ 67 Wally Moon	1.50	.70	.15
☐ 68 Jim Davis	1.25	.60	.12
☐ 69 Ed Bailey	1.25	.60	.12
☐ 70 Al Rosen	3.25	1.50	.32
☐ 71 Ruben Gomez	1.25	.60	.12
☐ 72 Karl Olson	1.25	.60	.12
☐ 73 Jack Shepard	1.25	.60	.12
☐ 74 Robert Borkowski	1.25	.60	.12
☐ 75 Sandy Amoros	1.75	.85	.17
☐ 76 Howie Pollet	1.25	.60	.12
☐ 77 Arnold Portocarrero	1.25	.60	.12
☐ 78 Gordon Jones	1.25	.60	.12
☐ 79 Clyde Schell	1.25	.60	.12
☐ 80 Bob Grim	1.75	.85	.17
☐ 81 Gene Conley	1.25	.60	.12
☐ 82 Chuck Harmon	1.25	.60	.12
☐ 83 Tom Brewer	1.25	.60	.12
☐ 84 Camilo Pascual	1.50	.70	.15
☐ 85 Don Mossi	1.75	.85	.17

	MINT	VG-E	F-G
☐ 86 Bill Wilson	1.25	.60	.12
☐ 87 Frank House	1.25	.60	.12
☐ 88 Bob Skinner	1.50	.70	.15
☐ 89 Joe Frazier	1.25	.60	.12
☐ 90 Karl Spooner	1.50	.70	.15
☐ 91 Milt Bolling	1.25	.60	.12
☐ 92 Don Zimmer	2.50	1.15	.25
☐ 93 Steve Bilko	1.25	.60	.12
☐ 94 Reno Bertoia	1.25	.60	.12
☐ 95 Preston Ward	1.25	.60	.12
☐ 96 Chuck Bishop	1.25	.60	.12
☐ 97 Carlos Paula	1.25	.60	.12
☐ 98 John Riddle	1.25	.60	.12
☐ 99 Frank Leja	1.25	.60	.12
☐ 100 Monte Irvin	4.50	2.10	.45
☐ 101 Johnny Gray	1.25	.60	.12
☐ 102 Wally Westlake	1.25	.60	.12
☐ 103 Chuck White	1.25	.60	.12
☐ 104 Jack Harshman	1.25	.60	.12
☐ 105 Chuck Diering	1.25	.60	.12
☐ 106 Frank Sullivan	1.25	.60	.12
☐ 107 Curt Roberts	1.25	.60	.12
☐ 108 Al Walker	1.25	.60	.12

	MINT	VG-E	F-G
☐ 109 Ed Lopat	2.50	1.15	.25
☐ 110 Gus Zernial	1.50	.70	.15
☐ 111 Bob Milliken	1.25	.60	.12
☐ 112 Nelson King	1.25	.60	.12
☐ 113 Harry Brecheen	1.25	.60	.12
☐ 114 Louis Ortiz	1.25	.60	.12
☐ 115 Ellis Kinder	1.25	.60	.12
☐ 116 Tom Hurd	1.25	.60	.12
☐ 117 Mel Roach	1.25	.60	.12
☐ 118 Bob Purkey	1.25	.60	.12
☐ 119 Bob Lennon	1.25	.60	.12
☐ 120 Ted Kluszewski	3.00	1.40	.30
☐ 121 Bill Renna	1.25	.60	.12
☐ 122 Carl Sawatski	1.25	.60	.12
☐ 123 Sandy Koufax	80.00	37.00	8.00
☐ 124 Harmon Killebrew	40.00	18.00	4.00
☐ 125 Ken Boyer	5.00	2.35	.50
☐ 126 Dick Hall	1.25	.60	.12
☐ 127 Dale Long	1.50	.70	.15
☐ 128 Ted Lepcio	1.25	.60	.12
☐ 129 Elvin Tappe	1.25	.60	.12
☐ 130 Mayo Smith	1.25	.60	.12
☐ 131 Grady Hatton	1.25	.60	.12

	MINT	VG-E	F-G
□ 132 Bob Trice	1.25	.60	.12
□ 133 Dave Hoskins	1.25	.60	.12
□ 134 Joe Jay	1.25	.60	.12
□ 135 Johnny O'Brien	1.25	.60	.12
□ 136 Vernon Stewart	1.25	.60	.12
□ 137 Harry Elliott	1.25	.60	.12
□ 138 Ray Herbert	1.25	.60	.12
□ 139 Steve Kraly	1.25	.60	.12
□ 140 Mel Parnell	1.50	.70	.15
□ 141 Tom Wright	1.25	.60	.12
□ 142 Gerry Lynch	1.25	.60	.12
□ 143 John (Dick) Schofield	1.25	.60	.12
□ 144 John (Joe) Amalfitano	1.25	.60	.12
□ 145 Elmer Valo	1.25	.60	.12
□ 146 Dick Donovan	1.25	.60	.12
□ 147 Hugh Pepper	1.25	.60	.12
□ 148 Hector Brown	1.25	.60	.12
□ 149 Ray Crone	1.25	.60	.12
□ 150 Michael Higgins	1.25	.60	.12
□ 151 Ralph Kress	2.50	1.15	.25
□ 152 Harry Agganis	3.75	1.75	.37
□ 153 Bud Podbielan	2.50	1.15	.25
□ 154 Willie Miranda	2.50	1.15	.25

	MINT	VG-E	F-G
☐ 155 Eddie Mathews	12.50	5.75	1.25
☐ 156 Joe Black	3.75	1.75	.37
☐ 157 Robert Miller	2.50	1.15	.25
☐ 158 Tommy Carroll	3.00	1.40	.30
☐ 159 Johnny Schmitz	2.50	1.15	.25
☐ 160 Ray Narleski	3.00	1.40	.30
☐ 161 Chuck Tanner	4.50	2.10	.45
☐ 162 Joe Coleman	3.75	1.75	.37
☐ 163 Faye Throneberry	3.75	1.75	.37
☐ 164 Roberto Clemente	135.00	60.00	13.50
☐ 165 Don Johnson	3.75	1.75	.37
☐ 166 Hank Bauer	7.50	3.50	.75
☐ 167 Thomas Casagrande	3.75	1.75	.37
☐ 168 Duane Pillette	3.75	1.75	.37
☐ 169 Bob Oldis	3.75	1.75	.37
☐ 170 Jim Pearce DP	1.50	.70	.15
☐ 171 Dick Brodowski	3.75	1.75	.37
☐ 172 Frank Baumholtz DP	1.50	.70	.15
☐ 173 Johnny Kline	3.75	1.75	.37
☐ 174 Rudy Minarcin	3.75	1.75	.37
☐ 176 Norm Zauchin	3.75	1.75	.37
☐ 177 Al Robertson	3.75	1.75	.37
☐ 178 Bobby Adams	3.75	1.75	.37

	MINT	VG-E	F-G
☐ 179 Jim Bolger	3.75	1.75	.37
☐ 180 Clem Labine	4.50	2.10	.45
☐ 181 Roy McMillan	3.75	1.75	.37
☐ 182 Humberto Robinson	3.75	1.75	.37
☐ 183 Anthony Jacobs	3.75	1.75	.37
☐ 184 Harry Perkowski DP	1.50	.70	.15
☐ 185 Don Ferrarese	3.75	1.75	.37
☐ 187 Gil Hodges	35.00	16.50	3.50
☐ 188 Charlie Silvera DP	1.50	.70	.15
☐ 189 Phil Rizzuto	30.00	14.00	3.00
☐ 190 Gene Woodling	4.50	2.10	.45
☐ 191 Eddie Stanky	4.50	2.10	.45
☐ 192 Jim Delsing	3.75	1.75	.37
☐ 193 Johnny Sain	5.50	2.60	.55
☐ 194 Willie Mays	160.00	75.00	16.00
☐ 195 Ed Roebuck	3.75	1.75	.37
☐ 196 Gale Wade	3.75	1.75	.37
☐ 197 Al Smith	3.75	1.75	.37
☐ 198 Yogi Berra	45.00	20.00	4.50
☐ 199 Odbert Hamrick	3.75	1.75	.37
☐ 200 Jackie Jensen	5.00	2.35	.50
☐ 201 Sherman Lollar	4.25	2.00	.42

	MINT	VG-E	F-G
☐ 202 Jim Owens	3.75	1.75	.37
☐ 204 Frank Smith	3.75	1.75	.37
☐ 205 Gene Freese	3.75	1.75	.37
☐ 206 Pete Daley	3.75	1.75	.37
☐ 207 Bill Consolo	3.75	1.75	.37
☐ 208 Ray Moore	3.75	1.75	.37
☐ 210 Duke Snider	125.00	40.00	12.00

Fleer—1960

The cards in this 79-card set measure 2½ " x 3½ ". The cards from the 1960 Fleer series of Baseball Greats are sometimes mistaken for 1930s cards by collectors not familiar with this set. The cards each contain a tinted photo of a baseball immortal, and were issued in one series. There are no known scarcities, although a number 80 card (Pepper Martin reverse with either a Tinker, Collins, or Grove obverse) exists (this is not considered part of the set). The catalog designation for 1960 Fleer is R418-2.
Complete Set: M-90.00; VG-E-42.00; F-G-9.00

	MINT	VG-E	F-G
Common Player (1–79) ..	.75	.35	.07
☐ 1 Napoleon Lajoie	2.50	.50	.10
☐ 2 Christy Mathewson	2.00	.90	.20
☐ 3 George H. Ruth	9.00	4.25	.90
☐ 4 Carl Hubbell	1.20	.55	.12
☐ 5 Grover Alexander	1.50	.70	.15
☐ 6 Walter P. Johnson	2.50	1.15	.25

		MINT	VG-E	F-G
☐	7 Charles A. Bender	.75	.35	.07
☐	8 Roger P. Bresnahan	.75	.35	.07
☐	9 Mordecai P. Brown	.75	.35	.07
☐	10 Tristram Speaker	1.25	.60	.12
☐	11 Joseph (Arky) Vaughan ..	.75	.35	.07
☐	12 Zachariah Wheat	.75	.35	.07
☐	13 George Sisler	1.00	.45	.10
☐	14 Connie Mack	1.00	.45	.10
☐	15 Clark C. Griffith	.75	.35	.07
☐	16 Louis Boudreau	1.10	.50	.11
☐	17 Ernest Lombardi	.75	.35	.07
☐	18 Henry Manush	.75	.35	.07
☐	19 Martin Marion	.75	.35	.07
☐	20 Edward Collins	.75	.35	.07
☐	21 James Maranville	.75	.35	.07
☐	22 Joseph Medwick	.75	.35	.07
☐	23 Edward Barrow	.75	.35	.07
☐	24 Gordon Cochrane	1.00	.45	.10
☐	25 James J. Collins	.75	.35	.07
☐	26 Robert Feller	2.50	1.15	.25
☐	27 Lucius Appling	1.10	.50	.11
☐	28 Lou Gehrig	6.00	2.80	.60
☐	29 Charles Hartnett	.75	.35	.07

		MINT	VG-E	F-G
☐	30 Charles Klein	.75	.35	.07
☐	31 Anthony Lazzeri	.75	.35	.07
☐	32 Aloysius Simmons	.75	.35	.07
☐	33 Wilbert Robinson	.75	.35	.07
☐	34 Edgar Rice	.75	.35	.07
☐	35 Herbert Pennock	.75	.35	.07
☐	36 Melvin Ott	1.10	.50	.11
☐	37 Frank O'Doul	.75	.35	.07
☐	38 John Mize	1.10	.50	.11
☐	39 Edmund Miller	.75	.35	.07
☐	40 Joseph Tinker	.75	.35	.07
☐	41 John Baker	.75	.35	.07
☐	42 Tyrus Cobb	7.00	.25	.70
☐	43 Paul Derringer	.75	.35	.07
☐	44 Adrian Anson	1.10	.50	.11
☐	45 James Bottomley	.75	.35	.07
☐	46 Edward S. Plank	1.00	.45	.10
☐	47 Denton (Cy) Young	2.00	.90	.20
☐	48 Hack Wilson	1.00	.45	.10
☐	49 Edward Walsh	.75	.35	.07
☐	50 Frank Chance	.75	.35	.07
☐	51 Arthur Vance	.75	.35	.07
☐	52 William Terry	1.00	.45	.10

		MINT	VG-E	F-G
☐	53 James Foxx	2.00	.90	.20
☐	54 Vernon Gomez	1.00	.45	.10
☐	55 Branch Rickey	.75	.35	.07
☐	56 Raymond Schalk	.75	.35	.07
☐	57 John Evers	.75	.35	.07
☐	58 Charles Gehringer	1.00	.45	.10
☐	59 Burleigh Grimes	.75	.35	.07
☐	60 Robert (Lefty) Grove	1.25	.60	.12
☐	61 George Waddell	.75	.35	.07
☐	62 John (Honus) Wagner	2.00	.90	.20
☐	63 Charles (Red) Ruffing	.75	.35	.07
☐	64 Kenesaw M. Landis	.75	.35	.07
☐	65 Harry Heilmann	.75	.35	.07
☐	66 John McGraw	1.00	.45	.10
☐	67 Hugh Jennings	.75	.35	.07
☐	68 Harold Newhouser	.75	.35	.07
☐	69 Waite Hoyt	.75	.35	.07
☐	70 Louis (Bobo) Newsom . . .	.75	.35	.07
☐	71 Howard (Earl) Averill	.75	.35	.07
☐	72 Theodore Williams	6.00	2.80	.60
☐	73 Warren Giles	.75	.35	.07
☐	74 Ford Frick	.75	.35	.07
☐	75 Hazen (Kiki) Cuyler	.75	.35	.07

		MINT	VG-E	F-G
☐	76 Paul Waner	.75	.35	.07
☐	77 Harold (Pie) Traynor	1.00	.45	.10
☐	78 Lloyd Waner	.75	.35	.07
☐	79 Ralph Kiner	1.25	.60	.12
☐	80 Pepper Martin* .... (Collins, Tinker or Grove pictured)	65.00	30.00	6.50

Bowman—1950

The cards in this 252-card set measure 2¹/₁₆″ by 2½″. This set, marketed in 1950 by Bowman, represented a major improvement in terms of quality over their previous efforts. Each card was a beautifully colored line drawing developed from a simple photograph. The first 72 cards are the scarcest in the set while the final 72 cards may be found with or without the copyright line. This was the only Bowman sports set to carry the famous "5-Star" logo.

Complete Set: M-1350.00; VG-E-600.00; F-G-120.00

		MINT	VG-E	F-G
	Common Player (1–72) ..	8.00	3.75	.80
	Common Player (73–252)	3.00	1.40	.30
☐	1 Mel Parnell	35.00	5.00	1.00
☐	2 Vern Stephens	8.00	3.75	.80
☐	3 Dom DiMaggio	11.00	5.25	1.10
☐	4 Gus Zernial	9.00	4.25	.90
☐	5 Bob Kuzava	8.00	3.75	.80
☐	6 Bob Feller	32.00	15.00	3.20

		MINT	VG-E	F-G
☐	7 Jim Hegan	8.00	3.75	.80
☐	8 George Kell	13.00	6.00	1.30
☐	9 Vic Wertz	8.00	3.75	.80
☐	10 Tommy Henrich	9.00	4.25	.90
☐	11 Phil Rizzuto	25.00	11.00	2.50
☐	12 Joe Page	9.00	4.25	.90
☐	13 Ferris Fain	9.00	4.25	.90
☐	14 Alex Kellner	8.00	3.75	.80
☐	15 Al Kozar	8.00	3.75	.80
☐	16 Roy Sievers	9.00	4.25	.90
☐	17 Sid Hudson	8.00	3.75	.80
☐	18 Eddie Robinson	8.00	3.75	.80
☐	19 Warren Spahn	25.00	11.00	2.50
☐	20 Bob Elliott	8.00	3.75	.80
☐	21 Pee Wee Reese	25.00	11.00	2.50
☐	22 Jackie Robinson	75.00	35.00	7.50
☐	23 Don Newcombe	13.00	6.00	1.30
☐	24 Johnny Schmitz	8.00	3.75	.80
☐	25 Hank Sauer	9.00	4.25	.90
☐	26 Grady Hatton	8.00	3.75	.80
☐	27 Herman Wehmeier	8.00	3.75	.80
☐	28 Bobby Thomson	10.00	4.75	1.00
☐	29 Eddie Stanky	9.00	4.25	.90

		MINT	VG-E	F-G
☐	30 Eddie Waitkus	8.00	3.75	.80
☐	31 Del Ennis	9.00	4.25	.90
☐	32 Robin Roberts	18.00	8.50	1.80
☐	33 Ralph Kiner	16.00	7.50	1.60
☐	34 Murry Dickson	8.00	3.75	.80
☐	35 Enos Slaughter	15.00	7.00	1.50
☐	36 Eddie Kazak	8.00	3.75	.80
☐	37 Luke Appling	12.00	5.50	1.20
☐	38 Bill Wight	8.00	3.75	.80
☐	39 Larry Doby	10.00	4.75	1.00
☐	40 Bob Lemon	15.00	7.00	1.50
☐	41 Hoot Evers	8.00	3.75	.80
☐	42 Art Houtteman	8.00	3.75	.80
☐	43 Bobby Doerr	9.00	4.25	.90
☐	44 Joe Dobson	8.00	3.75	.80
☐	45 Al Zarilla	8.00	3.75	.80
☐	46 Yogi Berra	45.00	20.00	4.50
☐	47 Jerry Coleman	9.00	4.25	.90
☐	48 Lou Brissie	8.00	3.75	.80
☐	49 Elmer Valo	8.00	3.75	.80
☐	50 Dick Kokos	8.00	3.75	.80
☐	51 Ned Garver	8.00	3.75	.80
☐	52 Sam Mele	8.00	3.75	.80

		MINT	VG-E	F-G
☐	53 Clyde Vollmer	8.00	3.75	.80
☐	54 Gil Coan	8.00	3.75	.80
☐	55 Buddy Kerr	8.00	3.75	.80
☐	56 Del Crandall	9.00	4.25	.90
☐	57 Vern Bickford	8.00	3.75	.80
☐	58 Carl Furillo	11.00	5.25	1.10
☐	59 Ralph Branca	9.00	4.25	.90
☐	60 Andy Pafko	8.00	3.75	.80
☐	61 Bob Rush	8.00	3.75	.80
☐	62 Ted Kluszewski	11.00	5.25	1.10
☐	63 Ewell Blackwell	9.00	4.25	.90
☐	64 Al Dark	10.00	4.75	1.00
☐	65 Dave Koslo	8.00	3.75	.80
☐	66 Larry Jansen	8.00	3.75	.80
☐	67 Willie Jones	8.00	3.75	.80
☐	68 Curt Simmons	9.00	4.25	.90
☐	69 Wally Westlake	8.00	3.75	.80
☐	70 Bob Chesnes	8.00	3.75	.80
☐	71 Red Schoendienst	11.00	5.25	1.10
☐	72 Howie Pollett	8.00	3.75	.80
☐	73 Willard Marshall	3.00	1.40	.30
☐	74 Johnny Antonelli	4.00	1.85	.40
☐	75 Roy Campanella	45.00	20.00	4.50

	MINT	VG-E	F-G
☐ 76 Rex Barney	3.00	1.40	.30
☐ 77 Duke Snider	32.00	15.00	3.20
☐ 78 Mickey Owen	3.00	1.40	.30
☐ 79 Johnny VanderMeer	4.00	1.85	.40
☐ 80 Howard Fox	3.00	1.40	.30
☐ 81 Ron Northey	3.00	1.40	.30
☐ 82 Whitey Lockman	3.00	1.40	.30
☐ 83 Sheldon Jones	3.00	1.40	.30
☐ 84 Richie Ashburn	8.50	4.00	.85
☐ 85 Ken Heintzleman	3.00	1.40	.30
☐ 86 Stan Rojek	3.00	1.40	.30
☐ 87 Bill Werle	3.00	1.40	.30
☐ 88 Marty Marion	4.00	1.85	.40
☐ 89 Red Munger	3.00	1.40	.30
☐ 90 Harry Brecheen	3.00	1.40	.30
☐ 91 Cass Michaels	3.00	1.40	.30
☐ 92 Hank Majeski	3.00	1.40	.30
☐ 93 Gene Bearden	3.00	1.40	.30
☐ 94 Lou Boudreau	9.00	4.25	.90
☐ 95 Aaron Robinson	3.00	1.40	.30
☐ 96 Virgil Trucks	3.00	1.40	.30
☐ 97 Maurice McDermott	3.00	1.40	.30
☐ 98 Ted Williams	100.00	45.00	10.00

	MINT	VG-E	F-G
☐ 99 Billy Goodman	3.50	1.65	.35
☐ 100 Vic Raschi	4.00	1.85	.40
☐ 101 Bobby Brown	5.00	2.35	.50
☐ 102 Billy Johnson	3.00	1.40	.30
☐ 103 Eddie Joost	3.00	1.40	.30
☐ 104 Sam Chapman	3.00	1.40	.30
☐ 105 Bob Dillinger	3.00	1.40	.30
☐ 106 Cliff Fannin	3.00	1.40	.30
☐ 107 Sam Dente	3.00	1.40	.30
☐ 108 Ray Scarborough	3.00	1.40	.30
☐ 109 Sid Gordon	3.00	1.40	.30
☐ 110 Tommy Holmes	3.50	1.65	.35
☐ 111 Walker Cooper	3.00	1.40	.30
☐ 112 Gil Hodges	18.00	8.50	1.80
☐ 113 Gene Hermanski	3.00	1.40	.30
☐ 114 Wayne Terwilliger	3.00	1.40	.30
☐ 115 Roy Smalley	3.00	1.40	.30
☐ 116 Virgil Stallcup	3.00	1.40	.30
☐ 117 Bill Rigney	3.00	1.40	.30
☐ 118 Clint Hartung	3.00	1.40	.30
☐ 119 Dick Sisler	3.00	1.40	.30
☐ 120 John Thompson	3.00	1.40	.30
☐ 121 Andy Seminick	3.00	1.40	.30

	MINT	VG-E	F-G
☐ 122 Johnny Hopp	3.00	1.40	.30
☐ 123 Dino Restelli	3.00	1.40	.30
☐ 124 Clyde McCullough	3.00	1.40	.30
☐ 125 Del Rice	3.00	1.40	.30
☐ 126 Al Brazle	3.00	1.40	.30
☐ 127 Dave Philley	3.00	1.40	.30
☐ 128 Phil Masi	3.00	1.40	.30
☐ 129 Joe Gordon	3.50	1.65	.35
☐ 130 Dale Mitchell	3.00	1.40	.30
☐ 131 Steve Gromek	3.00	1.40	.30
☐ 132 James Mickey Vernon	4.00	1.85	.40
☐ 133 Don Kolloway	3.00	1.40	.30
☐ 134 Paul Trout	3.00	1.40	.30
☐ 135 Pat Mullin	3.00	1.40	.30
☐ 136 Warren Rosar	3.00	1.40	.30
☐ 137 Johnny Pesky	3.50	1.65	.35
☐ 138 Allie Reynolds	5.00	2.35	.50
☐ 139 Johnny Maze	11.00	5.25	1.10
☐ 140 Pete Suder	3.00	1.40	.30
☐ 141 Joe Coleman	3.00	1.40	.30
☐ 142 Sherman Lollar	4.00	1.85	.40
☐ 143 Eddie Stewart	3.00	1.40	.30
☐ 144 Al Evans	3.00	1.40	.30

	MINT	VG-E	F-G
☐ 145 Jack Graham	3.00	1.40	.30
☐ 146 Floyd Baker	3.00	1.40	.30
☐ 147 Mike Garcia	4.00	1.85	.40
☐ 148 Early Wynn	11.00	5.25	1.10
☐ 149 Bob Swift	3.00	1.40	.30
☐ 150 George Vico	3.00	1.40	.30
☐ 151 Fred Hutchinson	3.50	1.65	.35
☐ 152 Ellis Kinder	3.00	1.40	.30
☐ 153 Walt Masterson	3.00	1.40	.30
☐ 154 Gus Niarhos	3.00	1.40	.30
☐ 155 Frank Shea	3.00	1.40	.30
☐ 156 Fred Sanford	3.00	1.40	.30
☐ 157 Mike Guerra	3.00	1.40	.30
☐ 158 Paul Lehner	3.00	1.40	.30
☐ 159 Joe Tipton	3.00	1.40	.30
☐ 160 Mickey Harris	3.00	1.40	.30
☐ 161 Sherry Robertson	3.00	1.40	.30
☐ 162 Eddie Yost	3.00	1.40	.30
☐ 163 Earl Torgeson	3.00	1.40	.30
☐ 164 Sibby Sisti	3.00	1.40	.30
☐ 165 Bruce Edwards	3.00	1.40	.30
☐ 166 Joe Hatton	3.00	1.40	.30
☐ 167 Preacher Roe	5.00	2.35	.50

	MINT	VG-E	F-G
☐ 168 Bob Scheffing	3.00	1.40	.30
☐ 169 Hank Edwards	3.00	1.40	.30
☐ 170 Dutch Leonard	3.00	1.40	.30
☐ 171 Harry Gumbert	3.00	1.40	.30
☐ 172 Peanuts Lowrey	3.00	1.40	.30
☐ 173 Lloyd Merriman	3.00	1.40	.30
☐ 174 Hank Thompson	3.50	1.65	.35
☐ 175 Monte Kennedy	3.00	1.40	.30
☐ 176 Sylvester Donnelly	3.00	1.40	.30
☐ 177 Hank Borowy	3.00	1.40	.30
☐ 178 Eddie Fitzgerald	3.00	1.40	.30
☐ 179 Chuck Diering	3.00	1.40	.30
☐ 180 Harry Walker	3.00	1.40	.30
☐ 181 Marino Pieretti	3.00	1.40	.30
☐ 182 Sam Zoldak	3.00	1.40	.30
☐ 183 Mickey Haefner	3.00	1.40	.30
☐ 184 Randy Gumpert	3.00	1.40	.30
☐ 185 Howie Judson	3.00	1.40	.30
☐ 186 Ken Keltner	3.50	1.65	.35
☐ 187 Lou Stringer	3.00	1.40	.30
☐ 188 Earl Johnson	3.00	1.40	.30
☐ 189 Owen Friend	3.00	1.40	.30
☐ 190 Ken Wood	3.00	1.40	.30

	MINT	VG-E	F-G
☐ 191 Dick Starr	3.00	1.40	.30
☐ 192 Bob Chipman	3.00	1.40	.30
☐ 193 Pete Reiser	3.50	1.65	.35
☐ 194 Billy Cox	3.50	1.65	.35
☐ 195 Phil Cavaretta	3.50	1.65	.35
☐ 196 Doyle Lade	3.00	1.40	.30
☐ 197 Johnny Wyrostek	3.00	1.40	.30
☐ 198 Danny Litwiler	3.00	1.40	.30
☐ 199 Jack Kramer	3.00	1.40	.30
☐ 200 Kirby Higbe	3.00	1.40	.30
☐ 201 Pete Castiglione	3.00	1.40	.30
☐ 202 Cliff Chambers	3.00	1.40	.30
☐ 203 Danny Murtaugh	3.50	1.65	.35
☐ 204 Granny Hamner	3.00	1.40	.30
☐ 205 Mike Goliat	3.00	1.40	.30
☐ 206 Stan Lopata	3.00	1.40	.30
☐ 207 Max Lanier	3.00	1.40	.30
☐ 208 Jim Hearn	3.00	1.40	.30
☐ 209 Johnny Lindell	3.00	1.40	.30
☐ 210 Ted Gray	3.00	1.40	.30
☐ 211 Charley Keller	3.50	1.65	.35
☐ 212 Gerry Priddy	3.00	1.40	.30
☐ 213 Carl Scheib	3.00	1.40	.30

	MINT	VG-E	F-G
☐ 214 Dick Fowler	3.00	1.40	.30
☐ 215 Ed Lopat	5.00	2.35	.50
☐ 216 Bob Porterfield	3.00	1.40	.30
☐ 217 Casey Stengel MGR	25.00	11.00	2.50
☐ 218 Cliff Mapes	3.00	1.40	.30
☐ 219 Hank Bauer	6.50	3.00	.65
☐ 220 Leo Durocher MGR	8.50	4.00	.85
☐ 221 Don Mueller	3.50	1.65	.35
☐ 222 Bobby Morgan	3.00	1.40	.30
☐ 223 Jim Russell	3.00	1.40	.30
☐ 224 Jack Banta	3.00	1.40	.30
☐ 225 Eddie Sawyer MGR	3.00	1.40	.30
☐ 226 Jim Konstanty	7.00	3.25	.70
☐ 227 Bob Miller	3.00	1.40	.30
☐ 228 Bill Nicholson	3.00	1.40	.30
☐ 229 Frank Frisch	9.00	4.25	.90
☐ 230 Bill Serena	3.00	1.40	.30
☐ 231 Preston Ward	3.00	1.40	.30
☐ 232 Al Rosen	9.00	4.25	.90
☐ 233 Allie Clark	3.00	1.40	.30
☐ 234 Bobby Shantz	5.50	2.60	.55
☐ 235 Harold Gilbert	3.00	1.40	.30

	MINT	VG-E	F-G
☐ 236 Bob Cain	3.00	1.40	.30
☐ 237 Bill Salkeld	3.00	1.40	.30
☐ 238 Vernal Jones	3.00	1.40	.30
☐ 239 Bill Howerton	3.00	1.40	.30
☐ 240 Eddie Lake	3.00	1.40	.30
☐ 241 Neil Berry	3.00	1.40	.30
☐ 242 Dick Kryhoski	3.00	1.40	.30
☐ 243 Johnny Groth	3.00	1.40	.30
☐ 244 Dale Coogan	3.00	1.40	.30
☐ 245 Al Papai	3.00	1.40	.30
☐ 246 Walt Dropo	3.50	1.65	.35
☐ 247 Irv Noren	3.50	1.65	.35
☐ 248 Sam Jethroe	3.50	1.65	.35
☐ 249 Snuffy Stirnweiss	3.00	1.40	.30
☐ 250 Ray Coleman	3.00	1.40	.30
☐ 251 John Moss	3.00	1.40	.30
☐ 252 Billy DeMars	10.00	2.00	.40

Football Cards

Topps—1961

The 1961 Topps set of 198 contains NFL players (1–132) and AFL players (133–197). The cards measure 2½" by 3½". Card number 198 is a checklist card. The fronts are very similar to the Topps 1961 baseball issue. The card backs were printed in light blue on white card stock. Statistical information from the immediate past season and career totals are given on the reverse. A "coin-rub" picture was featured on the right of the reverse.

		MINT	VG-E	F-G
Complete Set		175.00	80.00	18.00
Common Player (1–132)		.35	.15	.03
Common Player (133–198)		.55	.25	.05
☐	1 Johnny Unitas, Baltimore Colts	11.00	3.50	.75
☐	2 Lenny Moore, Baltimore Colts	2.50	1.15	.25
☐	3 Alan Ameche, Baltimore Colts	.90	.40	.09
☐	4 Raymond Berry, Baltimore Colts	2.75	1.25	.27
☐	5 Jim Mutscheller, Baltimore Colts	.35	.15	.03
☐	6 Jim Parker, Baltimore Colts	1.75	.85	.17
☐	7 Gino Marchetti, Baltimore Colts	2.25	1.00	.22

		MINT	VG-E	F-G
☐	8 Gene Lipscomb, Baltimore Colts	.90	.40	.09
☐	9 Baltimore Colts Team Card	.90	.40	.09
☐	10 Bill Wade, Chicago Bears	.55	.25	.05
☐	11 Johnny Morris, Chicago Bears	.90	.40	.09
☐	12 Rick Casares, Chicago Bears	.60	.28	.06
☐	13 Harlon Hill, Chicago Bears	.45	.20	.04
☐	14 Stan Jones, Chicago Bears	.35	.15	.03
☐	15 Doug Atkins, Chicago Bears	1.50	.70	.15
☐	16 Bill George, Chicago Bears	1.50	.70	.15
☐	17 J. C. Caroline, Chicago Bears	.35	.15	.03
☐	18 Chicago Bears Team Card	.90	.40	.09
☐	19 Big Time Football Comes To Texas (Eddie LeBaron)	.90	.40	.09
☐	20 Eddie LeBaron, Dallas Cowboys	.90	.40	.09
☐	21 Don McIlhenny, Dallas Cowboys	.45	.20	.04
☐	22 L.G. Dupre, Dallas Cowboys	.45	.20	.04
☐	23 Jim Doran, Dallas Cowboys	.45	.20	.04

		MINT	VG-E	F-G
☐	24 Bill Howton, Dallas Cowboys	.50	.22	.05
☐	25 Buzz Guy, Dallas Cowboys	.45	.20	.04
☐	26 Jack Patera, Dallas Cowboys	.90	.40	.09
☐	27 Tom Frankhauser, Dallas Cowboys	.45	.20	.04
☐	28 Dallas Cowboys Team Card	2.25	1.00	.22
☐	29 Jim Ninowski, Detroit Lions	.55	.25	.05
☐	30 Dan Lewis, Detroit Lions	.35	.15	.03
☐	31 Nick Pietrosante, Detroit Lions	.55	.25	.05
☐	32 Gail Cogdill, Detroit Lions	.45	.20	.04
☐	33 Jim Gibbons, Detroit Lions	.35	.15	.03
☐	34 Jim Martin, Detroit Lions	.35	.15	.03
☐	35 Alex Karras, Detroit Lions	3.00	1.40	.30
☐	36 Joe Schmidt, Detroit Lions	2.00	.90	.20
☐	37 Detroit Lions Team Card	.90	.40	.09
☐	38 Packers' Hornung Sets NFL Scoring Record	2.00	.90	.20
☐	39 Bart Starr, Green Bay Packers	6.50	3.00	.65
☐	40 Paul Hornung, Green Bay Packers	5.00	2.35	.50

	MINT	VG-E	F-G
☐ 41 Jim Taylor, Green Bay Packers	3.50	1.65	.35
☐ 42 Max McGee, Green Bay Packers	.65	.30	.06
☐ 43 Boyd Dowler, Green Bay Packers	.55	.25	.05
☐ 44 Jim Ringo, Green Bay Packers	1.75	.85	.17
☐ 45 Henry Jordan, Green Bay Packers	.90	.40	.09
☐ 46 Bill Forester, Green Bay Packers	.60	.28	.06
☐ 47 Green Bay Packers Team	1.00	.45	.10
☐ 48 Frank Ryan, Los Angeles Rams	.90	.40	.09
☐ 49 Jon Arnett, Los Angeles Rams	.55	.25	.05
☐ 50 Ollie Matson, Los Angeles Rams	2.25	1.00	.22
☐ 51 Jim Red Phillips, Los Angeles Rams	.35	.15	.03
☐ 52 Del Shofner, Los Angeles Rams	.50	.22	.05
☐ 53 Art Hunter, Los Angeles Rams	.35	.15	.03
☐ 54 Gene Brito, Los Angeles Rams	.35	.15	.03

	MINT	VG-E	F-G
☐ 55 Lindon Crow, Los Angeles Rams	.35	.15	.03
☐ 56 Los Angeles Rams Team Card	.90	.40	.09
☐ 57 Colts' Unitas 25 TD Passes	2.75	1.25	.27
☐ 58 Y.A. Tittle, San Francisco 49ers	5.00	2.35	.50
☐ 59 John Brodie, San Francisco 49ers	6.50	3.00	.65
☐ 60 J.D. Smith, San Francisco 49ers	.35	.15	.03
☐ 61 R.C. Owens, San Francisco 49ers	.35	.15	.03
☐ 62 Clyde Conner, San Francisco 49ers	.35	.15	.03
☐ 63 Bob St. Clair, San Francisco 49ers	.35	.15	.03
☐ 64 Leo Nomellini, San Francisco 49ers	1.75	.85	.17
☐ 65 Abe Woodson, San Francisco 49ers	.45	.20	.04
☐ 66 San Francisco 49ers Team Card	.90	.40	.09
☐ 67 Checklist	6.00	.60	.10
☐ 68 Milt Plum, Cleveland Browns	.90	.40	.09
☐ 69 Ray Renfro, Cleveland Browns	.50	.22	.05

		MINT	VG-E	F-G
☐	70 Bobby Mitchell, Cleveland Browns	2.50	1.15	.25
☐	71 Jim Brown, Cleveland Browns	20.00	9.00	2.00
☐	72 Mike McCormack, Cleveland Browns	1.50	.70	.15
☐	73 Jim Ray Smith, Cleveland Browns	.35	.15	.03
☐	74 Sam Baker, Cleveland Browns	.45	.20	.04
☐	75 Walt Michaels, Cleveland Browns	.75	.35	.07
☐	76 Cleveland Browns Team Card	.90	.40	.09
☐	77 Jimmy Brown Gains 1257 Yards	6.50	3.00	.65
☐	78 George Shaw, Minnesota Vikings	.45	.20	.04
☐	79 Hugh McElhenny, Minnesota Vikings	2.25	1.00	.22
☐	80 Clancy Osborne, Minnesota Vikings	.35	.15	.03
☐	81 Dave Middleton, Minnesota Vikings	.35	.15	.03
☐	82 Frank Youso, Minnesota Vikings	.35	.15	.03
☐	83 Don Joyce, Minnesota Vikings	.35	.15	.03

	MINT	VG-E	F-G
☐ 84 Ed Culpepper, Minnesota Vikings	.35	.15	.03
☐ 85 Charley Conerly, New York Giants	2.50	1.15	.25
☐ 86 Mel Triplett, New York Giants	.35	.15	.03
☐ 87 Kyle Rote, New York Giants	2.25	1.00	.22
☐ 88 Roosevelt Brown, New York Giants	1.75	.85	.17
☐ 89 Ray Wietecha, New York Giants	.35	.15	.03
☐ 90 Andy Robustelli, New York Giants	1.75	.85	.17
☐ 91 Sam Huff, New York Giants	2.25	1.00	.22
☐ 92 Jim Patton, New York Giants	.45	.20	.04
☐ 93 New York Giants Team Card	.90	.40	.09
☐ 94 Charlie Conerly Leads Giants For 13th Year	2.00	.90	.20
☐ 95 Sonny Jurgensen, Philadelphia Eagles	3.50	1.65	.35
☐ 96 Tommy McDonald, Philadelphia Eagles	.55	.25	.05
☐ 97 Bill Barnes, Philadelphia Eagles	.35	.15	.03

	MINT	VG-E	F-G
☐ 98 Bobby Walston, Philadelphia Eagles	.35	.15	.03
☐ 99 Pete Retzlaff, Philadelphia Eagles	.45	.20	.04
☐ 100 Jim McCusker, Philadelphia Eagles	.35	.15	.03
☐ 101 Chuck Bednarik, Philadelphia Eagles	2.50	1.15	.25
☐ 102 Tom Brookshier, Philadelphia Eagles	1.00	.45	.10
☐ 103 Philadelphia Eagles Team Card	.90	.40	.09
☐ 104 Bobby Layne, Pittsburgh Steelers	5.00	2.35	.50
☐ 105 John Henry Johnson, Pittsburgh Steelers	.90	.40	.09
☐ 106 Tom Tracy, Pittsburgh Steelers	.45	.20	.04
☐ 107 Buddy Dial, Pittsburgh Steelers	.55	.25	.05
☐ 108 Jimmy Orr, Pittsburgh Steelers	.55	.25	.05
☐ 109 Mike Sandusky, Pittsburgh Steelers	.35	.15	.03
☐ 110 John Reger, Pittsburgh Steelers	.35	.15	.03
☐ 111 Junior Wren, Pittsburgh Steelers	.35	.15	.03

	MINT	VG-E	F-G
☐ 112 Pittsburgh Steelers Team Card	.90	.40	.09
☐ 113 Bobby Layne Sets New Passing Record	2.25	1.00	.22
☐ 114 John Roach, St. Louis Cardinals	.35	.15	.03
☐ 115 Sam Etcheverry, St. Louis Cardinals	.50	.22	.05
☐ 116 John David Crow, St. Louis Cardinals	.50	.22	.05
☐ 117 Mal Hammack, St. Louis Cardinals	.35	.15	.03
☐ 118 Sonny Randle, St. Louis Cardinals	.50	.22	.05
☐ 119 Leo Sugar, St. Louis Cardinals	.35	.15	.03
☐ 120 Jerry Norton, St. Louis Cardinals	.35	.15	.03
☐ 121 St. Louis Cardinals Team	.90	.40	.09
☐ 122 Checklist	6.00	.60	.10
☐ 123 Ralph Guglielmi, Washington Redskins	.45	.20	.04
☐ 124 Dick James, Washington Redskins	.35	.15	.03
☐ 125 Don Bosseler, Washington Redskins	.35	.15	.03
☐ 126 Joe Walton, Washington Redskins	.75	.35	.07

	MINT	VG-E	F-G
☐ 127 Bill Anderson, Washington Redskins	.35	.15	.03
☐ 128 Vince Promuto, Washington Redskins	.35	.15	.03
☐ 129 Bob Toneff, Washington Redskins	.35	.15	.03
☐ 130 John Paluck, Washington Redskins	.35	.15	.03
☐ 131 Washington Redskins Team Card	.90	.40	.09
☐ 132 Browns' Plum Wins NFL Passing Title	.55	.25	.05

AFL Players

	MINT	VG-E	F-G
☐ 133 Abner Haynes, Dallas Texans	1.75	.85	.17
☐ 134 Mel Branch, Dallas Texans	.75	.35	.07
☐ 135 Jerry Cornelison, Dallas Texans	.55	.25	.05
☐ 136 Bill Krisher, Dallas Texans	.55	.25	.05
☐ 137 Paul Miller, Dallas Texans	.55	.25	.05
☐ 138 Jack Spikes, Dallas Texans	.75	.35	.07
☐ 139 Johnny Robinson, Dallas Texans	1.25	.60	.12
☐ 140 Cotton Davidson, Dallas Texans	1.00	.45	.10
☐ 141 Dave Smith, Houston Oilers	.55	.25	.05

	MINT	VG-E	F-G
☐ 142 Bill Groman, Houston Oilers	.90	.40	.09
☐ 143 Rich Michael, Houston Oilers	.55	.25	.05
☐ 144 Mike Dukes, Houston Oilers	.55	.25	.05
☐ 145 George Blanda, Houston Oilers	7.00	3.25	.70
☐ 146 Billy Cannon, Houston Oilers	2.25	1.00	.22
☐ 147 Dennit Morris, Houston Oilers	.55	.25	.05
☐ 148 Jacky Lee, Houston Oilers	.90	.40	.09
☐ 149 Al Dorow, New York Titans	.75	.35	.07
☐ 150 Don Maynard, New York Titans	6.50	3.00	.65
☐ 151 Art Powell, New York Titans	1.00	.45	.10
☐ 152 Sid Youngelman, New York Titans	.55	.25	.05
☐ 153 Bob Mischak, New York Titans	.55	.25	.05
☐ 154 Larry Grantham, New York Titans	.75	.35	.07
☐ 155 Tom Saidock, New York Titans	.55	.25	.05

	MINT	VG-E	F-G
☐ 156 Roger Donnahoo, New York Titans	.55	.25	.05
☐ 157 Lavern Torczon, Buffalo Bills	.55	.25	.05
☐ 158 Archie Matsos, Buffalo Bills	.75	.35	.07
☐ 159 Elbert Dubenion, Buffalo Bills	1.00	.45	.10
☐ 160 Wray Carlton, Buffalo Bills	.75	.35	.07
☐ 161 Rich McCabe, Buffalo Bills	.55	.25	.05
☐ 162 Ken Rice, Buffalo Bills ...	.55	.25	.05
☐ 163 Art Baker, Buffalo Bills ..	.55	.25	.05
☐ 164 Tom Rychlec, Buffalo Bills	.55	.25	.05
☐ 165 Mack Yoho, Buffalo Bills	.55	.25	.05
☐ 166 Jack Kemp, San Diego Chargers	16.00	7.50	1.60
☐ 167 Paul Lowe, San Diego Chargers	2.00	.90	.20
☐ 168 Ron Mix, San Diego Chargers	3.00	1.40	.30
☐ 169 Paul Maguire, San Diego Chargers	1.25	.60	.12
☐ 170 Volney Peters, San Diego Chargers	.55	.25	.05
☐ 171 Ernie Wright, San Diego Chargers	.55	.25	.05

	MINT	VG-E	F-G
☐ 172 Ron Nery, San Diego Chargers	.55	.25	.05
☐ 173 Dave Kocourek, San Diego Chargers	.55	.25	.05
☐ 174 Jim Colclough, Boston Patriots	.55	.25	.05
☐ 175 Babe Parilli, Boston Patriots	1.00	.45	.10
☐ 176 Billy Lott, Boston Patriots	.55	.25	.05
☐ 177 Fred Bruney, Boston Patriots	.55	.25	.05
☐ 178 Ross O'Hanley, Boston Patriots	.55	.25	.05
☐ 179 Walt Cudzik, Boston Patriots	.55	.25	.05
☐ 180 Charley Leo, Boston Patriots	.55	.25	.05
☐ 181 Bob Dee, Boston Patriots	.55	.25	.05
☐ 182 Jim Otto, Oakland Raiders	6.50	3.00	.65
☐ 183 Eddie Macon, Oakland Raiders	.55	.25	.05
☐ 184 Dick Christy, Oakland Raiders	.55	.25	.05
☐ 185 Alan Miller, Oakland Raiders	.55	.25	.05
☐ 186 Tom Flores, Oakland Raiders	2.50	1.15	.25

	MINT	VG-E	F-G
☐ 187 Joe Cannavino, Oakland Raiders	.55	.25	.05
☐ 188 Don Manoukian, Oakland Raiders	.55	.25	.05
☐ 189 Bob Collbaugh, Oakland Raiders	.55	.25	.05
☐ 190 Lionel Taylor, Denver Broncos	2.00	.90	.20
☐ 191 Bud McFadin, Denver Broncos	.55	.25	.05
☐ 192 Goose Gonsoulin, Denver Broncos	.75	.35	.07
☐ 193 Frank Tripucka, Denver Broncos	.90	.40	.09
☐ 194 Gene Mingo, Denver Broncos	.55	.25	.05
☐ 195 Eldon Danenhauer, Denver Broncos	.55	.25	.05
☐ 196 Bob McNamara, Denver Broncos	.55	.25	.05
☐ 197 Dave Rolle, Denver Broncos	.55	.25	.05
☐ 198 Checklist	9.00	.90	.15

INDEX

The HOUSE OF COLLECTIBLES Series

☐ Please send me the following price guides—
☐ I would like the most current edition of the books listed below.

THE OFFICIAL PRICE GUIDES TO:

☐ 753-3	American Folk Art (ID) 1st Ed.	$14.95
☐ 199-3	American Silver & Silver Plate 5th Ed.	11.95
☐ 513-1	Antique Clocks 3rd Ed.	10.95
☐ 283-3	Antique & Modern Dolls 3rd Ed.	10.95
☐ 287-6	Antique & Modern Firearms 6th Ed.	11.95
☐ 755-X	Antiques & Collectibles 9th Ed.	11.95
☐ 289-2	Antique Jewelry 5th Ed.	11.95
☐ 362-7	Art Deco (ID) 1st Ed.	14.95
☐ 447-X	Arts and Crafts: American Decorative Arts, 1894–1923 (ID) 1st Ed.	12.95
☐ 539-5	Beer Cans & Collectibles 4th Ed.	7.95
☐ 521-2	Bottles Old & New 10th Ed.	10.95
☐ 532-8	Carnival Glass 2nd Ed.	10.95
☐ 295-7	Collectible Cameras 2nd Ed.	10.95
☐ 548-4	Collectibles of the '50s & '60s 1st Ed.	9.95
☐ 740-1	Collectible Toys 4th Ed.	10.95
☐ 531-X	Collector Cars 7th Ed.	12.95
☐ 538-7	Collector Handguns 4th Ed.	14.95
☐ 748-7	Collector Knives 9th Ed.	12.95
☐ 361-9	Collector Plates 5th Ed.	11.95
☐ 296-5	Collector Prints 7th Ed.	12.95
☐ 001-6	Depression Glass 2nd Ed.	9.95
☐ 589-1	Fine Art 1st Ed.	19.95
☐ 311-2	Glassware 3rd Ed.	10.95
☐ 243-4	Hummel Figurines & Plates 6th Ed.	10.95
☐ 523-9	Kitchen Collectibles 2nd Ed.	10.95
☐ 080-6	Memorabilia of Elvis Presley and The Beatles 1st Ed.	10.95
☐ 291-4	Military Collectibles 5th Ed.	11.95
☐ 525-5	Music Collectibles 6th Ed.	11.95
☐ 313-9	Old Books & Autographs 7th Ed.	11.95
☐ 298-1	Oriental Collectibles 3rd Ed.	11.95
☐ 761-4	Overstreet Comic Book 18th Ed.	12.95
☐ 522-0	Paperbacks & Magazines 1st Ed.	10.95
☐ 297-3	Paper Collectibles 5th Ed.	10.95
☐ 744-4	Political Memorabilia 1st Ed.	10.95
☐ 529-8	Pottery & Porcelain 6th Ed.	11.95
☐ 524-7	Radio, TV & Movie Memorabilia 3rd Ed.	11.95
☐ 081-4	Records 8th Ed.	16.95
☐ 763-0	Royal Doulton 6th Ed.	12.95
☐ 280-9	Science Fiction & Fantasy Collectibles 2nd Ed.	10.95
☐ 747-9	Sewing Collectibles 1st Ed.	8.95
☐ 358-9	Star Trek/Star Wars Collectibles 2nd Ed.	8.95
☐ 086-5	Watches 8th Ed.	12.95
☐ 248-5	Wicker 3rd Ed.	10.95

THE OFFICIAL:

☐ 760-6	Directory to U.S. Flea Markets 2nd Ed.	5.95
☐ 365-1	Encyclopedia of Antiques 1st Ed.	9.95
☐ 369-4	Guide to Buying and Selling Antiques 1st Ed.	9.95
☐ 414-3	Identification Guide to Early American Furniture 1st Ed.	9.95
☐ 413-5	Identification Guide to Glassware 1st Ed.	9.95
☐ 412-7	Identification Guide to Pottery & Porcelain 1st Ed.	$9.95
☐ 415-1	Identification Guide to Victorian Furniture 1st Ed.	9.95

THE OFFICIAL (SMALL SIZE) PRICE GUIDES TO:

☐ 309-0	Antiques & Flea Markets 4th Ed.	4.95
☐ 269-8	Antique Jewelry 3rd Ed.	4.95
☐ 085-7	Baseball Cards 8th Ed.	4.95
☐ 647-2	Bottles 3rd Ed.	4.95
☐ 544-1	Cars & Trucks 3rd Ed.	5.95
☐ 519-0	Collectible Americana 2nd Ed.	4.95
☐ 294-9	Collectible Records 3rd Ed.	4.95
☐ 306-6	Dolls 4th Ed.	4.95
☐ 762-2	Football Cards 8th Ed.	4.95
☐ 540-9	Glassware 3rd Ed.	4.95
☐ 526-3	Hummels 4th Ed.	4.95
☐ 279-5	Military Collectibles 3rd Ed.	4.95
☐ 764-9	Overstreet Comic Book Companion 2nd Ed.	4.95
☐ 278-7	Pocket Knives 3rd Ed.	4.95
☐ 527-1	Scouting Collectibles 4th Ed.	4.95
☐ 494-1	Star Trek/Star Wars Collectibles 3rd Ed.	3.95
☐ 088-1	Toys 5th Ed.	4.95

THE OFFICIAL BLACKBOOK PRICE GUIDES OF:

☐ 092-X	U.S. Coins 27th Ed.	4.95
☐ 095-4	U.S. Paper Money 21st Ed.	4.95
☐ 098-9	U.S. Postage Stamps 11th Ed.	4.95

THE OFFICIAL INVESTORS GUIDE TO BUYING & SELLING:

☐ 534-4	Gold, Silver & Diamonds 2nd Ed.	12.95
☐ 535-2	Gold Coins 2nd Ed.	12.95
☐ 536-0	Silver Coins 2nd Ed.	12.95
☐ 537-9	Silver Dollars 2nd Ed.	12.95

THE OFFICIAL NUMISMATIC GUIDE SERIES:

☐ 254-X	The Official Guide to Detecting Counterfeit Money 2nd Ed.	7.95
☐ 257-4	The Official Guide to Mint Errors 4th Ed.	7.95

SPECIAL INTEREST SERIES:

☐ 506-9	From Hearth to Cookstove 3rd Ed.	17.95
☐ 504-2	On Method Acting 8th Printing	6.95

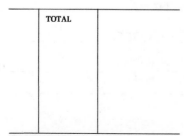

TOTAL	

SEE REVERSE SIDE FOR ORDERING INSTRUCTIONS

FOR IMMEDIATE DELIVERY

VISA & MASTER CARD CUSTOMERS

ORDER TOLL FREE!
1-800-733-3000

This number is for orders only; it is not tied into the customer service or business office. Customers not using charge cards must use mail for ordering since payment is required with the order—sorry, no C.O.D's.

OR SEND ORDERS TO

THE HOUSE OF COLLECTIBLES
201 East 50th Street
New York, New York 10022

_____ POSTAGE & HANDLING RATES _____

First Book	$1.00
Each Additional Copy or Title	$0.50

Total from columns on order form. Quantity_____ $_____

☐ Check or money order enclosed $_____ (include postage and handling)

☐ Please charge $_____to my: ☐ MASTERCARD ☐ VISA

Charge Card Customers Not Using Our Toll Free Number
Please Fill Out The Information Below

Account No. _____Expiration Date_____
(All Digits)

Signature_____

NAME (please print)_____PHONE_____

ADDRESS_____APT. #_____

CITY_____STATE_____ZIP_____